LINCOLN
AND BOOTH

LINCOLN AND BOOTH

MORE LIGHT ON THE CONSPIRACY

H. Donald Winkler

CUMBERLAND HOUSE

NASHVILLE, TENNESSEE

PUBLISHED BY
CUMBERLAND HOUSE PUBLISHING, INC.
431 Harding Industrial Drive
Nashville, Tennessee 37211

Cover design by Gore Studio, Nashville, Tennessee.

Library of Congress Cataloging-in-Publication Data

Winkler, H. Donald, 1932–
    Lincoln and Booth : more light on the conspiracy / H. Donald Winkler.
        p.   cm.
    Includes bibliographical references (p.) and index.
    ISBN 1-58182-342-8 (pbk. : alk. paper)
    1. Lincoln, Abraham, 1809–1865—Assassination. 2. Booth, John Wilkes,
1838–1865. 3. Conspiracies—United States—History—19th century. I. Title.
E457.5.W77 2003
973.7'092—dc21

2002155045

Printed in Canada

1 2 3 4 5 6 7 8 9 10 — 07 06 05 04 03

For Amy and Namri,

two angels on Earth

I do not consider that I have ever accomplished anything without God; and if it is His will that I must die by the hand of an assassin, I must be resigned.

I must do my duty as I see it, and leave the rest with God.

Abraham Lincoln

CONTENTS

———◆—◆◆◆—◆———

ACKNOWLEDGMENTS

Grateful acknowledgment and special thanks are due to:

Amy Cooper, special collections librarian at the University of Iowa Libraries, for searching for rare documents.

Danny Fluhart, president of the Dr. Samuel A. Mudd Society, Waldorf, Maryland, for photographic assistance and up-to-date information on many legal aspects of the Mudd case.

Ray A. Neff, emeritus professor, Indiana State University, for information on Lafayette C. Baker and the George W. Julian diary.

Laurie Verge, director of the Surratt House Museum, Clinton, Maryland, for pinning down facts about the Surratts and providing valuable criticism.

Betty Webb, librarian at the Anna Porter Public Library, Gatlinburg, Tennessee, for locating and obtaining countless books through the inter-library loan program.

Azile T. Winkler, my wife and the 1992 Virginia DAR Outstanding Teacher of American History, for researching various items and reviewing the manuscript.

INTRODUCTION

I remember four things I learned in school about the assassination of Abraham Lincoln:

1. John Wilkes Booth murdered the president at Ford's Theatre in Washington, D.C., on Good Friday, April 14, 1865, five days after Robert E. Lee surrendered his army at Appomattox Court House.

2. Booth was a mentally unbalanced actor solely responsible for the evil deed.

3. The leaders of the Confederacy were not involved in the plot to kill Lincoln.

4. A country doctor, Samuel A. Mudd, was unfairly found guilty of aiding and abetting Booth because he treated the assassin's broken leg.

I was badly misinformed about items 2, 3, and 4. In fact, most Americans have been more misinformed about Lincoln's assassination than about any other event in American history. The problem did not stop with the items cited above. Since the mid-1930s several sensational books have spread speculations about grand conspiracies, often jumping to unproven conclusions based on distorted evidence.

My own curiosity about the assassination skyrocketed after reading Otto Eisenschiml's *Why Was Lincoln Murdered?* This 1937 volume by a Chicago chemist resulted from substantial research that led to electrifying questions that captured the public's imagination. The culprit, readers were led to conclude, was none other than Lincoln's secretary of war, Edwin M. Stanton. He had betrayed the president and, with Northern industrialists and Radical Republicans in the Congress, arranged to have him killed.

Eisenschiml's book spawned volumes by other authors, such as Theodore Roscoe's *The Web of Conspiracy* (1959) as well as television and Hollywood dramas, all elaborating on and further sensationalizing Eisenschiml's thesis. Most historians have little regard for these "grand conspiracy" theories, but the eminent Harvard scholar David Herbert Donald wrote in his Pulitzer Prize–winning *Lincoln* that "much useful information" is found in the Eisenschiml and Roscoe books, "but both are marred by attempts to link

Stanton to the assassination." Stanton, it seems, was and remains a sacred cow. He is an untouchable giant—at least as far as most historians are concerned. Many nonhistorians, however, have continued their attempts to turn this sacred cow into bad hamburger.

Generally regarded by scholars as among the best books on the assassination published before the mid-1980s are George S. Bryan's *The Great American Myth* (1940), Thomas R. Turner's *Beware the People Weeping* (1982), and William Hanchett's *The Lincoln Murder Conspiracies* (1983). Bryan exposed what he regarded as invented stories, including the popular belief that Booth escaped and that someone was buried in his place. Turner, the first professional historian to deal with the assassination, provided an excellent account based on the information then available to him. Hanchett served up a superb guide to the growing literature on the subject, exposed the defects in facts and logic in all of the previous theories, and opened the door for further investigations.

Until 1988 historians tended to cling to the long-prevailing assumption that Booth was a crazed loner. They called it the "simple conspiracy" theory. That theory, however, began to crumble in 1988 with the publication of *Come Retribution* by CIA official William A. Tidwell with historian James O. Hall, perhaps the leading authority on the assassination, and David Winfred Gaddy, a career intelligence officer. General Tidwell applied his twenty-three-year background with the CIA to scrupulous research that uncovered a Confederate Secret Service operation in which one of the key players was none other than John Wilkes Booth. Threads Tidwell followed led him to other Confederate plots to capture Lincoln and/or to blow up the White House and kill Lincoln and his cabinet. Tidwell backed up his astonishing conclusions with painstaking scholarship that was difficult to dispute, even though much of the evidence was circumstantial. Among the handful of intelligence operatives and historians who assisted him was my uncle, Wallace Winkler, who during World War II was part of the highly classified Ultra operation that cracked the Nazi coding machine, Enigma, and greatly aided the Allies in defeating Germany. Tidwell's second book, *April '65* (1995), buttressed his "grand conspiracy" theory focused on the Confederate government and described how Southerners skillfully influenced and altered the true history of the assassination.

Ironically, immediately after the assassination, Stanton had taken the lead in placing the blame on the Confederate government, but lacking the information known today and relying on witnesses who perjured them-

selves, he was unable to prove his case. Confederate propagandists capitalized on these failures, discredited Stanton's theory, and persuaded the world
that their government had no involvement in Lincoln's death. They falsely
claimed they had nothing to gain from the heinous act and everything to lose
and that Booth was solely to blame. In reality, Lincoln's forcible removal, by
whatever means, was the Confederacy's last desperate measure to save that
sinking nation. Nevertheless, the Confederate position prevailed among historians for 123 years.

Two books published after 1990 helped to dispel other misconceptions
associated with Lincoln's assassination. Both were written by Edward Steers
Jr.: *His Name Is Still Mudd: The Case Against Dr. Samuel Alexander Mudd*
(1997) and *Blood on the Moon* (2001). These books should put to rest forever the misconception that Samuel Mudd was an innocent victim of vindictive Northern wrath whose only involvement with Booth was treating his
broken leg on the night of the assassination.

History is the drama of individuals in conflict. John Wilkes Booth so
despised Abraham Lincoln that he turned his back on his own family,
became an agent of the Confederate government, and engaged in covert
operations sanctioned by Richmond. Intelligent, meticulous, and careful,
Booth may not have been the James Bond of the Civil War, but he was certainly the man his superiors singled out for what Bill Miller described in
The Surratt Courier as "a daring act requiring careful planning and considerable courage."

This book attempts to understand Booth's motives and actions from his
viewpoint—what he would and would not have done and why.

Of the eight "conspirators" charged by the government in the crime
against Lincoln, the most controversial is Mary Elizabeth Surratt, a deeply
religious, forty two year old widow who was hanged along with Lewis
Paine, David Herold, and George Atzerodt. She was the first woman executed by the federal government. Numerous books and articles about her
case are listed in the bibliography at the end of this book. Her boarding
house in Washington and her tavern at Surrattsville were havens, or "safe
houses," for Confederate spies, smugglers, and dispatch carriers, and her
son John was a close associate of Booth. Whether or not she was part of the
conspiracy is the subject of a chapter in this book.

If, as historians tell us, Secretary of War Stanton was not involved in the
conspiracy against Lincoln, there is considerable evidence that Stanton
resorted to political devilry on numerous other occasions, from refusing to

comply with Lincoln's request for a specific protector at Ford's Theatre to managing the death of Mary Surratt, smearing the reputation of Gen. William T. Sherman, and placing himself at the center of the effort to impeach President Andrew Johnson. This book also examines Stanton's actions, motives, and decisions related to concealing Booth's diary, intimidating witnesses, and naming and pursuing certain conspirators while allowing others to go free.

Wars make heroes, and the Civil War was no exception. The South especially produced a significant crop, from Jefferson Davis and Robert E. Lee to Stonewall Jackson, Jeb Stuart, and John S. Mosby. This last Southerner is of great interest to this narrative of the Lincoln assassination. Well known is Mosby's talent for irregular warfare, but his participation in clandestine operations associated with the death of the president has been one of the South's best kept secrets. For this reason, an entire chapter is devoted to this colorful character who, figuratively, almost became Booth's best friend and who was one of the Union's most hated Confederate commanders.

I have approached the Lincoln assassination from the perspective of a professional journalist who has researched Lincoln for ten years. Drawing and building upon the latest scholarship, I have investigated the people and events related to the assassination. During this process I have found many unanswered questions as well as lies, betrayals, deceptions, obstructions of justice, subterfuges, trickeries, clandestine schemes, and other shameful acts. I have raised several questions never before explored and suggested answers never before considered. I have also asked and examined questions that have never been convincingly explained. I do not pretend to have definitive answers.

I ask you, the reader, to ponder and to look for the truth, however it may come. Raise your own questions and draw your own conclusions. You are studying one of the great mysteries of our national history. I hope you enjoy the journey as much as I have enjoyed mine.

LINCOLN
AND BOOTH

1

PROVOCATION

Shortly after returning from Gettysburg in November 1863, Abraham Lincoln reviewed a troubling report from a committee of seven surgeons who had recently been released from Libby and Belle Isle prisons in the capital of the Confederacy. "No prison or penitentiary ever seen by [this committee] in a Northern state equaled in cheerlessness, unhealthiness, and paucity of rations these two military prisons in Richmond," they asserted. At Libby Prison the committee noted "brutal treatment" and "upon the most trivial charges . . . confinement for several days in damp dungeons" where the inmates are "fed only on bread and water." Lack of food for all prisoners led to debilitation, disease, and high mortality, the surgeons concluded.

Letters and statements from others who had experienced Libby supported these allegations. Former inmates called the prison dark, dirty, unheated, and poorly ventilated and sanitized. Prisoners, they said, were sometimes shot just for looking out of the windows. Pennsylvanian Clarence Wilson recalled lying down at night "dovetailed together like sardines in a box, on the bare floor, without anything to cover us." He weighed only ninety pounds when he was released. Ohioan George Pitt wrote of being jammed into one room of the prison hospital with 110 other patients on

19

mats of straw. He described "daily battles with maggots and filth." Others reported fighting disease by drinking castor oil from pint bottles shared among the detainees. More than fifty thousand men—primarily officers—passed through Libby during the war, and many died there. Except for Andersonville in Georgia, Libby was regarded by many Northerners as the most notorious prison in the Confederacy. Poet Julia A. Moore wrote:

> Fathers, brothers, young husbands dear
> Went through that prison door—
> Some lived to return home, we hear,
> And others are no more.
> Many a noble soldier died
> In Libby prison cell,
> And comrades perish'd side by side,
> As many a man can tell.
> No loving hand was near a couch
> To bathe an aching head—
> No loving friend to watch the hours,
> Or soothe their dying bed;
> No friend to wipe the fallen tears
> From off the dewy face—
> No loving kindred was there near
> To mark their resting place.

With an attitude of "enough is enough," many inmates in the Richmond prisons focused on escape efforts. Some succeeded. The most spectacular attempt occurred at Libby on February 9, 1864, when 109 officers crawled through a fireplace, slid down a chimney, cut through a hospital room, scampered down a closed stairway leading to the basement, and wormed themselves through a fifty-three-foot-long tunnel. They had carved out the tunnel using only a pocket knife, a wooden spittoon, a piece of rope, a rubber cloth, and some chisels smuggled into the prison by Elizabeth Van Lew, a Union spy in Richmond. The tunneling was dangerous work. Sandy ground could have caved in the tunnel during a rainstorm, or the prisoners could have tapped into the high water table. Despite the hazards, the escapees emerged safely outside the prison grounds, but forty-eight were recaptured in or near Richmond and two drowned. Fifty-nine reached Union lines.

Some of the escapees made their way to Washington, where they gave firsthand accounts of the hellish life inside the infamous prison. These accounts further demoralized an already war-weary populace as well as the Union army, which was being weakened by desertion after the horrendous loss of life during the 1863 campaigns. Many in the North demanded that the Lincoln administration negotiate an end to the war. This sentiment carried over into the political maneuvering of the election year of 1864. Lincoln knew his job was on the line. Aggressive action—something dramatic—was necessary to boost morale and rally the troops.

While the Union and Confederate armies were somewhat dormant during the winter months of early 1864, Lincoln was approached by swash-buckling twenty-eight-year-old Gen. H. Judson Kilpatrick. He bragged that he could execute a successful raid on Richmond, destroy railroads, and liberate Union prisoners of war at the Libby and Belle Isle prisons. With Robert E. Lee's army in winter camps, Kilpatrick reasoned that Richmond was not only accessible but conquerable. Union intelligence reported weak defenses for the Confederate capital—about three thousand Virginia militia.

Not one to turn a deaf ear to an interesting plan, Lincoln arranged a meeting in the White House with Kilpatrick and Secretary of War Edwin M. Stanton. When the meeting ended, the general's instructions were clear: The

Notorious Libby Prison in Richmond, Virginia, was the site of one of the most remarkable escapes in American history.

H. Judson Kilpatrick (*left*) and Ulric Dahlgren (*right*) devised and led a cavalry raid on Richmond designed to release Union prisoners.

daring raid would proceed. Kilpatrick would lead four thousand cavalrymen to Richmond, free thousands of prisoners, and distribute broadly an amnesty proclamation offering full pardons to Southerners who wished to come back into the Union.

Lincoln, however, had reservations about Kilpatrick's leadership. The cavalryman was known to be rash and ruthless, erratic and tempestuous—a man likely to lose his head in a moment of peril. Later, Gen. William T. Sherman called Kilpatrick "a hell of a damned fool" but added, "I want just that sort of man to command my cavalry." To others Kilpatrick was either heroic and noble or, as one Union officer wrote, "a frothy braggart without brains." He drove his men so roughly, without regard for their well-being, that he earned the nickname, "Kilcavalry." Always in a hurry to do something great, the horse general was intent on a political future: a governorship then possibly the presidency.

To offset Kilpatrick's shortcomings, a twenty-one-year-old one-legged colonel, Ulric Dahlgren, was made second in command and charged with the responsibility for preparing detailed plans for the mission. Dahlgren's father was a man Lincoln greatly admired for modernizing the navy's weaponry—Adm. John A. Dahlgren, then commanding the Federal fleet lying off Charleston, South Carolina. The young Dahlgren, regarded as vigorous and capable, had a spotless military and personal record. He had lost his leg during an aggressive pursuit of Lee's army after the battle of Gettysburg, but he was still eager to "smell hell" and felt his wooden leg would not hinder him as a cavalryman.

Artist Edwin Forbes sketched Kilpatrick's force of four thousand men as they departed their camps north of the Rapidan River on Sunday evening, February 28. Under a clear sky and a bright moon, the men rode toward Richmond.

The young Dahlgren welcomed the opportunity to help lead the daring raid. "If successful," he said, "it will be the grandest thing on record. . . . It is an undertaking that if I were not in, I should be ashamed to show my face again." In the end, he proposed a two pronged raid, attacking Richmond simultaneously from opposite directions. Lincoln and Stanton approved. The venture, however, looked good on paper but proved to be a costly mistake.

Kilpatrick's cavalry moved out on February 28—thirty-five hundred men under Kilpatrick, five hundred under Dahlgren—and soon ran into complications. Spies infiltrated Dahlgren's force and delivered his plans to Confederate Gen. Wade Hampton. Dahlgren and Kilpatrick intended to communicate by signals, but the flat, wooded country provided few observation points, and the two forces lost contact with each other. Then rain, snow, and sleet slowed their advance.

Both forces were repulsed on the outskirts of Richmond, and while galloping away, Dahlgren's men were ambushed. Some escaped, some were captured. Dahlgren was killed. When the Confederates searched his body, they found a notebook and some sensitive papers. The papers revealed startling information. One document was the draft of an address Dahlgren apparently planned to read to his men. A portion of it read: "We hope to release the prisoners from Belle Island first, and having seen them fairly started, we will cross the James River into Richmond, destroying the bridges after us and exhorting the released prisoners to destroy and burn the hateful city; and do not allow the rebel leader Davis and his traitorous crew to escape." A special

A map of the Kilpatrick-Dahlgren Raid (February 28–March 2, 1864) highlights the routes followed by the two segments of the attack on Richmond. Dahlgren's route is indicated by the dashed line.

order added: "The men must keep together and well in hand, and, once in the city, it must be destroyed and Jeff. Davis and Cabinet killed."

These papers, along with Dahlgren's artificial leg, were sent to Richmond and shown to President Jefferson Davis, military adviser Gen. Braxton Bragg, and Secretary of State Judah P. Benjamin. "Easier said than done," Davis allegedly commented after hearing of the plan to kill him and burn the city. Gen. Robert E. Lee, outraged by the notes, urged publication in the press so "that our people & the world may know the character of the war our enemies wage against us, & the unchristian & atrocious acts they plot & perpetrate." The notes were published, further fanning the flames of hatred against Lincoln and the Union.

To add to the furor, Dahlgren's artificial leg was displayed in a store window, and one of his fingers was cut off by someone who admired a ring he wore. His body was buried in an unmarked grave, where Elizabeth Van Lew and friends found it and sneaked it out of Richmond in a wagon filled with fruit trees. His artificial limb, however, remained in the South. Confederate Lt. James Pollard, head of the unit that ambushed Dahlgren, claimed it after he lost his own leg. When he realized it was the wrong size and not adaptable, he gave the prosthetic to amputee John N. Ballard, one of Col. John S. Mosby's partisan rangers, who wore it for the duration of the war.

Meanwhile, Confederate leaders sent copies of the damning papers to Union Gen. George G. Meade and pointedly asked if Dahlgren's words reflected Lincoln's current policy. Kilpatrick and Dahlgren had served formerly under Meade, but Meade had not been involved in planning the raid. Kilpatrick, however, responded through Meade and repudiated the documents. Yet Kilpatrick lacked integrity and loved to make speeches to his own troopers. It is highly probable that, as head of the mission, he helped to compose the notes for Dahlgren to use. Meade, of course, questioned the notes' authenticity. He attempted to assure Lee that neither he nor the U.S. government sanctioned assassination. He said the notes must have been planted on Dahlgren's body by the Confederates themselves, but added that if they were authentic, they must have originated with the dead colonel. Privately, to his wife, Meade acknowledged that Kilpatrick and Dahlgren probably had intended to burn the capital and murder the Confederate leaders.

Indeed, these objectives may have had Lincoln's support. Ten months earlier, when Kilpatrick's brigade had advanced to within two miles of Richmond but retreated after encountering resistance, the president had telegraphed a message similar to Dahlgren's message to Gen. Joseph Hooker: "[T]here was not a sound pair of legs in Richmond. . . . [O]ur men, had they known it, could have safely gone in and burnt everything & brought us Jeff Davis." Such drastic measures as the Kilpatrick-Dahlgren Raid certainly reflected the president's determination to do whatever was necessary to end the rebellion. There would be serious repercussions.

Despite Meade's assurances, Jefferson Davis was convinced that the Dahlgren papers originated with Lincoln and that he, therefore, had targeted the leaders of the Confederacy. Such a view was consistent with Davis's regard for Lincoln as "a bloodthirsty despot." Many Southerners agreed and wanted to retaliate in kind—to kill or capture the much-hated president responsible for bringing so much misery and death throughout the South. They blamed Lincoln for atrocities committed by Union troops, and they detested the Union president's policy of recruiting freed slaves into the army—a policy Confederates feared would foster a massive slave rebellion and the killing of thousands of women and children. To Southerners, Lincoln was a tyrant, and the Dahlgren mission was the irrefutable confirmation.

The audacity of the aborted mission could not be ignored. Editors of the *Richmond Examiner* urged retribution: "To the Washington authorities we are simply criminals awaiting punishment, who may be hanged or who may be pardoned. In their eyes our country is not ours, but theirs. The hostilities which they carry on are not properly war, but military execution and coercion. . . . What then would we practically suggest? First, to put to death all 'raiders' caught in the act; secondly, to insist upon the most scrupulous carrying out of retaliation for murders, robberies, and other outrages."

Earlier, Confederate Secretary of War James A. Seddon had opposed all proposals to capture or kill Lincoln. "The laws of war and morality, as well as Christian principles and sound policy," he announced, "forbid the use of such means." But after the Kilpatrick-Dahlgren Raid, Seddon scrapped that philosophy. Retaliation was uppermost in Confederate minds. "The enormity of [Lincoln's] offense was not forgotten!" Davis wrote in his memoirs.

Ten months after the raid, an infamous advertisement appeared in the *Selma (Ala.) Dispatch*. It solicited one million dollars from Confederate citizens to underwrite the assassinations of three "cruel tyrants": Lincoln, Secretary of State William H. Seward, and Vice President–elect Andrew Johnson. Such a proposal clearly demonstrates the escalating hatred and possible intentions of some Southerners, regardless of Christian principles and the laws of war and morality.

By 1864 clandestine operations were commonplace for the Confederacy, which entrusted such affairs to a cluster of ten organizations. The War Department alone had a secret service, a signal corps, a strategy bureau, and a torpedo bureau (which pioneered the use of land and sea mines as well as delayed-action fuses). There was furthermore a well-organized espionage network in Washington and an operation in Canada to support couriers and other tasks. After the Kilpatrick-Dahlgren Raid, however, more was required. Confederate leaders became more aggressive and transformed the

The Confederacy's team of clandestine operatives in Canada was headed by Jacob Thompson of Mississippi (*left*), formerly secretary of the interior in the Buchanan administration, and Clement C. Clay (*right*), a former senator from Alabama. Thompson, the senior "commissioner," represented Jefferson Davis and Secretary of State Judah Benjamin. Clay represented the War Department.

Canadian office into a terrorist organization and "a clandestine operation of unprecedented size and importance," according to William A. Tidwell in his well-researched book *April '65*.

Canadians apparently did not object to the presence of Confederate operatives, at least not at first. Their border was already riddled with spies, agents, and counteragents, and their country had become a safe haven for fifteen thousand Southerners and eighteen thousand fugitive slaves. Lincoln's blockade of Southern ports had severely curtailed the cotton trade between Canada and the South, causing Canadian ships to lie idle. Confederate agents, with money from Richmond, pumped up Canada's economy by contracting ship construction in the yards of Nova Scotia, New Brunswick, and Quebec. The ships would be used as blockade-runners to carry arms to the beleaguered Confederate armies and cotton to England and Canada. Agents also bought the friendship of newspaper publishers and received favorable editorials in return. Some Canadians feared the Union might attack Canada, but Lincoln assured them he would never do that. He believed in the age-old military maxim: Never get involved with enemies in your front and rear simultaneously.

In the spring and summer of 1864 Jefferson Davis and Judah P. Benjamin beefed up their operation in Canada with new personnel and an operating budget of a million dollars in gold. The agents were to develop and carry out complex covert operations against the Union. Among their assignments: organize antiwar and anti-Lincoln movements in the North to secure Lincoln's defeat in the fall election, set fires and start epidemics in Northern cities, sabotage railroads and steamers, foster prison riots as a cover to help Confederate prisoners escape, and develop a plan to capture Lincoln and use him as a hostage to be exchanged for thousands of Confederate prisoners.

These clandestine operatives were headed by Jacob Thompson of Mississippi, a former U.S. congressman who had been secretary of the interior during the administration of James Buchanan. His associate, Clement C. Clay, a former senator from Alabama, represented the Confederate War Department. Davis directed them to "carry out such instructions as you have received from me verbally, in such manner as shall seem most likely to be conducive to the furtherance of the interests of the Confederate States of America." A key member of the so-called Canada Cabinet was George N. Sanders, a radical activist described by Lincoln secretary John Hay as "a seedy-looking rebel with grizzled whiskers and a flavor of old clothes." Sanders had supported revolutionary movements in Europe and had recommended the assassination of Napoleon III.

One of Thompson's subversive schemes was known as the Great Northwest Conspiracy. He sent a band of sixty-two terrorists from Canada to liberate eight thousand prisoners of war from Camp Douglas in Chicago and

Confederate terrorists based in Montreal raided St. Albans, Vermont, and robbed the town's three banks. As a parting touch, they required all the bank tellers to take an oath of allegiance to the Confederacy.

LESLIE'S

to call "true patriots to arms" to take control of Illinois and parts of Ohio and Indiana. The "true patriots" he hoped to involve were Northerners who opposed the war and/or openly sympathized with or supported the Confederacy. Most of them belonged to the Knights of the Golden Circle or the Sons of Liberty and were popularly known as Copperheads. Their peak membership was alleged to be as many as thirty-five thousand. Yet the plan was foiled by Union agent Thomas Keefe, who learned of the plot aboard a train from Canada while he kept company with some of the raiders. Keefe alerted the commander of the prison camp, who immediately brought in two thousand soldiers to reinforce his guards. Also, prominent Copperheads were arrested, and the expected five thousand volunteers from the various chapters of the Sons of Liberty ignored the summons to action. Thompson's grand "explosion to shake the Union" simply fizzled out.

One of the covert actions devised by Clement Clay to enrich Confederate coffers and disrupt Lincoln's reelection campaign was a raid on St. Albans, a small Vermont town within a three-hour ride of the Canadian border. Twenty-one Confederate soldiers in civilian clothes meandered into St. Albans in the late summer of 1864. Ten of them had been involved in the Chicago plot. They pretended to be Canadian horse buyers or members of a hunting and fishing club planning an outing on Lake Champlain. On October 19 they emerged from their hotels with guns drawn, herded the townspeople together on the village green, then robbed the town's three banks of about two hundred thousand dollars. With the famous Rebel Yell echoing down the main street, the Confederates took off for the Canadian border, throwing incendiary bombs intended to destroy the town. The bombs, however, missed their targets and did little damage. Canadian authorities caught and imprisoned fourteen of the raiders and confiscated ninety thousand dollars from them; the others escaped with the rest of the money. Clement Clay provided six thousand dollars to defend the raiders, and George N. Sanders initiated propaganda efforts to influence opinion in Canada and help secure freedom for the defendants. It took several months, but eventually all the raiders were freed, and the confiscated money was returned to them.

Meanwhile, Thompson's Confederate operation continued to grow larger and more sophisticated. His actions kept alive the threat of terrorist activities in the North and spread alarm throughout the Northern home front. The role of the Southern agents did not end until several months after Lincoln's assassination and after a successful propaganda effort to manipulate people and information to assure the public that the Confederacy was not responsible for the American president's murder.

Another prominent Confederate in the Canada office was Dr. Luke P. Blackburn, a well-educated Kentuckian who tried to use his medical expertise to engage in a kind of biological warfare against the North and especially against Lincoln. Although Blackburn was an expert on the treatment of yellow fever, he, like other physicians of the period, believed it was highly infectious, not realizing it was spread only by mosquitoes. With the full knowledge of the Confederate government, Blackburn initiated a plot to create epidemics of the deadly disease in Northern urban populations, among Union troops in Southern coastal towns, and even in the White House by redistributing clothing that had belonged to yellow fever victims.

The scheme was revealed at the trial of the Lincoln conspirators by Godfrey Joseph Hyams, who was responsible for the distribution. The plot was "directed against the masses of northern people solely to create death," Hyams testified. While some historians have questioned Hyams's story, eight witnesses supported it, including two high-ranking Confederate officials.

Blackburn conceived the plot in April 1864 after sailing to Bermuda to treat casualties of a devastating yellow fever epidemic. The island served as a critical base of operations for Confederate blockade-runners, whose survival was important to the South. Blackburn packaged the clothing and bedding of diseased victims in eight trunks. He shipped them to Halifax, Nova Scotia, and employed Hyams to import them into the United States, specifically to Washington, D.C.; Norfolk, Virginia; and New Bern, North Carolina, where they were to be sold at auction and subsequently create epidemics. Further, Hyams was ordered to deliver a small black valise filled with infected dress shirts to the White House as a gift to the president from an anonymous admirer. For whatever reason, Hyams refused to carry out that order. He claimed the task was too risky. Under the alias of J. W. Harris, however, he did ship the trunks, even though he had to bribe a ship's captain and customs officers to get them into the United States. He also secured an auction house to sell the clothing. Blackburn, still in Bermuda, filled three more trunks, which were to be held until the spring of 1865, then shipped to New York City and sold at auction.

Meanwhile, Hyams, fuming over not being paid for his work—except for a one-hundred-dollar deposit from Jacob Thompson—visited the U.S. consul's office in Toronto and offered to divulge what he knew of the plot in exchange for money and a pardon. The consul agreed after Hyams correctly revealed the location of a Confederate "bomb house" in the city. Hyams gave a detailed statement on April 12—two days before Lincoln was assassinated. When federal prosecutors learned of Hyams's statement, they brought him to Washington to testify in the conspiracy trial, but they were unable to prove that Jefferson Davis knew of Blackburn's plots.

Overlooked among Davis's papers was a letter from one of the Canadian agents, a former Episcopal priest, Kensey Johns Stewart. In December 1864 Stewart wrote to Davis and lambasted "unhuman and cruel" activities carried out by certain agents. "Your Excellency is aware that when a negro is slightly chastised, he hates you," Stewart wrote, "but a just and thorough whipping humbles him." The former cleric suggested that Thompson and several others needed a "thorough whipping." Stewart added:

> As our country has been and is entirely dependent upon God, we cannot afford to displease him. Therefore, it cannot be our policy to employ wicked men to destroy the persons and property of private citizens, by inhumane and cruel acts. I name only one. *$100 of public money has been paid here to one 'Hyams,' a shoemaker, for services rendered by convening and causing to be sold . . . at auction,*

Northerners who opposed the war and/or openly sympathized with or supported the Confederacy were known as Copperheads. An illustrator from *Harper's Weekly* drew them as snakes who would strike without warning.

boxes of small-pox clothing. . . . It is only a matter of surprise that God does not forsake us and our cause when we are associated with such misguided friends.

Thus, Davis knew of Blackburn's and Hyams's activities at least by this date, but four months later the plot was still in operation.

Strangely, in one of the cities targeted by Blackburn—the coastal town of New Bern—more than two thousand people died of yellow fever after the auction of clothing there, even though the clothing could not have caused it. A New Bern newspaper commented: "This hideous . . . plan to deliberately murder innocent men, women, and children . . . is regarded here as an act of cruelty without a parallel."

Tracing the shipment of clothing, governmental officials made an interesting discovery. When they learned that the trunks were shipped through the port of Boston, an official of the Boston customhouse checked hotel registers to see if the hired carrier, J. W. Harris (an alias of Hyams), had been in the city in July or August. He did not find Harris, but he did come across the names of John Wilkes Booth and three men from Canada and one from Baltimore registered at the Parker House on July 26, 1864.

In the book *Come Retribution,* the authors concluded that this gathering in Boston was no coincidence. They reasoned that the men from Canada were undoubtedly Confederate agents using aliases and that they were in Boston for a secret meeting with Booth, a person whose credentials greatly appealed to them.

The well-known young actor grew up near Baltimore and attended the finest private academies. He was from a famous theatrical family. His brother Edwin and his father, Junius, were regarded as America's finest actors. Except for Wilkes (as he preferred to be called), his family was loyal

Nine years before the war, Booth participated in a North-South confrontation at St. Timothy's Hall, a military school in Catonsville, Maryland. With many students fiercely Southern in their temperament and the faculty predominately Northern, trouble was unavoidable. The incident started when some students killed chickens belonging to the school and the faculty reacted by suspending holidays. In retaliation, Booth, his young brother Joseph, and other students armed themselves, camped out in some nearby woods, and claimed they were prepared to defend themselves unless the holidays were restored. The headmaster relented three days later. Booth remembered that day as one on which the South had fought the North and won.

While working with several members of the Confederate operation in Canada, John Wilkes Booth gained the respect of their leaders. When the time came, they offered his services to Richmond.

to the Union. His conflicting position may be partly traced to the early days of his acting career. His first performances, in a stock theater in Philadelphia, were imperfect and crude. On one occasion he entered to the roll of drums, began his lines, then blanked out and lost his composure. Turning to a fellow actor, he blurted, "Drat it! Who the hell am I?" Guffaws and hisses sent him racing to the wings.

It was only after Booth moved south around 1859 that he matured as an actor and could express both the fiercest and the tenderest passion and emotion on stage. A daring man who demanded realism, he delighted in leaps and bounds, sword thrusts, and fisticuffs. Southerners loved the handsome, flamboyant actor with jet-black hair, big black eyes, neatly cropped black mustache, and heavy eyelids that "gave him an Oriental touch of mystery." With impeccable manners and courtly demeanor, Booth was quickly accepted into the upper-crust social structure of the South. He dressed elegantly. He loved music and played the flute. He was an expert fencer, a gifted swordsman, a crack shot, a fine horseman, and a superb billiards player—skills appreciated by Southern gentlemen. Clara Laughlin, a writer for *McClure's* magazine, described him as "too easy to love and too hard to scold; too quick to charm and too charming to be judged." Clara Morris, an actress who once appeared with him, said, "It was impossible to see him and not admire him; it was equally impossible to know him and not love him." His extraordinary presence and magnetism made him the idol of countless women, not the least of whom were his mother and his pretty sister, Asia.

Returning to the North after the outbreak of war, Booth condemned abolitionists for what he called their treasonable activities and Lincoln for his efforts "to crush out slavery, by robbery, rapine, slaughter, and bought armies." Booth himself regarded slavery as "one of the greatest blessings that God ever bestowed upon a favored nation." But while swearing allegiance to the South, he refused to enlist in the Confederate army. He had promised his mother he would never take up arms against the Union she and all her other children staunchly supported.

Booth instead joined the Knights of the Golden Circle, a network of spies that operated between Richmond and Montreal. Performing in cities throughout the North, the actor could travel unquestioned and relay messages to and from Confederate agents. He also is believed to have participated in the Confederate underground, smuggling badly needed medicines such as quinine and laudanum from Canada through Union lines to Confederate forces. He gained the respect of Confederate agents and spies, and they viewed him as "hot property"—so hot that early in July 1864 the Confederate operatives in Canada offered Booth's services to the Richmond government. The meeting in Boston on July 26 was likely a follow-up to that offer.

Booth's first two recruits in his plot to capture Lincoln were boyhood friends Michael O'Laughlin (*left*) and Samuel B. Arnold (*right*). They had both served in the Confederate infantry.

Booth was perceived as manna from heaven. Here was a Secessionist who could move around Washington with access to almost anything. Here was a meticulous schemer who could plan and carry out Lincoln's abduction. Sanders and Clay undoubtedly urged such action, and the government seemingly approved it. Thus this clandestine operation proceeded with Booth in charge. Before July 26 Booth was primarily interested in acting and oil investments, but after the Boston discussions he was focused on assembling a team to kidnap the Yankee president. The scheme, the idea of trading Lincoln for Confederate prisoners, especially appealed to him because his childhood friend Jesse Wharton had died in a Union prison, probably from starvation or abuse, like many captives on both sides.

Around September 1, 1864, Booth met with two boyhood friends at Barnum's Hotel in Baltimore. Twenty-nine-year-old Samuel B. Arnold and twenty-four-year-old Michael O'Laughlin had served in the Confederate army and were looking for excitement. Arnold, discharged for a disability, was an unemployed clerk and farmhand who was inclined to be lazy. He had attended school with Booth at St. Timothy's Hall in Catonsville, Maryland. O'Laughlin, skilled at handling horses, worked in a Baltimore stable and had a reputation for holding his liquor. He was a small, quiet, delicate-looking man with thick black hair and a heavy black mustache. Both men were poor and more dumb than bright. They regarded Booth as rich and influential. In the actor's hotel room, they talked about the war and the steady swelling of Northern prisons with thousands and thousands of Southern prisoners. Booth spoke of Gen. Ulysses S. Grant's halting the exchanging of prisoners of war. His order crippled the South, which was running out of manpower. Booth then unfolded a stupendous scheme to capture Lincoln. He chose the word "capture" instead of "kidnap" deliberately. He knew that kidnapping was a crime, but in wartime, capturing enemy soldiers was proper and expected. Thus Lincoln as a commander in chief was liable to capture.

Booth's plan was to "hurry him out of Washington, down through intensely disloyal counties of [southern] Maryland to the Potomac, ferry him into Virginia, and carry him to Richmond." Lincoln would be a bargaining chip to blackmail the North into granting terms proposed by the Confederacy, or he could be exchanged for thousands of Confederate prisoners of war—enough possibly to help the South win the war.

Booth convinced Arnold and O'Laughlin of the plan's feasibility. He explained that Lincoln often moved about Washington unattended or with a single guard, and it would be easy to seize him—perhaps when he was en route to his summer retreat at the Soldiers Home on the outskirts of Washington. Another option would be to capture him on one of his unguarded nightly walks from the White House to the War Department. They could hide him temporarily in the cellar of an old house on Seventeenth Street. It was surrounded by two acres of high trees and shrubbery and a high brick wall. The cellar, reached by a trap door, was once used as a slave prison. Booth assured Arnold and O'Laughlin that others were willing to help. He emphasized the glory in it for all of them—the likelihood of the Confederacy's winning the war on its own terms, and the handsome rewards for the men who had saved it. Persuaded by Booth's magnetism, money, and enthusiasm, Arnold and O'Laughlin joined the "enterprise."

Interestingly, Booth seemed to be an authority on the president's habits and movements, even though the actor had been in Washington less than a year. A Washington insider likely kept him well briefed, along with the Confederate authorities in Richmond. Booth's plan and a plan approved in Richmond that same month were identical.

In September, Confederate cabinet members and probably George N. Sanders of the Canada office met and launched a team of agents to determine the feasibility of abducting Lincoln. The team was headed by Capt. Thomas Nelson Conrad, a spy and cavalry scout. He was paid four hundred dollars in gold to cover his expenses. Having lived in Washington for more than five years, Conrad knew the city well. He would be assisted by Daniel Cloud, a former classmate at Dickinson College; John "Bull" Frizzell, described by Conrad as a "broad-shouldered, rawboned . . . six-footer . . . always ready to 'cuss' out the Yankees and knock down a guard"; and Conrad's "halfbreed" servant, William, who he said was "bold as a lion."

For military support, Conrad was given papers directing Col. John S. Mosby and Lt. Charles H. Cawood "to aid and facilitate [his] movements." Cawood was the senior signal corps officer in northern Virginia. He would assist the kidnappers in crossing the Potomac and keep Richmond informed. Mosby, a small, thin man known as the "Gray Ghost," possessed one of the most brilliant minds in the history of guerrilla warfare. On his splendid gray horse, he led assaults with eyes flashing and a satirical smile showing his perfect white teeth. His cavalry, the Forty-third Battalion Virginia Partisan Rangers—commonly called Mosby's Rangers—specialized in overnight raids and in collecting intelligence on Union activities. In a famous raid on March 8, 1863, Mosby infiltrated Union lines in Fairfax County, Virginia, and captured a general and thirty-two soldiers without firing a shot. Mosby would be important not just to Conrad but also to John Wilkes Booth.

Conrad and three associates wrangled their way through Union lines and entered Washington in late September 1864. Their mission was to reconnoiter the White House and "ascertain Mr. Lincoln's customary movements," Conrad wrote twenty-eight years later. "We had to determine at what point it would be most expedient to capture the carriage and take possession of Mr. Lincoln," he added, "and then whether to move him through [southern] Maryland to the lower Potomac [Charles County] . . . or to the upper Potomac [Montgomery County] and deliver the prisoner to Mosby's [Rangers] for transportation to Richmond. . . . Having scouted the country pretty thoroughly . . . we finally concluded to take the lower Potomac." That route was also chosen by Booth.

Conrad may have been doing preparatory work for Booth, or possibly the Confederates were so intent on capturing Lincoln that two teams were sent. It is also possible that the Canadian office endorsed Booth's plan without clearing it with Richmond. Regardless, having determined that Lincoln's trips to the Soldiers Home afforded the best opportunity to abduct him, the agents positioned themselves in Lafayette Square across from the White House so they could observe his travels. Just when Conrad was ready to act, he was stunned to see Lincoln's carriage accompanied by a heavy guard. Believing his plans had been discovered, Conrad aborted the scheme.

A few days earlier, Lincoln had received an anonymous letter warning him about a likely attack on September 26. Lincoln usually ignored such threats, but an incident that occurred a month earlier may have motivated him to forward this letter to the War Department, resulting in increased protection. While headed for the Soldiers Home one evening in August,

In a memoir of Booth written by his sister, Asia, she described a troubling incident from a time when she and her mother visited his boarding school around 1850. Booth told her that he had met a gypsy in the woods who read his palm and predicted a gloomy future for him. The fortuneteller forecast: "Ah, you've a bad hand. It's full enough of sorrow. Full of trouble. You'll break hearts, they'll be nothing to you. You'll die young. . . . You're born under an unlucky star. You've got in your hand a thundering crowd of enemies. . . . You'll make a bad end. . . . You'll have a fast life—short, but a grand one. . . . I've never seen a worse hand, and I wish I hadn't seen it. . . . You'd best [become] a missionary or a priest and try to escape it."

someone had fired a shot at the president. The bullet pierced the crown of his hat as his frightened horse sped for safety.

Conrad stayed in Washington until at least November 10 and possibly met Booth near that date and handed the initiative over to him. Conrad called his own mission "a humiliating failure."

Booth, after seeing Arnold and O'Laughlin in Baltimore, was "laid up" in New York with erysipelas of the arm before traveling to Franklin, Pennsylvania, to dispose of his oil investments at a loss of six thousand dollars. He checked in at the St. Lawrence Hall in Montreal, Canada, on October 18, 1864, ostensibly to ship his theatrical wardrobe from Montreal to a Southern port, through the blockade. But he remained there ten days—much longer than necessary for finalizing these arrangements. The hotel, Montreal's best, was the unofficial headquarters of the Confederate operation in Canada. Here the so-called Canada Cabinet of the Confederacy conducted business. Booth knew these men well. His conversations with some of them were described at the conspirators' trial after the assassination.

Among the Confederate fanatics with whom Booth met in Canada were Patrick C. Martin, a blockade-runner who was the principal Confederate Secret Service agent in Montreal before Thompson arrived, and George N. Sanders, who, like Booth, regarded Lincoln as a bloody tyrant. Through Martin, Booth secured letters of introduction to two prominent Confederate sympathizers in southern Maryland: Dr. William Queen and Dr. Samuel A. Mudd—men who would secure local support and develop escape routes. Martin also accompanied Booth to the Ontario bank in Montreal where the

Booth's and Lincoln's paths crossed several times. When the actor heard that Lincoln's son Tad said (about Booth), "He makes me thrill," he sent the small boy a rose. On another occasion, when Lincoln attended the theater with some of his wife's relatives, Booth stepped near the president's box and shook his finger at him. Mary's half-sister Emilie Todd Helm commented, "He looks as if he meant that for you." The president replied, "Well, he does look pretty sharp at me, doesn't he?" On November 9, 1863, the president took Mary and a few friends to see Booth in *Marble Heart.* Lincoln applauded the actor rapturously and sent word backstage that he would like to meet him. Booth declined the interview and told the messenger he would rather have "the applause of a nigger" than that of Lincoln. Reviewing Booth's performance, the *Washington Chronicle* said he "appears to have taken our citizens by storm." Lincoln apparently agreed.

actor purchased a bank draft with $300 in gold—a substantial amount at the time—and opened an account with Montreal bills and a $255 check from a Mr. Davis, a Confederate money broker. These transactions suggest that Booth was being prepaid for a covert operation and that the money came from Confederates in Canada with approval from Richmond. The bank draft would later be recovered from Booth's body at the Garrett farm, and the account book would be found in conspirator George Atzerodt's room at the hotel in which Vice President Johnson resided.

Three credible witnesses in the later assassination investigation testified that they saw Booth and Sanders together in Montreal on various occasions, including mid-October. What the two men discussed is unknown, but given Sanders's background, he likely proposed killing Lincoln. Sanders probably assured Booth that political assassination was permissible during wartime.

An idealist, Sanders believed in political assassinations and the exploitation of chaos and disorder to topple governments. Four months earlier, in July 1864, Sanders, Clay, and James Holcombe attempted to embarrass Lincoln and influence the November election by arranging a peace conference at a hotel on the Canadian side of Niagara Falls. Lincoln ignored it but sent a Secret Service agent in civilian clothes. The agent found the hotel filled with Confederate sympathizers, one of whom—a Confederate peace commissioner—was urging a plan to assassinate Lincoln before the election to cause electoral chaos. The commissioner undoubtedly was George N. Sanders.

On October 28, 1864, Booth left Montreal and returned to New York. Whatever was discussed in Richmond, Boston, and Montreal before November obviously took into account the presidential election. Until late summer it was widely assumed that Lincoln would be defeated by Democrat George B. McClellan. If McClellan won, the South had little to fear. Peace Democrats called for the repeal of the Emancipation Proclamation, and McClellan pledged to suspend it and seek an immediate armistice.

Lincoln himself had all but conceded defeat. On September 8 Lincoln's long-time friend Leonard Swett wrote to his wife: "We are in the midst of conspiracies equal to the French Revolution." Journalist Clara Laughlin commented in 1909: "Buzzing about everybody's ears [in 1864] was the sound of conspiracy and discontent, and nearly every heart that knew bitterness blamed Lincoln as its cause."

The president's precarious political situation reached an all-time low in August. His own party was badly divided. Radical Republicans had pushed through Congress a reconstruction bill abolishing slavery and treating the

South as a conquered foe. Lincoln did not believe it was constitutional, and all cabinet members agreed with him. His pocket veto—not signing the legislation within the required time—killed the bill. The president insisted that reconstruction was a matter for him to determine, not Congress.

In response, on August 5, two Radical Republicans—Sen. Benjamin F. Wade and Rep. Henry Winter Davis—issued a manifesto that amounted to a declaration of war on the president by members of his own party. Attacking what they called Lincoln's "personal ambitions" and "sinister" motives, Wade and Davis claimed "the right and duty to check the encroachments of the Executive on the authority of Congress."

Republican political boss Thurlow Weed met with Lincoln on August 12 and told him bluntly that the president's reelection was impossible. On August 14, a secret council of Republican Party leaders met to select an alternate candidate "to save us from utter overthrow," as Horace Greeley bluntly stated. "Mr. Lincoln," Greeley asserted, "is already beaten." But the cabal could agree on only one man—Ulysses S. Grant—and he was not available. Grant was not about to challenge his commander in chief.

It was no wonder that a late-summer visitor found Lincoln deeply depressed, "indeed quite paralyzed and wilted down." To a friend Grant wrote: "I think . . . for [the president] to attempt to answer all the charges the opposition will bring against him will be like setting a maiden to work to prove her chastity." Only significant military conquests could save Lincoln's presidency.

That summer Confederate Gen. Jubal Early came dangerously close to advancing on Washington. Finally repelled, he returned to the Shenandoah Valley, an important supply area for the South. Lincoln, determined to avoid another attack from Early, pressured Grant in August to send Gen. Philip H. Sheridan's cavalry to the Valley to destroy Early's army. Sheridan did just that and more. When his campaign ended, much of the Shenandoah Valley lay in smoldering ruins, and the region was unfit to supply further Confederate operations. Sheridan's victories in September and October followed Gen. William T. Sherman's conquest of Atlanta on September 2 after a four-month campaign.

Sherman and Sheridan gave Lincoln exactly what he needed. Politics in Washington changed almost overnight. Radical Republicans abandoned their plans to choose another candidate and rallied around Lincoln. Support for the president soared and carried him from certain defeat to a landslide victory.

Election day in 1864 was dark and rainy in Washington and equally unpleasant in Richmond and Montreal after the results were known. Lincoln-haters in both the North and the South regarded his reelection as intolerable. If Lincoln could not be removed by the ballot, they would need to find other means. Shortly before the election, a Wisconsin newspaper (the *La Crosse Democrat*) edited by a Peace Democrat observed: "And if he is elected . . . for another four years, we trust some bold hand will pierce his heart with [a] dagger point for the public good."

More than ever, Southern leaders were motivated to move forward as fast as possible with their clandestine operations against Lincoln. Abduction was now crucial. With Lincoln snatched and spirited away to Richmond, the Union would surely agree to trading two hundred thousand Confederates captives for him.

Shortly after the election, Booth addressed a letter to his mother and placed it inside a safe at his sister's home in Philadelphia. It was discovered two days after the assassination. In the letter he asked for his mother's

During two weeks in November 1864, Booth rehearsed for a November 25 benefit performance of *Julius Caesar* at the Winter Garden in New York. With all three Booth brothers performing, the benefit was proclaimed the greatest theatrical event in the city's history. It was the only time the three brothers ever appeared together, and their proud mother watched them from a stage box. Ironically, John Wilkes Booth's terrorist friends from Montreal almost inadvertently wiped out the Booth family that night. Midway through the performance, smoke began to fill the theater from a hotel fire the terrorists ignited next door. The audience of nearly three thousand might have panicked and trampled performers and patrons to death had it not been for the pleading of Edwin Booth, who assured them that they were not in danger. The fire was part of a vast incendiary plot to burn twenty-two hotels in the city—a scheme that originated from the Canada Cabinet in Montreal. Fortunately for New Yorkers, the plot failed. After setting the fires, the perpetrators had closed the doors and transoms to their hotel rooms. Those actions shut off the supply of oxygen, and the fires went out. Jacob Thompson, leader of the Canada Cabinet in Montreal, lamented the failure in a December 3, 1864, letter to Secretary of State Judah P. Benjamin. The arson squad was commanded by Col. Robert M. Martin of the Tenth Kentucky Cavalry. Imprisoned a year later, Martin told two other prisoners, who happened to be errant Union soldiers, that he drank with Booth in Toronto and had been involved in discussions of actions against Lincoln.

forgiveness for breaking his pledge to her not to take up arms for the Confederacy. He wrote, "Knowing the vile and savage acts committed on my countrymen, their wives, and helpless children, . . . I have cursed my wilful idleness, and begun to deem myself a coward and to despise my own existence."

Encouraged and supported by the Confederate operatives in Canada, and possibly by Richmond, Booth was about to prove his courage. While in New York much of November to rehearse for a benefit performance of *Julius Caesar* with his two brothers, he purchased two hard-to-find weapons—seven-shot Spencer carbines—for his dreadful mission. He also picked up three pistols, several daggers, ammunition, and two sets of handcuffs. He dropped off much of this arsenal in Baltimore with his old school chum and recently acquired gang member, Samuel Arnold.

After spending more time in Canada in December, Booth stopped briefly in Baltimore to advise Arnold to buy a horse and buggy and bring them and the weapons to Washington. Returning to the capital city, Booth acquired a swift, one-eyed horse in southern Maryland and stabled it near Ford's Theatre. His preparations for the kidnapping were well under way. The Kilpatrick-Dahlgren Raid, the covert operation in Canada, and Lincoln's reelection had placed Booth at a critical juncture from which there was no turning back.

2

NABBING
LINCOLN

No man was more indispensable to Booth's plan than John H. Surratt Jr. On December 23, 1864, the two men met through one of Booth's primary contacts in southern Maryland, Dr. Samuel A. Mudd, in Washington. After Booth met with Mudd in the saloon of the National Hotel—a hangout for Secessionist gentlemen of leisure—they walked toward the boarding house operated by Surratt's widowed mother, Mary, at 541 H Street near the city's federal district. On the way, they encountered John Surratt and his close friend Louis J. Weichmann, a boarder at the house.

Twenty-year-old Surratt and twenty-two-year-old Weichmann had been schoolmates at a Catholic seminary. Surratt, five feet nine inches tall, had long hair and a goatee. He worked for an express company but was singled out by Mudd for Booth's attention because of his success as a Confederate Secret Service courier whose route included Montreal, other Northern cities, and Richmond. He was also well acquainted with the Confederate underground in southern Maryland. Surratt knew the territory and the right people. Since he was the only unmarried man on the route, he performed most of the hard riding, going often to Richmond through the thick of Federal detectives. Years afterward he explained that he had "devised various ways to carry the dispatches: sometimes in the heels of my boots, sometimes between the planks of my buggy. It was a fascinating life to me. It seemed as if I could not do too much or run too great a risk." Because of Surratt's experience, Mudd and Booth regarded him as critical to the enterprise.

Surratt's friend Weichmann was a handsome, somewhat effeminate, self-possessed young man who handled prisoners' records as a clerk in the War Department in Washington. He may have assisted Surratt in his clandestine activities. They shared a room and a bed at the boarding house when Surratt was in town. Weichmann was treated as a member of the Surratt family.

The four men convened in Booth's room at the National Hotel, where he ordered a milk punch apiece and four cigars. Surratt reported Booth's conversation with him that day in a lecture five years later in Rockville, Maryland. He quoted Booth:

> I will confide my plans to you; but before doing so I will make known to you [my] motives. In the Northern prisons are many thousands of our men whom the United States Government refuses to exchange. You know as well as I the efforts that have been made to bring about the desired exchange. Aside from the great suffering they are compelled to undergo, we are sadly in want of soldiers. We cannot spare one man, whereas the United States Government is willing to let their own soldiers remain in our prisons because she has no need of them. I have a proposition to submit to you which I think, if we can carry out, would bring about the desired exchange.

Surratt commented that "a long and ominous silence" followed Booth's preamble. Finally, Surratt asked, "What is your proposition?" Booth did not answer at first but "arose and looked under the bed, into the wardrobe, in the doorway and the passageway, and then said: 'We will have to be careful; walls have ears.' He then drew his chair close to me and in a whisper said, 'It is to capture President Lincoln, and carry him off to Richmond.'"

Surratt claimed that he exclaimed, "KIDNAP PRESIDENT LINCOLN!" and stood aghast at the proposition. He told Booth it sounded "foolhardy" and "foolish." He could not imagine "successfully seizing Mr. Lincoln in the capital of the United States, surrounded by thousands of his soldiers, and carrying him off to Richmond." But Booth was persistent. According to Surratt, he "went on to tell with what facility he could be seized in and about Washington, as, for example, in his various rides to and from the Soldiers Home, his summer residence. He entered into minute details of the proposed capture, and of the various parts to be performed by the actors in the performance." Surratt's first reaction was that he "was amazed—thunderstruck—and, in fact, frightened at the unparalleled audacity of his scheme."

LIBRARY OF CONGRESS

John H. Surratt's success as a Confederate Secret Service courier and his knowledge of the Rebel underground made him indispensable to Booth.

Later, during the trial of the Lincoln conspirators, Weichmann testified that Booth drew lines on an envelope, as if drawing a map, and that the other three men commenced a long whispered discussion around a table at a distance from which he could not hear them. Weichmann's statement, however, may not be accurate but rather an effort to separate him from culpability in the plot. Was Weichmann ordered to a corner of the room while the others met around a table? Possibly, but not likely.

After two days' reflection following the meeting, Surratt told Booth he "was willing to try it," because he believed it "practical at the time." Surratt further justified his decision: "Where is there a young man in the North, with one spark of patriotism in his heart, who would not have with enthusiastic ardour joined in any undertaking for the capture of Jefferson Davis, and brought him to Washington? There is not one who would not have done so! So I was led on by a desire to assist the South in gaining her independence. I had no hesitation in taking part in anything honorable that might tend toward the accomplishment of that object."

Surratt quit his job at the express company and gave full attention to the abduction plot, with the exception of courier services for the Confederate government—errands that may have been directly related to the plot.

During a brief break for Christmas with his family in Baltimore, Booth unsuccessfully attempted to recruit actor-friend Samuel Chester to join the conspiracy. Booth told Chester the abduction might take place at Ford's Theatre, and if so, he needed someone who, on signal, would open the back door so the captors might rush out quickly. Chester refused to participate.

Booth spent New Year's Eve in the capital city, and shortly thereafter Surratt introduced him to his mother and sister at their boarding house. Both were impressed by the actor's charm, fame, and passion to save the South.

Booth's meticulous planning and Surratt's commitment to the cause led to the following:

1. Surratt and Thomas Harbin (another Confederate Secret Service agent introduced to Booth by Mudd) purchased a flat-bottomed boat at Port Tobacco, Maryland, on January 14. With a capacity of fifteen persons, it would be used to transport Lincoln across the river and into Virginia. To conceal the boat and serve as its captain, Harbin and Surratt recruited German-born George Atzerodt, a wiry thirty-year-old carriage painter at Port Tobacco. As a part-time ferryman, Atzerodt had often assisted Surratt and other Confederate spies in crossing the Potomac with contraband mail and dispatches. Atzerodt's knowledge of all the creeks and inlets in the area made him a valuable asset.

2. Booth rented a stable in the alley behind Ford's Theatre and hired carpenter Edman Spangler to put in two stalls and raise the roof to accommodate the buggy Samuel Arnold was bringing down from Baltimore. Spangler was a thirty-nine-year-old scene-shifter, carpenter, and stagehand at Ford's. He was also a long-time friend of the Booth family.

3. Surratt recruited a close friend, David E. Herold, age twenty-two. Herold was familiar with the poorly mapped roads of southern Maryland that Booth would need to use. While pursuing the sport of bird hunting, Herold had visited the Surratt tavern—a small inn thirteen miles from Washington at Surrattsville, Maryland. Mary Surratt had vacated it when she moved to Washington; she rented it to John M. Lloyd, a former policeman. Herold renewed his friendship with John Surratt in the capital city, where Herold lived with his mother and seven sisters. His recently deceased father had for twenty years been principal clerk of the store at the navy yard. Herold himself was an unemployed pharmacy clerk, and he had once worked at Thompson's Drug Store in Washington and delivered a bottle of castor oil to the White House. Easygoing and easily bored, Herold appeared dimwitted and timid, and he had an annoying habit of shifting from foot to foot when someone was talking to him. Actually he was very clever and had attended Georgetown College.

4. In need of a strong man who could overcome any resistance from Lincoln, Booth and Surratt were handed twenty-year-old Lewis Powell (a.k.a. Paine) by Col. John S. Mosby at the direction of a high official in the Confederacy, presumably Secretary of State Judah P. Benjamin. Powell stood six feet one and a half inches tall and had a brawny chest and muscles like iron. Naturally violent, he placed no value on anyone's life, including his own. He used a skull as an ash tray and claimed that it was the head of a Union soldier he had killed. Often portrayed as a monster, Powell was regarded by his contemporaries as personable, gentlemanly, and a practical joker. A Confederate general called him "chivalrous, generous, and gallant"—characteristics one might expect of the son of a Baptist clergyman who had had a strict religious upbringing. Powell was even considering the ministry as a career at the time the Civil War broke out. Instead he lied about his age (he was seventeen but said that he was nineteen), joined the Florida infantry, and saw action at Yorktown, Seven Pines, Gaines's Mill, Antietam, and Chancellorsville before being shot through the right wrist and captured at Gettysburg. With probable assistance from a nurse who had Southern sympathies—Maggie Branson—Powell escaped from a military field hospital at Gettysburg and headed south in search of his Florida regiment. Instead he joined Mosby's Rangers, a special unit of regular soldiers tremendously effective in carrying out hit-and-run raids and ambushes behind enemy lines. A year and a half later, in January 1865, Mosby handpicked Powell to be part of the team to carry out the abduction of Lincoln. Powell later admitted he had worked with the Confederate Secret Service on the plot. While housed at the Baltimore boarding house of the Branson family, Powell was introduced to John Surratt, and Surratt later introduced him to Booth. Shortly, Powell got into a fracas with a black maid at the Branson home and almost beat her to death. Brought before a provost marshal, he was ordered to sign an oath of allegiance to the United States. He did, using the name Lewis Paine, an alias he had permanently adopted.

Although Paine had been hardened by combat, he did have certain values. Before joining Mosby's Rangers, he briefly served with Harry S. Gilmore's raiders but deserted them after they robbed and roughed up a group of Jewish peddlers. He told Maggie Branson he was above such simple thievery. On the other hand, he once robbed a store after sending the shopkeeper in pursuit of an innocent passerby.

Booth and Surratt now had an action team. Each man had a specific skill or knowledge. They were tied together by Southern loyalties and

Booth's magnetism and money. The actor showered them with food, housing, new clothes, and liberal quantities of drink when they were in Washington. Paine, Booth, and Surratt apparently developed an especially close camaraderie. With his only desire that of pleasing Booth, Paine would be a dependable hit man available for any duty Booth assigned to him. All members, in fact, were ready to serve their leader.

Perhaps more than anything else, Booth wanted to be a Confederate hero. To bolster that image, he explained his kidnapping rationale in an impassioned letter he sealed and entrusted to his brother-in-law. With the subtlety of a sledgehammer, Booth attacked Lincoln, applauded the South, and defended his upcoming plans. Among other things he wrote:

> This country was formed for the white, not for the black, man. And looking upon African slavery from the same standpoint held by the noble framers of our Constitution, I, for one, have ever considered it one of the greatest blessings (both for themselves and us) that God ever bestowed upon a favoured nation. Witness heretofore our wealth and power, witness their elevation and enlightenment above their race elsewhere. I have lived among it most of my life, and have seen less harsh treatment from master to man than I have beheld in the North from father to son. Yet heaven knows, no one would be more

George Atzerodt (*left*) possessed a knowledge of the creeks and inlets of the Potomac River that would be valuable to Booth in transporting the captured president across the river to Virginia. Lewis Paine (a.k.a Powell, *right*), a Baptist preacher's son, brought strength, courage, and fierce loyalty to Booth's team.

willing to do for the Negro race than I, could I but see a way to better their condition. But Lincoln's policy is only preparing the way for their total annihilation. . . . My love (as things stand today) is for the South alone. Nor do I deem it a dishonour in attempting to make for her a prisoner of this man, to whom she owes so much of her misery.

Surratt presumably reported the completion of Booth's team to Confederate leaders in Richmond in late January 1865. He met with Secretary of State Benjamin and possibly Mosby to finalize strategies and logistics. The government would alert operatives on the chosen escape route, especially those managing clandestine signal stations. Mosby would organize the Virginia side of the Potomac to receive the hostage and his captors.

Benjamin, who was close to Jefferson Davis, was probably a central figure in the enterprise. Unlike other members of the Confederate cabinet, he was not particularly interested in preserving slavery. In early January 1865 Benjamin had sent a diplomatic emissary to England with the promise that the South would grant a general emancipation of the slaves in exchange for British intervention in the war. For this action, he narrowly escaped censure by the Confederate Senate. Outspoken but clear-sighted, this former Yale student and U.S. senator from Louisiana once quipped that many Confederate soldiers were barefoot not because the army hadn't supplied them with shoes but because they had traded them for whiskey. While he was almost universally disliked in the South, Benjamin pressed forward with plans to save the South by any means available.

With Petersburg then under siege by Grant and the likely need for the government to withdraw from Richmond, Davis and Benjamin were indeed desperate. According to Robert E. Lee's nephew, Fitzhugh Lee, it was hoped that Lee's army, "rapidly moving from his lines, could form a junction with General Joseph E. Johnston . . . and all troops in the Department of South Carolina, Georgia, and Florida. Lee and Johnston were then to assail Sherman before Grant could get to his relief, as the question of supplying his enormous army, moving from its base to the interior, would retard him after the first few days' march."

Davis later recalled a conference with Lee on February 26 or March 4:

He [Lee] stated that the circumstances had forced upon him the conclusion that the evacuation of Petersburg was but a question of time. . . . If we had to retreat it should be in a southwardly direction toward the country from which we were drawing supplies, and from which a large portion of our forces had been

derived. . . . The programme was to retire to Danville, at which place supplies
should be collected and a junction made with the troops under General J. E.
Johnston, the combined force to be hurled upon Sherman in North Carolina,
with the hope of defeating him before Grant could come to his relief. Then the
more southern States, freed from pressure and encouraged by this success, it
was expected, would send large reinforcements to the army, and Grant, drawn
far from his base of supplies into the midst of a hostile population, it was hoped
might yet be defeated.

Davis knew that timing was critical. Grant would be holed up during the
winter, but with the arrival of spring, Grant could be expected to overpower
the Confederate positions at Petersburg and Richmond. The Confederate
president expected that to occur between late March and late April. Thus
Lincoln had to be captured before late March, while Richmond was still controlled by the Confederacy. Once Lincoln was in hand, negotiations favorable
to the South were likely. In addition, the action would surely throw Washington into turmoil, stymie or interrupt communications between Grant and
Sherman, and improve Lee's chance of success.

Mud, or the lack thereof, was another factor. The last freeze in the Richmond area normally occurred in early April, after which the roads would
become usable for supply trains to feed the troops. Author William A. Tidwell pointed out that Lee could be more flexible because he could move
along a railroad in Confederate territory while Grant would need to bring
his supplies with him, slowing his movement under muddy conditions. For
Lee, the best time to move his army would be around the first of April.

That meant that Lincoln had to be captured no later than the end of
March. The authors of *Come Retribution* indicated that by early March, at the
latest, everything was ready in Virginia for this operation. Escape routes
were protected, and a special train was available. Further, it was hoped that
Lincoln's capture would make it unnecessary to evacuate Richmond.

Apparently, Booth's first plan was to capture Lincoln at Ford's Theatre
on or about January 18. The theater was like a second home to the actor,
and he roamed the building at will. He had earned the friendship of the
stage crew and others who worked there by buying them drinks after
shows, complimenting them, and generally treating them like friends. As a
result, they respected him and would gladly help him when asked. Booth
could count on them to bring down the lights and to clear a path backstage.

Thus Booth devised a plan to abduct the president and assigned various
tasks to his team. At a signal Surratt would shut off the master gas valve

under the stage, extinguishing the lights. Arnold would seize the president in his box seat. Atzerodt would handcuff him and secure him with ropes. Arnold, Atzerodt, and Booth would lower Lincoln onto the stage into the hands of Lewis Paine. The others would jump down, and together they would load the president into a waiting carriage and escape over the Navy Yard Bridge and head for Port Tobacco, Maryland, twenty-nine miles away. There Atzerodt would ferry the party across the Potomac to Virginia.

Reportedly, Surratt regarded the plan as impractical. Did Booth actually expect the spectators to remain seated while the traitorous scheme was carried out? Still, Booth gave the go-ahead. Unfortunately for the schemers, one of two things happened, depending on the exact night the capture was to have occurred. Historians disagree on the date. Either Mother Nature intervened with a ferocious storm that kept Lincoln in the White House, or Lincoln went to Grover's Theatre instead of Ford's that night.

What evolved later in Booth's mind was a more practical plan based on the one conceived by Thomas N. Conrad—capture Lincoln on his way to or from the Soldiers Home. It was a plan all of the conspirators counted on. The scheme called for intercepting the carriage, overpowering the coachman, and chloroforming or gagging Lincoln. Disguised in Yankee uniforms, they would take over the carriage and rush Lincoln out of the city, into southeastern Maryland, and across the Potomac into Virginia. In Maryland they would stop at Mary Surratt's tavern for supplies and weapons. To trip up any pursuers, they would stretch wires across the road near the tavern. At Port Tobacco, where Atzerodt waited with a flatboat, the kidnappers would cross into Virginia. Once in Confederate territory, Booth expected the spy network to channel them safely to Richmond. It was a careful, well-thought-out plan.

When Surratt's buddy Weichmann returned to the boarding house from his work at the War Department on Wednesday, March 15, he went up to the attic over his room and saw Surratt and Paine "sitting together on the bed surrounded by spurs, bowie knives, and revolvers." When he told Mary Surratt what he had seen, she supposedly reminded him that since her son John was in the habit of "going into the country he had to have those things as a protection." Weichmann's own involvement in, or knowledge of, the plot is unclear. He later stated that his observations convinced him that "something devious" was going on. Some writers believe that Weichmann wanted to join the plot, but both Surratt and Booth turned him down because he could neither ride nor shoot, and after being rejected, Weichmann was motivated to betray the Surratts.

Anderson Cottage at the Soldiers Home was Lincoln's summer residence. It was three miles north of the White House. Only a last-minute change in Lincoln's plans prevented him from being kidnapped near there.

At a meeting of the conspirators that week, Surratt expressed his fear that the plot was known in Washington and suggested they abandon the effort. He noted that the government was building a stockade on the Navy Yard Bridge, with the gates opening toward the south, "as though they expected danger from within, and not from without." Everyone but Booth seemed inclined to agree. The actor rose, slammed his fist onto the table, spewed some obscenities, and exclaimed: "Well, gentlemen, if the worst comes to the worst, I shall know what to do." Harsh words and even threats then passed among the group, according to Surratt's version of the meeting. Four of the six rose to leave, one saying, "If I understand you to intimate anything more than the capture of Mr. Lincoln, I, for one, will bid you goodbye." Surratt claimed that the others nodded their acquiescence and prepared to leave. Booth, perceiving probably that he had gone too far, asked their pardon, saying he "had drunk too much champagne." Arnold was ready to withdraw from the group unless they executed their plan that week. After some wrangling, Surratt recalled, "everything was amicably arranged, and we separated at five o'clock in the morning."

On March 17, with time fast running out for the Confederacy, Booth learned on short notice that Lincoln was to visit Campbell General Hospital to attend an afternoon performance of *Still Waters Run Deep* for invalid servicemen. The hospital was near the Soldiers Home, north of Washington and off a deserted stretch of road. Booth regarded the setting as suitable. With less than an hour's notice, according to Surratt, six of the seven conspirators—Booth, Arnold, Atzerodt, O'Laughlin, Paine, and Surratt—gathered at a restaurant near the hospital. They would lie in wait for the president's carriage as it was returning, spring from the bushes by the roadside at a lonely spot, overpower and handcuff Lincoln and his carriage driver, and drive swiftly toward southern Maryland, the Potomac, and the boat secured by Atzerodt. Somewhere in Maryland, Herold would meet them with weapons.

There are two versions of what actually happened. In one, Booth rode to the hospital to be sure Lincoln was there. He wasn't and wasn't expected, and Booth returned to the restaurant disgusted. In the other version—told by Surratt—the conspirators waited patiently in the woods near the hospital. Shortly, an elegant carriage approached. Thinking it must be Lincoln's, Booth and another rider, probably Surratt, rode alongside and peered inside. Surratt later said, "To our great disappointment, the president was not there, but one of the government officials—Mr. Chase, if I mistake not." That would be Salmon P. Chase, the chief justice of the Supreme Court.

Whichever version is accurate, the outcome was the same. Booth was as angry as a wolf denied its prey. He had been foiled again. His painstaking plans had gone for naught. At the last minute Lincoln had changed his mind. He had decided to speak to an Indiana regiment newly arrived from the front and to present a captured Confederate flag to the state's governor. The ceremony took place at Booth's hotel!

Weichmann later testified that when he returned home for dinner that evening, he found nobody there except a mulatto boy and Mary Surratt. The boy reported that John Surratt had gone horseback riding with six other gentlemen, including Booth, Paine, Atzerodt, Herold, and two others he did not know. Mary Surratt, said Weichmann, was "weeping bitterly," and he tried to console her. She told him, "John is gone away; go down to dinner, and make the best of your dinner you can." Perhaps he had left her a note about the abduction plan and indicated he would be leaving the country.

To her surprise, about 6:30, Surratt, Paine, and Booth returned. Weichmann said that they came into his room one at a time. Surratt, "very much excited," arrived first. "He rushed into the room. He had a revolver in his hand—a four-barreled revolver." The boarder asked, "What is the matter?"

Surratt replied, "I will shoot anyone that comes into this room. My prospects are gone; my hopes are blighted; I want something to do; can you get me a clerkship?"

The others entered the room within minutes, and all seemed wild and anxious. "Booth . . . walked around the room three or four times very frantically," Weichmann noted, "and did not notice me. He had a whip in his hand. I spoke to him, and, recognizing me, he said, 'I did not see you.' The three then went upstairs into the back room, in the third story, and must have remained there about thirty minutes, when they left the house together."

Arnold, Paine, and O'Laughlin headed back to Baltimore, feeling the "enterprise" was over. Paine would not return to the boarding house until after the assassination.

Activities at the Surratt house before and on March 17 aroused Weichmann's suspicions, or so he said. He made a confidant of Capt. Daniel H. L. Gleason, a fellow clerk at a desk next to his in the War Department. Weichmann claimed to have told Gleason before March 17 that Booth was a "secesh" sympathizer and mentioned snatches of conversations he had overheard. "Captain, what do you think of all this?" Weichmann asked. "Do you think they could be blockade-runners? Do you think any party could attempt the capture of President Lincoln?" Gleason reportedly "laughed and hooted at the idea."

On the morning of March 18, Weichmann repeated Surratt's comments to Gleason, by which he inferred that "Surratt's mysterious and incomprehensible business had failed." They pondered what Surratt and the others might have been up to, perhaps bearing dispatches or breaking open the Old Capitol Prison. "But," said Weichmann, "we hit upon nothing." The two men agreed that strange things were happening with Surratt and perhaps the information needed to be reported, but they apparently decided only "to keep an eye on [the conspirators] and if anything again came up to report it promptly to the authorities, secure horses if need be, and pursue them."

After the assassination, Gleason allegedly advised Stanton to summon Weichmann as a witness, but Gleason himself was never called to the stand. Thus there was no confirmation of Weichmann's statement that the two clerks had conferred and decided not to alarm the government.

In a 1911 memoir Gleason recalled several discussions with Weichmann about Booth and other Confederate sympathizers who came and went at the boarding house at all hours of the day and night. Gleason said that Weichmann told him he had discovered pistols and knives at the house, and that when he confronted Surratt about them, Surratt said they would be used in a plan to kidnap Lincoln and his cabinet on inauguration day, March 4. Gleason said that he was "stunned and amazed" and that further talks with

Weichmann convinced him that "the only thing to do was to see Mr. Stanton." Instead, knowing that Stanton "was rather explosive in his language and overbearing in his temper," Gleason passed the information to his roommate, who was on the staff of the military commander of Washington, Gen. Christopher C. Augur. The roommate then arranged through channels to inform Stanton, who immediately ordered two companies of cavalry to accompany Lincoln's carriage.

Weichmann also reported his suspicions to a U.S. enrolling officer, known only as McDavitt, "who in turn had notified the authorities," according to Gleason's report of what Weichmann told him. But when nothing unusual happened at the inauguration, Gleason and Weichmann assumed they had been misled. If true, it explains their reluctance to report the suspicions they discussed on March 18 after the failed kidnap attempt.

Was Stanton informed of these suspicions? Were names given to him? Gleason's memoir suggests that the secretary of war was informed. Yet historians have debated these questions for more than a century. Many see no reason to doubt Gleason's reminisces. In fact, nearly all those who have investigated the assassination state unequivocally that the War Department was aware of Booth's conspiracy to kidnap Lincoln. Some say that Stanton was aware of the rumors, but no one in the War Department took them seriously. Yet if they didn't take them seriously, why, after the assassination, did they quickly seek and arrest those involved only in the abduction plot?

In the highly praised book *Kennedy and Lincoln*, John K. Lattimore concluded that Weichmann's earlier warnings enabled authorities to go directly to the Surratt boarding house after the assassination. In *Twenty Days*, authors Dorothy and Philip Kunhardt claim that Stanton knew of the plot but "paid it no heed," except to keep an eye on Arnold and O'Laughlin. If Stanton did know about Booth's plan and failed to round up the plotters or keep them under surveillance, he was guilty of remarkably poor judgment—judgment poor enough to get Lincoln killed. At the conspirators'

Guerrilla leader William C. Quantrill and a band of men set out for Washington in early 1864 to kidnap or kill Lincoln. Federal troops intercepted them in Kentucky on May 10, and in the ensuing battle Quantrill was mortally wounded. He survived for twenty days. When Quantrill's lover, Kate Clarke, visited him, he handed her everything he had—five hundred dollars in gold. She did not wait for him to die. Instead, she took the first coach to St. Louis and used the gold to set up a brothel.

trial after the assassination—when Stanton unquestionably was aware of the kidnapping efforts—he chose to ignore the abduction and focus only on the assassination. Did he do so, at least in part, to mask his own incompetence?

Historian William Hanchett is more critical of Gleason's 1911 memoir, because it differs markedly from a deposition Gleason made for the War Department under oath on April 18, 1865. At that time Gleason reported that Weichmann told him he was acquainted with some young blockade-runners who were engaged in a different, suspicious enterprise. "He never gave me to understand what the nature of the plot was," Gleason asserted. Then he advised Weichmann to join the group and find out what they were about, but to get the provost marshal's approval before doing so. Weichmann regarded the idea as too risky. Then Weichmann later reported to him that the group had dispersed and that their plans apparently had been abandoned. The key sentence in this disposition followed: "*After* the assassination of Mr. Lincoln, I told the authorities of this." In his 1865 statement, Gleason made no reference to passing any information to Stanton weeks before the assassination, which he claimed to have done in his 1911 memoir.

Is it not possible—even likely—that in 1865 Gleason was intimidated by Stanton and would not say anything that embarrassed the secretary? For Gleason to state publicly that he had informed Stanton of a plot and that Stanton ignored the information would come perilously close to implicating Stanton in the conspiracy. By 1911 Stanton had been dead for forty-two years, and Gleason had nothing to fear.

In 1865 Gleason's first objective was undoubtedly self-protection. If the truth served his best interests, then he could have stated it without fear. If, however, the truth risked endangering him, it would have to be replaced with a safer version. The evidence shows that Gleason congratulated Weichmann for his trial testimony, which "completely changed my opinion [of you]." At the trial, Weichmann testified that he and Gleason had speculated only casually about the activities at the Surratt house and that Gleason "laughed and hooted" at the possibility of a kidnapping. Taking the whole matter lightly, there was no reason to tell Stanton or any other authority figure. That position got both men off the hook.

Author Osborn H. Oldroyd, however, took a somewhat different view, based on Weichmann's account of the conversations. In his *Assassination of Abraham Lincoln,* Oldroyd asserted that Gleason was alarmed by whatever Weichmann told him, and that it was Gleason who made the decision not to inform Stanton, despite being convinced "something wrong" was taking place. Under that scenario, Gleason's failure to communicate made him partly responsible for Lincoln's murder, if one assumes that Stanton would have acted upon a report from Gleason. Booth biographer Francis Wilson went a step further, calling Gleason's decision "as brilliant a bit of stupidity as could be imagined."

Weichmann wrote his own history in 1901 (not published until 1975) and repeated the version of the conversations he gave at the trial: "My only regret in this whole affair is that . . . he [Gleason] and I did not then [March 18] go to Secretary Stanton and inform him." They didn't go, Weichmann said, because he could not believe that his friends, the Surratts, could be involved in any plan to harm the president.

So what did Stanton know, and when did he know it? The answers to these questions remain elusive.

On March 18—the night after the Campbell Hospital kidnap failure— Booth gave his last stage performance—a benefit at Ford's Theatre for his actor-friend John McCullough. Booth handed Surratt two tickets, and Surratt invited Weichmann to go with him. Atzerodt and Herold also were there and dined afterward with the other two. Three days later Booth caught a train for New York, one of the nerve centers for the Confederacy's clandestine activities. John Surratt, meanwhile, was escorting Confederate courier Sarah Slater on the final leg of a trip from Montreal to Richmond with dispatches. She had arrived in Montreal on March 17 with urgent messages from Secretary of State Benjamin. The required responses were given to Slater, and she left with them for Richmond. Slater stayed often in Washington, spent at least two nights at the Surratt boarding house, reportedly saw Booth "a good deal" according to Atzerodt, and apparently brought communications to him from Richmond and Canada. She was never apprehended.

Back in Washington from New York, Booth telegraphed O'Laughlin and urged him to return to the capital with Samuel Arnold. "Come on, with or without him. . . . Don't fail," Booth urged. Whatever scheme the actor had in mind, it must have fallen through. Arnold and O'Laughlin were not interested in any further kidnapping attempts. Arnold wrote to Booth on Monday, March 27:

When I left you, you stated we would not meet in a month or so. Therefore I made application for employment, an answer to which I shall receive during the week. I told my parents I had ceased with you. Can I, then, under existing circumstances, come as you request? You know full well that the G—t

[Government] suspicions something is going on there; therefore, the undertaking is becoming more complicated. Why not, for the present, desist, for various reasons, which, if you look into, you can readily see, without my making any mention thereof. . . . Time more propitious will arrive yet. Do not act rashly or in haste. I would prefer your first query, go and see how it will be taken in R—d [Richmond] and ere long I shall be better prepared to be with you again.

The letter was signed, "Your friend, Sam." It was discovered in Booth's hotel room a few hours after the assassination.

At a meeting with Arnold and O'Laughlin on March 31, Booth too seemed to be disgusted with the whole affair. According to Arnold, Booth told them he had given up the kidnapping plan forever. By March 31 Lincoln wasn't even in Washington; he was at City Point, Virginia, conferring with Grant. Kidnapping was no longer a viable option. Something else had to be done to disrupt the Union command and cause confusion in Washington. Booth hinted at the possibility of murder, but Arnold, O'Laughlin, and Surratt wanted no part of that. They had come aboard for kidnapping, not murder. Booth was furious with them for deserting him and with himself for wasting time and money. He began to drink excessively, reportedly guzzling a quart of brandy daily to calm his nerves. He could still depend on three important men—Atzerodt, Herold, and Paine—as well as the Confederate spy network in Maryland and Virginia and John Surratt's mother, Mary, who provided a headquarters for the conspirators in two locations: her boarding house in Washington and the tavern she owned at Surrattsville.

From April 2 through April 7 Booth was in New York and Boston, the latter for an apparent meeting with Confederate officials from Canada—a meeting at which Lincoln's assassination probably was the major topic. Atzerodt later revealed that around April 8 Booth's group talked seriously of ways to *eliminate* the tyrant Lincoln. Thus assassination appeared to be emerging as the only option for the Confederacy and for John Wilkes Booth.

3

EXPLOSIVE
MEASURES

LOUD, BELLIGERENT, AND INTOXICATED, Booth struck a table with his fist and complained to actor-friend Samuel K. Chester that he had missed "a splendid chance to kill the president on the 4th of March," the date of Lincoln's second inauguration. Booth had attended the event by securing an official pass through the assistance of his secret fiancée, Lucy Hale, daughter of Sen. John P. Hale of New Hampshire. The Hales and their two daughters lived in the same hotel where Booth stayed—the National. On Inauguration Day, Booth stood in the rotunda of the Capitol as Lincoln passed through to the portico, and during the ceremony he stood no more than fifty feet above Lincoln on the balustrade.

As a drizzle fell on that raw, wet Saturday, Booth heard only the parts of Lincoln's speech that would have antagonized Southerners and revitalized their desire for retribution: "Yet, if God wills that [the war] continue until all the wealth piled by the bondsman's two hundred and fifty years of unrequited toil shall be sunk, and until every drop of blood drawn with the lash shall be paid by another drawn with the sword, as was said three thousand years ago, so still it must be said, 'the judgments of the Lord are true and righteous altogether.'" For those who found that sentence offensive, the next sentence, a magnanimous statement of tolerance, probably fell on deaf ears:

"With malice toward none, with charity for all, with firmness in the right as God gives us to see the right, let us strive on to finish the work we are in, to bind up the nation's wounds, to care for him who shall have borne the battle and for his widow and his orphan, to do all which may achieve a just and lasting peace among ourselves and with all nations." As the president finished, he kissed the Bible, and the sun broke out, as if the heavens were sending a message.

Booth's thoughts were not heaven-sent, however. In early April he had begun to ponder Lincoln's demise. John Surratt, meanwhile, had again escorted Confederate courier Sarah Slater to Richmond, arriving during the night of March 31 with responses from Montreal to Judah P. Benjamin's messages. Surratt reported to Benjamin and was given more dispatches to carry to Canada and two hundred dollars in gold for expenses. On the return trip he stopped briefly in Washington to change clothes, dine on oysters at a downtown eatery with Weichmann, and tell him good-bye, saying he would sleep at the National Hotel that night and leave by an early morning train for Montreal. That was the last they would see of each other for two years. Surratt would soon be on the run.

It is unknown what Benjamin discussed with Surratt, what was contained in the messages to Montreal, or whether Surratt met with Booth before the actor left for New York to meet with some Confederate operatives. Supposedly, Booth departed Washington on April 2, and Surratt arrived in Washington on April 3, the day on which the fall of Richmond was celebrated with great rejoicing. Beyond any doubt, Surratt conferred with Confederate officials in Richmond near the time when they determined that their desperate situation required desperate measures. They knew they would have to evacuate Richmond momentarily and that two climactic battles were imminent—between Lee and Grant in Virginia, and between Joseph E. Johnston and William T. Sherman in North Carolina. The last remaining hope for Confederate victory required a massive disruption of the Union leadership and communication. If that could be achieved, then perhaps Lee, after evacuating Richmond, could link up with Johnston's army in North Carolina and defeat Sherman and Grant. Under this scenario, the target window for Lincoln's assassination would be April 10 to 15, during the time of the anticipated evacuation. This projection, however, proved to be off by more than a week.

The desperate situation led to a plan to infiltrate a select team of soldiers and explosive experts into Washington to work with Booth and/or to

LIBRARY OF CONGRESS

On April 9 Robert E. Lee surrendered his army, which at the time amounted to less than one-sixth of the Confederates then under arms. Neither Jefferson Davis nor, for that matter, John Wilkes Booth believed that Lee's capitulation was the end of the Confederacy. In Booth's mind "something decisive and great" had to be done to offset Lee's surrender.

blow up the White House at a time when Lincoln and his cabinet were in session. If that did not disrupt the North, nothing would. Apparently regarded earlier as a contingency plan should the kidnapping effort fail, the bombing of the White House was likely the subject of the memorandums going back and forth between Richmond and Montreal.

George Atzerodt mentioned the project during his confession after the assassination.

> Booth said he had met a party in New York who would get the president certain. They were going to mine the end of the President's House near the War Department. They knew an entrance to accomplish it through. Spoke about getting friends of the president to get up an entertainment and they would mix in it, have a serenade and thus get at the president and party. These were understood to be projects. Booth said if he did not get him quick the New York crowd would. Booth knew the New York party apparently by a sign. He [Atzerodt] saw Booth give some kind of sign to two parties on the Avenue who he said were from New York.

Needing money to fund a clandestine operation to blow up the White House, Judah P. Benjamin secured Jefferson Davis's signature on April 1 for the issuance of a treasury warrant for fifteen hundred dollars in gold from the Secret Service account. Of the total, two hundred dollars probably went to Surratt and the remainder to explosives expert Sgt. Thomas F. "Frank" Harney and Col. John S. Mosby. As a key figure in the Confederate Torpedo Bureau, Harney had successfully used explosive devices—mines, subterra shells, and hand grenades—to inflict Union casualties and destroy supplies and equipment. Mosby headed a unit that not only supported Lee but also undertook special missions for the government with great skill and ingenuity. After Lee's surrender, Mosby's troops and the Confederate Signal Corps' secret line continued to carry out their responsibilities and were prepared to assist Booth after the assassination.

A few days before the fall of Richmond on April 3, there were two significant departures from Richmond: John Surratt returned to Montreal by way of Washington, and a demolition team headed by Harney reported to Mosby in Fauquier County in northern Virginia. To infiltrate Harney and his special ordnance of fuses and detonators into Washington, Mosby created a force of about 150 men. Several of them were Marylanders who had recently joined the rangers. Harney and his escorts left Fauquier County on April 8 and within two days were fifteen miles from Washington, at Burke Station in Fairfax County. By then Lee had surrendered, but Mosby's men did not know that. Nor did they know that a detachment from the Eighth Illinois Cavalry was lurking in the area. The cavalry surprised and routed Harney's protectors and captured Harney and three others on April 10. They were taken to the Old Capitol Prison in Washington.

Had sexy gossip not been bypassed by the press, Booth's amorous conquests would have embarrassed a U.S. senator. Booth's favorite mistress was Ella Turner, a petite, nineteen-year-old redhead with whom he regularly slept naked while secretly engaged to a senator's daughter. When Turner heard that Booth had shot Lincoln, she placed his photograph under her pillow and a rag soaked with chloroform around her head. Luckily, a prostitute found her and called a physician, who revived her. After Booth had been killed, photographs of five women were found on his body. Four were actresses; the other was Lucy Hale, his secret fiancée. She was the daughter of Republican Sen. John P. Hale, a prominent abolitionist whom Booth naturally despised. Secretary of War Edwin M. Stanton kept Lucy's involvement with Booth a secret to avoid humiliating her family. She then shocked her parents by announcing that she and Booth had been engaged. Stanton again kept the revelation out of the press. Edwin Booth later released a letter Lucy wrote to him. In it she avowed she would have gladly married Booth on the gallows.

The purpose of Harney's mission was first published in 1907 in a memoir by Col. Edward H. Ripley of the Ninth Vermont Infantry. His troops were among the first to enter Richmond on April 3 after the evacuation. On April 4 a soldier, William H. Snyder, from the Confederate Torpedo Bureau told Ripley he viewed the war as over and had a problem of conscience. Under oath, he said that he was concerned about Lincoln's safety because he knew "that a party had just been dispatched from Raine's [George W. Rains's] torpedo bureau on a secret mission, which vaguely he understood was aimed at the head of the Yankee government, and he wished to put Mr. Lincoln on his guard [because he] was in great danger."

Ripley, who was impressed with Snyder's intelligence and appearance, met with Lincoln the following morning aboard the *Malvern,* anchored in the James River at Richmond. The Vermonter read Snyder's statement to the president and urged him to meet with the soldier. Lincoln declined, saying, "I cannot bring myself to believe that any human being lives who would do me harm."

Booth probably learned of Harney's capture through the notorious Old Capitol Prison grapevine. If not, he realized something was amiss when Harney and his men did not show up in the capital city. Without Harney, with Richmond evacuated a week earlier than expected—on April 2—and with Lee's having surrendered, Booth had a dilemma. Using a logic similar to that which motivated Jefferson Davis to move farther south and toward the

Rather than visit the White House, Sgt. Frank Harney was welcomed as a guest at the Old Capitol Prison.

west, Booth did not feel that Lee's surrender made the Confederacy a lost cause. He knew there were other Confederate armies in the field, including Johnston's in North Carolina. In fact, Lee had surrendered less than one-sixth of the Confederates in arms on April 9. As Lincoln's secretaries John Nicolay and John Hay later wrote: "The armies that still remained to them . . . were capable of strenuous resistance and of incalculable mischief. Leading minds on both sides thought the war might be indefinitely prolonged." Davis certainly favored that position.

With Harney derailed, perhaps Booth felt he could enhance Southern hopes and accomplish Harney's goal by killing Lincoln, Vice President Andrew Johnson, and Secretary of State William Seward. Strangely, the second most important official in Washington—Secretary of War Stanton—apparently was not on Booth's list. Regardless, since Booth originally planned to kidnap only one official—the president—his mental jump to murdering three officials logically followed his learning of the failure of Harney's mission.

Booth no longer had any source for new orders or suggestions to aid his conspiracy—at least not from the Confederate government, which was on the run. He still had the Confederate underground in Maryland and Virginia and whatever assistance might be available in Washington. He also had his inflamed imagination, a fervid desire for hero status, and a misguided belief that something decisive and great could still save the Confederacy.

Meanwhile, Confederate Secretary of State Judah P. Benjamin, who endorsed the scheme of blowing up the White House to create chaos in the Union government, burned all of his intelligence records and escaped to England.

4

A CHANGE
IN PLANS

NEWS OF LEE'S SURRENDER at Appomattox Court House generated unprecedented joy and celebration throughout the North. In Washington the announcement came at daybreak on the rainy morning of April 10 "as a great boom startled the misty air . . . shaking the very earth, and breaking the windows of houses about Lafayette Square," wrote journalist Noah Brooks. "Boom! Boom! went the guns, until five hundred were fired. . . . It was Stanton's way of telling the people that the Army of Northern Virginia had at last laid down its arms, and that peace had come again."

People gathered outside the War Department and showed their exhilaration by shouting and cheering. A band played patriotic airs. In response to calls from the crowd, Secretary of War Stanton, Vice President Johnson, and others made speeches. Unlike the others, Johnson was bitter and vindictive: "And what shall be done with the leaders of the rebel host? I know what I would do if I were president. I would arrest them as traitors, I would try them as traitors, and, by the Eternal, I would hang them as traitors!" It was a position held by the Radical Republicans, who regarded Johnson and Stanton as among their number.

On Tuesday night, April 11, several hundred jubilant Washingtonians pushed their way onto the White House grounds to hear the president

speak. Mary Lincoln's seamstress Elizabeth Keckley described the scene
from a second-floor window: "I looked out, and never saw such a mass of
heads before . . . and what added to the weird, spectral beauty of the scene
was the confused hum of voices that rose above the sea of forms. . . . It was
a grand and imposing scene."

Candles placed in all the windows provided illumination as Lincoln
appeared on a balcony to make a promised speech. He was greeted with
thunderous applause.

In the shadows, leaning against a tree, John Wilkes Booth grimly
watched the proceedings. Standing beside him were Lewis Paine and David
Herold. Heartsick and weary, Booth had been wandering through the streets
of Washington and was obviously irritated by the incessant cheering. He had
read and been haunted by an illuminated sign on the long facade of the
Capitol: "This is the Lord's doing; it is marvelous in our eyes." Erected to celebrate the fall of Richmond, it remained there after Lee's surrender.

The president raised his hand, the cheering slowly died down, and he
spoke. Lincoln projected his vision of a united America without slavery. In
sharp contrast to Vice President Johnson's remarks the night before, Lincoln
pressed upon his audience their sober responsibilities toward the conquered
states, and he said that he was grieved rather than gratified by any demon-
strations of joy that took no account of the sorrow of the defeated. He said of
the seceded states now conquered that "finding themselves safely at home, it
would be utterly immaterial whether they had ever been abroad."

Several minutes into his remarks he brought up a subject that made
Booth and Paine cringe and their tempers rise: "It is also unsatisfactory to
some that the elective franchise is not given to the colored man. I would
myself prefer that it were now conferred on the very intelligent, and on
those who serve our cause as soldiers."

Booth undoubtedly exploded with rage. He could not envision or toler-
ate African Americans having a say in the government of the white South. He
grumbled to Paine and Herold, "That means nigger citizenship." Fuming,
Booth vowed, "That's the last speech he'll ever make." Booth urged Paine to
shoot Lincoln immediately. Paine refused, and Booth turned away in disgust,
exclaiming, "Now, by God, I'll put him through."

Booth probably lingered to hear the second speaker, Sen. James Harlan
of Iowa, secretary-designate of the Department of the Interior. His daughter
later married Robert Lincoln. Booth, still shuddering over Lincoln's rather
moderate remarks, must have lost all mental control when Harlan made the

The residence of Secretary of State William H. Seward was checked out by conspirator Lewis Paine on both Thursday and Friday mornings, April 13 and 14. Thus Booth's assassination plan was being developed much earlier than previously thought.

LESLIE'S

mistake of asking: "What shall be done with these brethren of ours?" The crowd responded with cries of "Hang 'em! Hang 'em!" Then when Harlan suggested that Lincoln might pardon some of them, the crowd roared as one, "Never!" He explained that most Southerners were not guilty of anything and that he, for one, was willing to trust the future to the president of the United States. He was applauded enthusiastically. As he left the window, the Marine Corps band played "The Battle Hymn of the Republic."

The South was in disarray. It had lost more than 258,000 men in battle and by disease. Much of its countryside was in ruins. Harney's mission to blow up the White House had failed. Yet Booth knew that some Confederate armies were still in the field, and he felt that maybe the Confederacy could still be saved. He was unwilling to consider that the cause was lost. What Harney could not accomplish, perhaps he, Booth, could achieve in a different, dramatic way and turn the tide. Later in his diary he wrote: "For six months we had worked to capture, but our cause being almost lost, something decisive and great must be done." He would set about doing it—and quickly. Only four days after Harney's capture, Booth was determined to kill the president.

Booth now began to drink even more than normally—which was more than most people could handle. John Deery, who kept a bar in front of Grover's Theatre, saw Booth often during this time: "He sometimes drank at my bar as much as a quart of brandy in the space of less than two hours of an evening."

But the actor known for meticulous planning kept his wits about him as he worked out his fanatical scheme.

On Thursday, April 13, Gen. and Mrs. Ulysses S. Grant received a hero's welcome in Washington. Mary Lincoln invited the Grants to a theater party at Ford's on Friday night, and they accepted. On Thursday night there was a magnificent grand illumination of the city, with flashing rockets, waving banners, speeches, concerts, and receptions. Author Clara Laughlin later said that nearly everyone loyal to the Union was "drunk with the joy of victory." It may have been the most beautiful night in Washington's history. The *Evening Star* reported: "Washington was all ablaze with glory. . . . Far as the vision extended were brilliant lights, the rows of illuminated windows at a distance blending into one, and presenting an unbroken wall of flame. . . . High above all towered the Capitol, glowing as if on fire and seeming to stud the city below with gems of reflected glory as stars light upon the sea."

Booth's whereabouts that night are unknown, but that afternoon he had dropped in at Grover's Theatre and asked manager C. D. Hess if he were going to invite Lincoln to the play the following night. Hess thanked Booth for suggesting it and said he would do so immediately. Three men, probably Booth's associates, had mapped out the theater's layout and exits sometime that week.

Louis Weichmann had been a schoolmate of John Surratt at a Catholic seminary and, at the time of the Lincoln assassination, shared a room with John at the Surratt's boarding house. Weichmann later was a key witness for the prosecution of Mary Surratt. John Surratt denounced him as a "base-born perjurer" who "was a party to the plan to abduct Lincoln."

At the National Hotel early Friday morning—Good Friday—David Herold encountered the night clerk as the man was going off duty. "Going to see Booth?" asked the clerk, known only as Burton. Herold indicated he was. "Well, I don't think he's in," said Burton. "I didn't see him come in last night, and he always stops for a chat with me before he goes to bed. But you'd better look in his room and see."

Herold went to Room 228 and knocked but got no response. He opened the door and found the room unoccupied.

Whether or not the night clerk's report of the conversation is accurate, Booth did get together with some of his coconspirators by nine o'clock. He went to a barbershop for a shave and a haircut accompanied by Paine and Herold. Booth then casually entered Grover's Theater and asked if the Lincolns would be attending that evening. The answer was no.

Around eleven o'clock Booth stopped at Ford's Theatre to pick up his mail. The twenty-one-year-old proprietor, Henry Clay "Harry" Ford, later said that someone teasingly told the actor, "Your friends Lincoln and Grant are coming to the theater tonight, and we're fixin' to have Lee sit with them." Booth allegedly replied, "Lee would never do that. He would never let himself be paraded, like a conquered Roman, by his captors." Then, as the story goes, Booth walked away thoughtfully.

The anticipated attendance by the president and the general in chief was news that day. To guarantee a packed house, Ford placed notices in both afternoon dailies. The announcement in the *Washington Evening Star* listed Grant first: "Lieut.-Gen'l Grant, President and Mrs. Lincoln have secured the State Box at Ford's Theatre TONIGHT, to witness Miss Laura Keene's *American Cousin*."

While most historians have assumed Booth first learned of Lincoln's theater plans from Harry Ford, recent research strongly indicates Booth knew much earlier that Lincoln would be attending the theater somewhere Friday night. He was only in doubt as to which theater: Grover's or Ford's. Ford's Theatre personnel received the reservation at 10:30 A.M. Friday from Mary Lincoln, but Booth had relocated George Atzerodt from a Washington flophouse to Vice President Johnson's elegant hotel, Kirkwood House, around 8 A.M. so that he would be in place for the multiple crimes that night. Further, Booth secured a commitment from Mary Surratt early that morning for a critical afternoon trip to her tavern at Surrattsville. Booth assumed Lincoln would attend Grover's to see the exciting new play *Aladdin*. When he ruled that out, he was sure it would be Ford's. Booth's visit to Ford's late that morning confirmed it. Clearly, before April 14 Booth was planning the assassination at a theater on Friday night. He could only have learned of the president's plans from someone close to the White House.

Booth spent much of the day Friday finalizing logistics. His goal, like that of Davis, Benjamin, and Harney, was to disrupt the government and throw the nation into massive confusion. His method was murder—and not just the murder of Lincoln but also of other high officials—Vice President Andrew Johnson and Secretary of State William H. Seward. With both the president and vice president dead, federal law required the secretary of state to set in motion the process for the electoral college to provide a new president. With the secretary of state also dead, congressional infighting over his replacement and control of the electoral college would create a constitutional crisis.

Did Booth figure this out by himself, or was the idea suggested earlier by his Confederate connections in Canada, perhaps by the revolutionary George N. Sanders? If Booth's purpose had been solely to rid the government of those men most responsible for the war, then Secretary of War Edwin M. Stanton surely would have been a target. He was not on Booth's list.

Seward had been severely injured in a carriage accident on April 5 and was bedridden at his home on the east side of Lafayette Square near the White House. Booth sent strongman Lewis Paine to Seward's house to check out the situation. On both Thursday and Friday mornings the intimidating Paine spoke through a window to a male nurse to ask about Seward's condition—further proof of Booth's plans being in the works as early as Thursday morning. Paine also visited a chambermaid there, according to Atzerodt's confession, and "she was pretty [and] he had a great mind to give her his diamond pin."

If Booth did not spend Thursday night at the National Hotel, as the desk clerk claimed, where was he? Perhaps he was with his nineteen-year-old mistress, Ella Turner, at the bordello where she stayed, or at Mary Surratt's boarding house. On Friday morning he had to have met with Mary Surratt to initiate an important mission for her—a mission that only would have been necessary if Booth already was aware of Lincoln's plans to attend the theater on Friday night. Booth needed Mary Surratt to take field glasses and a message to John Lloyd, the man who leased her tavern at Surrattsville. She gladly accommodated him.

Through her, Booth instructed Lloyd to retrieve the weapons that had been concealed earlier at the tavern, because they would be called for *that*

HARPER'S WEEKLY

Mary Surratt's tavern at Surrattsville (to the left above) served as a safe house for Confederate couriers in southern Maryland. Per Booth's instructions, two carbines and other supplies were kept for him at the tavern. On the day of the assassination, Mary Surratt allegedly told the proprietor to "get the shooting irons out."

night. The day after the March kidnapping attempt, David Herold and John Surratt had hidden Booth's Spencer carbines and other equipment in the floorboards above the tavern's kitchen. Lloyd knew that and undoubtedly expected to be called upon to make the weapons available when Booth needed them.

To accomplish her assignment, Mary Surratt required transportation, and she asked Weichmann to rent a carriage and drive her there that afternoon. Weichmann's version of this episode further substantiates the timetable. He went to work as usual that morning, but around ten o'clock received a circular from Stanton permitting all employees to attend Good Friday services if they wished to do so; the handout indicated that the clerks "would be relieved from duty for the day." After attending mass, Weichmann returned to the boarding house at noon.

He was resting in his room when Mary Surratt knocked on his door between two and two-thirty. She said she needed to go into the country to see about a debt due her from John Nothey and asked if he would drive her. Weichmann commented that he would enjoy the drive, and she gave him ten dollars to rent a horse and buggy. As he was about to leave, Booth rang the doorbell. When Weichmann returned to the house, he saw Booth and Mary Surratt huddled in close conversation. Booth left shortly after that. When Mary Surratt entered the buggy, she carried a package wrapped in

coarse brown paper—the field glasses Booth had just brought to her. Weichmann later wondered how Booth knew that she was going to the country
just then. He testified at the conspirators' trial that it appeared to him as if the
journey to the country had been planned beforehand and Booth's afternoon
visit seemed to follow up an earlier visit he must have made in the morning,
which he construed from the comment of another boarder.

Further evidence that Mary Surratt's trip to Surrattsville was to help
Booth came from Atzerodt's confession, which was discovered many years
later: "Booth told me that Mrs. Surratt went to Surrattsville to get out the
guns [two carbines] which had been taken to that place by Herold. This
was Friday."

On the way to Surrattsville, Weichmann recalled an incident that he
described at John Surratt's 1867 trial:

> When about halfway down, we saw a group of [Union] cavalrymen to the left,
> a short distance from the roadside. The soldiers were lolling on the green and
> enjoying themselves. . . . Stopping the buggy, Mrs. Surratt hailed an old man,
> seemingly a farmer, and desired to know what those soldiers were doing there.
> "They are pickets," he replied. She then asked if they remained out all night,
> and he stated that they were generally called in at eight o'clock in the evening.
> "I am glad to know that," she said, and [we] drove on.

On that very night, Booth and Herold dashed down that same road and
past the spot where Weichmann and Mary Surratt had seen the pickets.
Weichmann concluded that it was important for Mary Surratt to know if the
road would be clear that night.

Accounts of Booth's hour-by-hour itinerary for much of the day cannot
be precisely reconstructed. Historians differ somewhat but generally agree
on what he accomplished during that fateful day. That afternoon he rented a
fast roan, stopped at the Herndon House to instruct Lewis Paine to check
out that afternoon, delivered the field glasses to Mary Surratt, visited Ford's
Theatre to make alterations in the presidential box, and wrote a two-page
letter to the editor of the *Washington National Intelligencer* with the reasons
for "our proceedings."

On his way to mail the letter, Booth encountered a friend, John Mathews, who had a minor role in *Our American Cousin,* the play being performed
at Ford's Theatre. Mathews was one of two actors Booth had sought unsuccessfully to recruit for the kidnapping scheme. Apparently on impulse,
Booth handed the stamped, sealed letter to Mathews and asked him to

deliver it to the newspaper office the following morning. The actor agreed to do it, but after witnessing the assassination that night, he tore open the envelope, read the letter twice, and burned it—or so he said. He kept the incident a secret for two years. The contents—a justification for the assassination—frightened him, and he feared his possession of the letter would result in his arrest. When he finally talked about it in 1867, he issued what he called a verbatim report of the letter's contents, a portion of which read:

> When Caesar had conquered the enemies of Rome and the power that was his menaced the liberties of the people, Brutus arose and slew him. The stroke of his dagger was guided by his love for Rome. It was the spirit and ambition of Caesar that Brutus struck at. "O then that we could come by Caesar's spirit, And not dismember Caesar! But Alas! Caesar must bleed for it!" I answer with Brutus.

Mathews also claimed that Booth signed the letter not just with his own name but also those of his three coconspirators: Atzerodt, Herold, and Paine. By doing so, he shared his sought-after hero status with them.

That Booth wrote the letter is not questioned. A stableman and a hotel clerk were aware of it. Mathews's word, however, is not entirely believable. First, one must concede that Mathews had an incredible memory to recall Booth's exact words two years later. Second, if Booth gave the letter to Mathews for delivery, he was taking a big chance, and Booth was known to be careful, thorough, and meticulous. Booth had damned Mathews for his earlier refusal to join the kidnapping conspiracy and had called him "unfit to live." Author Robert L. Mills in *It Didn't Happen the Way You Think* doubted that Booth would have been so careless as to endanger the success of his plot by risking the possibility of Mathews's reading the letter immediately and

Booth was "stung to the quick" by the president's reelection in 1864, wrote Lincoln's secretaries John Nicolay and John Hay in their 1890 biography of the president. The actor's hatred of Lincoln degenerated from schemes to kidnap him to plans to murder the president. In the end, Booth the actor sought to play the role of Brutus in real life and to strike down the Caesar he knew as the tyrant Lincoln (see the recollection of Booth's letter excerpted above). The beloved actor firmly believed he would be a hero by removing the much-reviled president—perhaps in 1864 the most denigrated president in American history up to that time.

reporting its contents to the authorities. Had that occurred, Booth would
have been arrested and hanged. Further, for public notoriety, Mathews could
have concocted some of the story to coincide with remarks in Booth's diary
(by then a public document) and related published testimonies.

    While such uncertainties exist, there is little doubt that Booth devoted
the entire day—starting early in the morning—to meticulously planning the
attacks on Lincoln, Johnson, and Seward that night. His schedule strongly
suggests that he had advance knowledge of Lincoln's plans—knowledge that
had to have come from Booth's intelligence system and its special contacts at
the highest levels of government.

5

INCOMPETENT
AND CARELESS

F OR THE FIRST TIME in his presidency, on Good Friday, April 14, 1865,
Abraham Lincoln seemed concerned about the possibility of assassi-
nation. The war was all but over. Robert E. Lee had surrendered to U. S.
Grant on April 9 at Appomattox Court House, Virginia. Confederate Gen.
Joseph E. Johnston, the only remaining Confederate commander with a siz-
able force in the field, was sandwiched between the armies of Grant and
William T. Sherman and expected to capitulate momentarily.

Throughout the war Lincoln had ignored concerns about his own safety,
even though hardly a day passed without hate mail threatening "a deadly
blow" against him. Horace Greeley guessed that Lincoln must have received
at least ten thousand vicious letters. The president kept in his office desk a
file marked "Assassination." It contained at least eighty threats.

"I know I am in danger," Lincoln told newspaperman John W. Forney,
"but I am not going to worry over threats like these." When Lincoln's friend
Leonard Swett warned him of the dangers of exposing himself to assassins,
the president brushed his apprehension aside: "I cannot be shut up in an
iron cage and guarded." To another friend, Charles G. Halpine, the president admitted no fear of political assassins. Believing firmly "what will be,
will be," no protection could stop his assassination if Providence willed it.

"If someone wants to take my life and is willing to give his own in return," he said, "it cannot be prevented." He could only die once, he commented to Secretary of the Navy Gideon Welles.

In the meantime, the president had made himself an easy target. He stole away for solitary walks, especially at night. He held public receptions where security was almost nonexistent. He conferred with generals in the field. He stood atop a parapet at Fort Stevens on the outskirts of Washington for a clear view of Jubal Early's approaching Confederate forces as soldiers around him were shot dead. He attended the theater frequently. He had walked virtually unguarded through the streets of the fallen Confederate capital. When he and his family stayed at his summer retreat at the Soldiers Home on the outskirts of Washington, he often rode back and forth to the White House in an unguarded carriage.

Nearly every night, before going to bed, he strolled without protection down a densely shaded path through the White House grounds to the War Department's telegraph office to learn the latest news from the war front. "It was impossible to induce him to forgo these lonely and dangerous [activities]," lamented Ward Hill Lamon, Lincoln's long-time friend and self-appointed bodyguard who was also the marshal of the District of Columbia. One night when Lincoln attended the theater accompanied only by Sen. Charles Sumner and an elderly Prussian minister, Lamon angrily offered to resign, concerned that neither of Lincoln's guests "could defend himself against an assault from any able-bodied woman in this city."

Secretary of War Edwin M. Stanton knew that the president was in danger. He called Lincoln's acts foolhardy and urged him to accept bodyguards. Stanton, who earlier had called Lincoln a long-armed baboon, was now regarded as one of the president's most ardent supporters. The short, paunchy man with gray, scented whiskers and an abrasive personality had efficiently manned and equipped the military while instituting harsh security measures.

Despite Lincoln's indifference toward his own safety, others prevailed—to a point. A body of cavalry detailed to escort the president on his rides to and from the Soldiers Home in 1862 was dismissed when Lincoln complained that the clatter of their sabers and spurs made it impossible for him to talk with Mary. The cavalry was replaced in 1863 by the Union Light Guard—well-trained Ohioans mounted on black steeds. Two of these guards were stationed around the clock at each gateway to the White House. An infantry company protected the southern approaches.

LESLIE'S

On April 4, 1865, after Richmond had been evacuated by the Confederate government, Lincoln walked and rode through the streets without a care for his safety. Former slaves, now free, cheered the president and knelt before him.

In addition, at Lamon's request, four officers from the Washington police were assigned special duty at the Executive Mansion in early 1865. They wore civilian clothing but carried concealed pistols. Two served from 8 A.M. until 4 P.M., the third from 4 P.M. until midnight, and the fourth from midnight to 8 A.M. They were to accompany Lincoln on his walks, escort him to the theater, and guard the Lincolns' private rooms in the White House. For the second inauguration—March 4, 1865—Stanton offered to appoint a select body of officers to keep watch over Lincoln day and night, especially when he went out. On this occasion, as on others, Lincoln dismissed Stanton's concerns. "It is useless," he told the secretary of war. "If it is the will of Providence that I should die by the hand of an assassin, it must be so."

Stanton always appeared to be anxious about the president's safety and scolded Lincoln for his careless disregard in early April 1865, two weeks

Ward Hill Lamon, Lincoln's long-time friend and self-appointed guard, was sent to Richmond by the president to resolve certain political problems after the city fell into Union hands. Before leaving, Lamon pleaded with the president to avoid the theater.

before the assassination. On March 23 Lincoln had sailed down the Potomac to Chesapeake Bay and up the James River to Grant's City Point headquarters, which was within ten miles of the besieged city of Petersburg—a city essential to Lee's defense of Richmond. When Lee evacuated Petersburg on April 3, Lincoln followed the soldiers into the city, and Stanton telegraphed the president: "Allow me respectfully to ask you to consider whether you ought to expose the nation to the consequences of any disaster to yourself in the pursuit of a treacherous and dangerous enemy like the rebel army." Lincoln thanked him for his concern but further irritated Stanton by wiring back: "It is certain now that Richmond is in our hands, and I think I will go there tomorrow. I will take care of myself."

The next day, walking through the streets of Richmond to the Confederate White House, Lincoln had a small escort of six sailors in front and six behind, two officers, his son Tad, and bodyguard William H. Crook. The city's blacks, now free, cheered Lincoln and knelt before him. "Don't kneel to me," the president admonished them. "You must kneel to God only and thank him for your freedom."

While Stanton worried about Lincoln's safety with good reason, Lincoln-haters seethed at the spectacle. This "triumphal entry into the fallen city breathed fresh air upon the fire which consumed [John Wilkes Booth]," Wilkes's sister, Asia, later wrote.

By Friday, April 14, 1865, Lincoln's refusal to fear death had done an about-face. For the first time something moved Lincoln to recognize the dangers that his bodyguards, his secretary of war, and his wife had long dreaded. That something was a dream, and the more he thought about it, the more alarmed he became. Lincoln believed that God spoke to people in dreams, usually in code. Common people, the president felt, were more capable of understanding dreams than were the highly educated. Dreams were part of the "workmanship of the Almighty," he once said. He took them seriously.

On Tuesday, April 11, Lincoln related a recent dream to Mary and a few friends: "There seemed to be a death-like stillness about me. Then I heard subdued sobs, as if a number of people were weeping. I thought I left my bed and wandered downstairs. . . . It was light in all the rooms; every object was familiar to me. . . . I kept on until I arrived at the East Room, which I entered. There I met with a sickening surprise. Before me was a catafalque, on which rested a corpse wrapped in funeral vestments. . . . 'Who is dead in the White House?' I demanded of one of the soldiers. 'The president,' was the answer, 'he was killed by an assassin!' Then came a loud burst of grief from the crowd, which awoke me from my dream. I slept no more that night."

The first time Lincoln opened the Bible after the dream, his eyes fell on Genesis 28, which relates one of Jacob's dreams. Lincoln said that he then turned to other passages "and seemed to encounter a dream or a vision wherever I looked." He said he kept on turning the leaves of the old book, and everywhere he was drawn to passages recording matters about super-natural visitations, dreams, and visions.

Shortly after that, Lincoln asked bodyguard Ward Hill Lamon to go to Richmond as his personal representative to iron out some problems that blocked the calling of Virginia's reconstruction convention. Before he left, Lincoln told him about the dream and the Bible readings:

It seems strange to me how much there is in the Bible about dreams. There are, I think, some sixteen chapters in the Old Testament and four or five in the New in which dreams are mentioned; and there are many other passages scattered throughout the book which refer to visions. If we believe in the Bible, we must accept the fact that in the old days, God and His angels came to men in their sleep and made themselves known in dreams. [My dream] has haunted me. Somehow the thing has got possession of me, and like Banquo's ghost, it will not let go.

Lamon, a huge and commanding-looking Virginian with brown wavy hair and beard, was one of Lincoln's most devoted friends. After studying law in Kentucky before the war, Lamon had settled in Danville, Illinois, where he was admitted to the bar. His association with Lincoln began in the 1850s when they traveled the circuit together. Increasingly concerned for the president's safety, Lamon often slept fully armed on the floor outside Lincoln's bedroom door. "You ought to know that your life is sought after," he once warned Lincoln, "and your life will be taken unless you and your friends are cautious." Now Lamon pleaded with the president: "Promise me you won't go out after nightfall while I'm gone, particularly to the theater." Lincoln would not fully agree.

Why Lincoln ordered his long-time bodyguard to Richmond remains an unsolved mystery in the story of the assassination. Someone from the State Department could have been equally or more effective in dealing with the problems related to the Virginia reconstruction convention. There were no persuasive reasons for sending Lamon, except that he was a native Virginian.

Keenly aware of Lincoln's dream and of the president's concern about it, Lamon did not want to be away from him. "I don't understand why I must go," he told the president, "but I am accustomed to obedience." Silent for a moment, Lincoln responded, "I know you have my interests at heart. That is why you must go to Virginia." The president's determination to send him to Richmond is especially puzzling in light of Lincoln's sudden concern for his own safety that week.

On Thursday night, April 13, Lincoln had a different dream, and he spoke of it at his cabinet meeting on Friday morning. He was on the water, "in some singular, indescribable vessel, and . . . he was moving with great rapidity towards an indefinite shore." This dream, he said, had come to him many times—before important Union victories—and he was sure something good was about to happen—presumably the surrender of Confederate Gen. Joseph E. Johnston and the last major Confederate force in the field. Still, Lincoln's earlier dream haunted him and frightened him.

Meanwhile, Grant was in Washington to finish a plan to reduce the size of the army to a peacetime level. On Friday morning, while conferring with Stanton, Grant mentioned an invitation from the White House to accompany the Lincolns to Ford's Theatre that night. The general said that he had accepted the invitation, but now neither he nor his wife felt like attending. What he did not say was that Julia Grant refused to sit in a theater box with "that crazy woman," meaning Mary Lincoln.

Julia's unease around Mary had climaxed in late March when both women were with their husbands at Grant's headquarters at City Point. During a review of the troops commanded by Edward O. C. Ord, the president rode on horseback to the main encampment in the company of several generals. Mary and Julia were conveyed by an ambulance over the rough, muddy roads. The first lady urged the driver not to fall too far behind, anxious not to miss the review. When the driver complied, the road was unforgiving and bounced the ladies from their seats. Mary's head struck the roof of the vehicle, and although her decorated hat cushioned the blow, she had a headache after the ordeal. The first lady had a bad history with headaches, and this one was one of her worst.

When the small party arrived at the reviewing stand, Mary saw that they had missed the beginning. She fumed and then noticed that the attractive young wife of General Ord accompanied Lincoln and the generals. Turning to Julia Grant, Mary Lincoln exclaimed, "*That woman* is pretending to be me. The soldiers will think that vile woman *is me!*"

Julia tried to point out that Mary Ord was accompanying her husband, not the president, but Mary insisted that the younger woman was flirting with Lincoln. "Does she suppose that *he* wants *her* by *his* side?" When Julia tried to convince her otherwise, Mary turned on her. "I suppose," she accused Julia, "you think you will get to the White House yourself, don't you?!" Momentarily, as Mary Ord entered the reviewing stand, Mary Lincoln accosted her as a whore and spewed a spate of vicious expletives before turning to Lincoln and demanding that he remove Ord from command.

Nothing appeased the first lady that day or that night, where her recriminations continued throughout a dinner hosted aboard the steamer *River Queen*. Embarrassed guests noted that the president bore her petulance "as Christ might have done, with an expression of pain and sadness that cut one to the heart, but with supreme calmness and dignity." Afterward, Mary remained in her cabin for three days before returning alone to Washington. Although no one could have predicted it, her actions contributed to her husband's assassination.

Julia Grant refused to socialize with Mary Lincoln after this affair. Thus U. S. Grant, in Washington less than three weeks later, was torn between pleasing his wife by rejecting the theater invitation or accepting it and pleasing the president. Stanton assured him that the Lincolns would not be distressed, that he and his wife always turned down such invitations. A religious man, Stanton did not approve of the theater.

Stanton also commented that it was dangerous and unwise for Grant to appear at public gatherings. He advised the general to wait until the cabinet meeting later that morning to tell Lincoln that he had a change of plans—the Grants could not accompany the Lincolns because they wanted to visit their two children in Burlington, New Jersey. The excuse was weak; the Grants could have taken a Saturday morning train with better connections than the six o'clock Friday evening train, which was much slower and necessitated a long wait in Philadelphia. The morning train would have reunited the Grants with their children just two hours later than the earlier train.

Strangely, even though Grant chose not to accompany the Lincolns to Ford's Theatre, it never occurred to him to assign any guards to watch over the president. The nation's two most powerful military figures, knowing the danger to the president, apparently did not discuss or even consider what they might do to protect Lincoln that night.

Attorney General James Speed put the matter in perspective in a letter to President Andrew Johnson dated July 1865: "At the time of assassination a civil war was flagrant . . . the principal policing of the city was by Federal soldiers . . . and the President's House and person were, or should have been, under the guard of soldiers."

Lincoln may have wanted Grant with him not only because it had been announced in the newspapers, and the people expected to see the man who had won the war, but also because Lincoln anticipated that Grant would have a military escort. Without Grant—and those guards—Lincoln surely felt doubly concerned about his own safety. He had not dismissed the dream of his assassination. He could not dismiss it. He made that perfectly clear to his wife and to Lamon.

Although Stanton had assured Grant that his rejection of the invitation would be of no concern to Lincoln, Stanton was wrong. Lincoln reportedly felt the affront keenly, and Grant could not have misinterpreted Lincoln's feelings. But Lincoln's plea for the Grants to reconsider fell on deaf ears. Grant chose to ignore the wishes of his commander in chief.

That afternoon, after the cabinet meeting and Grant's rejection of the invitation, Lincoln went to the War Department—immediately west of the White House—to seek something he had never sought before—special protection for the evening at Ford's Theatre. Daytime bodyguard William H. Crook accompanied the president, taking note of Lincoln's sad, melancholy face and unusually slow gait.

As they neared the turnstile dividing the White House grounds from the enclosure to the War Department, a few drunken men blocked their path. Crook stepped forward and cleared the way. Lincoln, speaking slowly and softly, observed: "Crook, do you know, I believe there are men who want to take my life? And I have no doubt they will do it."

Surprised, because the president had never mentioned anything like this to him before, Crook replied, "I hope you're mistaken."

Lincoln continued: "I have perfect confidence in those who are around me, in every one of you men. I know no one could do it and escape alive. But if it is to be done, it is impossible to prevent it."

At the War Department, Lincoln told Stanton he was "looking for someone to go to the theater with me tonight. . . . Grant says that he cannot attend, and neither can you. May I have your man Eckert?"

Maj. Thomas T. Eckert, chief of the War Department's Telegraph Office, was tall, muscular, and solidly built. One writer described him as "a bear of a man with a temper to match his size." Lincoln said that he had seen Eckert break five cast-iron pokers by striking them over his arm, one after the other.

"I'm thinking," Lincoln said to Stanton, "he would be the kind of man to go with me this evening."

Stanton shrugged. "I cannot spare him. I have important work for him this evening."

Julia Grant's unease around Mary Lincoln influenced her husband not to accept the president's invitation to join the Lincolns at Ford's Theatre. After earlier experiences in the company of the first lady, Julia simply refused to sit in a theater box with "that crazy woman."

Annoyed and possibly angry, Lincoln replied, "I will ask the major myself, and he can do your work tomorrow!" The president walked into the adjoining cipher room and extended the invitation to Eckert. "Now, Major," he cajoled, "come along. Mrs. Lincoln and I want you with us."

Eckert, however, knew Stanton's wishes and was not one to disappoint the secretary of war. He declined the president's request, citing the pressing work he had to do for Stanton, although he had no idea what it was.

"Very well," Lincoln said, "I will take Major Rathbone along, but I should much rather have you."

Henry R. Rathbone, slender and dapper, was a twenty-eight-year-old ladies' man who was far less imposing than Eckert. The Lincolns had already invited Rathbone and his fiancée, Clara Harris, daughter of New York Sen. Ira Harris. The major, however, would be unarmed, and his attentions would be centered not on Lincoln but on Clara.

Shortly after the president left the War Department, Stanton told Eckert that he had changed his mind about needing him to work that night. Stanton and Eckert both went home. Eckert was at his home when he received the tragic news of Lincoln's murder. For the rest of his life, this devoted, loyal bluecoat wondered why Stanton had lied to the president, and he regretted his lost opportunity to protect Lincoln.

Stanton, by his own account, dined at home that night then went to see the bedridden secretary of state, Seward. When he returned home, he spoke to a cluster of serenaders, locked up the house, and prepared for bed.

For whatever reason, Stanton had lied to Lincoln that afternoon. Neither he nor Eckert were guilty of insubordination, since Lincoln did not command Eckert's presence, but they were grossly inconsiderate and guilty of poor judgment. For years the secretary of war had demonstrated grave concern about the president's safety—had in fact been obsessive about it—but now he appeared oblivious to it.

Stanton's refusal to accommodate Lincoln's request for protection was both inconceivable and irresponsible. It remains one of the great mysteries of Lincoln's assassination. If Stanton had an important project that demanded Eckert's attention, which he didn't, the secretary of war had at his disposal the full manpower of the U.S. military forces in Washington, as well as the National Detective Police and the provost marshals. Stanton, however, did nothing to protect Lincoln on the night of April 14, 1865.

As a result of Stanton's unusual actions, some researchers have tried to link him with the conspiracy to kill Lincoln. Such efforts, however, have been discredited by most historians, who have concluded that Stanton was fiercely loyal to the president. They have also described him as emotional, stubborn, hard-working, and driven, but not as a conspirator.

Yet power and cruelty went hand in hand with Stanton. He made and broke men mercilessly. He was a master of deceit. Author Jim Bishop noted that Stanton "abhorred lying but he practiced it." Grant observed, "It seemed to be pleasanter to him to disappoint than to gratify." David Homer Bates, manager of the War Department's telegraph office, believed Stanton was by nature "haughty, severe, domineering, and often rude." Bates likened him to the characterization of Napoleon by Charles Phillips, the Irish orator: "Grand, gloomy, and peculiar." Such was the man who advised Lincoln to avoid the theater but failed to provide adequate protection when the president chose to go.

Lincoln, however, admired him. "Stanton," he said, "is the rock upon which are beating the waves of this conflict. . . . I do not see how he survives—why he is not crushed and torn to pieces. Without him, I should be destroyed." What Lincoln did not know—could not know—was that because of Stanton's inexplicable failure to honor the president's request for Eckert's company, Lincoln would indeed be destroyed.

Historians have advanced two reasons for Stanton's blatant lie to Lincoln and his refusal to provide protection: (1) It was Stanton's way of trying to convince Lincoln not to go to the theater; and (2) Stanton may have thought that Lincoln was joking. But Stanton surely knew from past experience that Lincoln could not be dissuaded when his mind was made up; Lincoln was definitely going to the theater. As for "joking," Lincoln definitely was not in a jovial mood, according to Crook, and the seriousness of Lincoln's request was amplified when he ignored Stanton's refusal and went directly to Eckert.

If Stanton had a valid excuse, why then did he later state publicly that this meeting with Lincoln never occurred? Historians suggest "poor memory" as an excuse, but Stanton, known for his attention to detail, would not likely forget a request from the president for protection—especially on the day Lincoln was shot. Still, Stanton testified under oath at a congressional investigation that Lincoln's last time in the War Department was on April 12—not Friday, April 14. A moment later he contradicted himself, admitting that Lincoln was there on April 13 but not on April 14. Yet two highly reputable men—William H. Crook and telegraph office manager David Homer Bates—both claimed that Lincoln requested Eckert's services on April 14. The request, in fact, could not have been made before April 14—the date Grant declined Lincoln's invitation to the theater. If Grant had accepted, army guards would probably have accompanied him, and Eckert would not have been needed. Further, at the congressional hearing, Stanton had no need to refer to the dates of Lincoln's visits. Congress was not investigating the Eckert matter. The committee's questions dealt with a proposed meeting of the Virginia legislators in early April 1865. Nevertheless, Stanton chose to emphasize that Lincoln had not been in the War Department on the day of the assassination.

Although Bates's account of the April 14 meeting was not published until 1907—forty-two years after the event—Crook recalled the incident emphatically. One should also note that Bates admired Stanton and was a lifelong friend of Eckert. The likelihood of this story being invented is highly improbable.

One hypothesis was developed by author Robert L. Mills in *It Didn't Happen the Way You Think.* Based on Stanton's desire to punish the South, in opposition to Lincoln's policy of "malice toward none and charity for all," Mills reasoned that Stanton needed some dramatic occurrence to steer public opinion toward harsh punishment for the South. Mills assumes that Stanton knew of Booth's earlier attempts to kidnap the president and reasoned that if Booth made a second attempt, Stanton could expose the heinousness of these efforts, secure public support for a military occupation of the South, and guarantee his own political power.

All Stanton had to do, according to Mills's theory, was to let Booth know he had secret allies in Washington who would clear his path at Ford's Theatre. An incompetent guard would be assigned, and he would leave his post at the right time. Eckert would not be allowed to accompany the president. Assuming Stanton did not want Lincoln to be hurt, all the pieces fit together until Booth switched his plans from kidnapping to assassination. It's an interesting theory, and it falls apart only if Stanton's loyalty to Lincoln was strong enough to make such a plan inconceivable.

The guard assigned to protect Lincoln at Ford's Theatre on the night of April 14 was a frail, sickly man—John F. Parker, an alcoholic, thirty-five-year-old native Virginian with questionable loyalty to Lincoln. He was a lowlife member of the Metropolitan Police. Notoriously unreliable, Parker had been cited for unbecoming conduct, insubordination, loafing, and drunkenness while on duty. He had been tried fourteen times by the police for violation of orders, inattention to duty, and other infractions. He also

Lincoln's assassination dream prompted him to ask Maj. Thomas T. Eckert to accompany him to the theater. Eckert was chief of the War Department's Telegraph Office and a man of considerable strength. He refused the president's invitation after Secretary of War Edwin M. Stanton contended that he had important work for him to do that evening.

habitually arrested streetwalkers who refused to grant him their favors gratis. Even though married, he once spent a week in a Washington bawdyhouse, later explaining he was there to protect the place.

How could a person of such low character become one of the four Metropolitan Police officers detailed for White House duty and charged with staying close to the president and keeping a sharp lookout for anyone who might have designs on his life or person? To a large extent, the blame can be placed on Mary Lincoln.

Earlier that month, Parker was up for the army draft, and he wanted to avoid it. He did, thanks to a letter Mary wrote on April 3 sponsoring his transfer to the White House guard, which was followed with another letter the next day to have him "exempted from the draft." Her handwritten authorization for Parker's appointment, scripted on paper headed "Executive Mansion," states: "This is to certify that John F. Parker, a member of the Metropolitan Police, has been detailed for duty at the Executive Mansion. By order of Mrs. Lincoln."

Through Mary Lincoln's involvement, Parker guarded the Lincolns' box at Ford's Theatre—until he decided to abandon his post, thereby leaving the box unguarded and providing easy access for John Wilkes Booth. Parker's absence has never been explained adequately. All facts related to his movements were conveniently "lost" in the files of the official investigation. When

Mary's sponsorship of Parker came to light, no one wanted to pursue it. Her actions, Stanton's inaction, and Parker's presumed incompetence made it incredibly easy for Booth, or anyone, to attack the president at Ford's Theatre that night. So why did Mary Lincoln apparently go out of her way to arrange for Parker's assignment to the White House? The answers are again fuzzy.

It may be significant that Mary Lincoln's letters sponsoring Parker's transfer to the White House guard and exempting him from the draft came just after her intemperate actions at City Point. Not only had she cursed Mary Ord for riding too close to the president, but at dinner that evening she also had lambasted her husband for flirting with the woman. When she returned to Washington in time to sponsor Parker's transfer to the White House guard, was she still blinded by her irrational rage? Was she capable of making such a decision?

The date of the first letter, April 4, was the same day that Federal forces marched into Richmond. Lincoln and his son Tad walked through the streets of the fallen capital and sat at Jefferson Davis's desk at the Confederate White House. "Thank God I have lived to see this," Lincoln said. "It seems to me I have been dreaming a horrid nightmare for four years, and now the nightmare is over." Mary, feeling left out of a great moment in history, rushed to Richmond on April 6 to see the fallen capital for herself—just two days after arranging Parker's White House assignment. She was accompanied by her frequent companion, Sen. Charles Sumner (a Radical Republican) and others.

Later, returning to Washington aboard the *River Queen* with her husband, Mary still smoldered with jealousy and resentment. She reportedly struck Lincoln in the face and cursed him. Was she in the same mood when she signed the papers that placed John Parker as the sole guard of the Lincolns' box at Ford's Theatre on the night of April 14, 1865—the guard who left his post, leaving Lincoln totally unprotected. Or was she part of something more sinister?

Mary's long history of emotional imbalance and physical abuse of her husband dated back to the early years of their marriage. She had struck him on the head with firewood, chased him from their home with a knife, thrown potatoes and tomatoes at him, flung hot coffee in his face, and grabbed and pulled out some of his whiskers. In the White House she entertained devious, unscrupulous men such as Henry Wikoff, a former secret agent for the British who was jailed for kidnapping and seducing an American woman in Europe. Lincoln's secretary John Hay called him a "branded social pariah." Yet Mary took him on long carriage rides and even leaked through him to the *New York Herald* an advance copy of Lincoln's State of the Union message, which resulted in a congressional investigation. She also had overspent in one year a four-year appropriation to redecorate the White House and tried to cover the overexpenditure by padding the household bills and certifying fake bills, such as one for 517 loads of manure for the White House lawn. Lincoln told a government official that her actions suggested "partial insanity."

During the first two weeks of April 1865, Mary was especially out of sorts. Was she at this time so distraught that she could have become, unwittingly or knowingly, a part of a conspiracy against her husband? Considering her previous acts of violence against him and her White House indiscretions and illegal activities, the answer is yes—but proof of any culpability is lacking because Mary Lincoln was never investigated.

The first lady was certainly capable of changing personalities in a matter of seconds. When, for example, a delegation of Republican leaders was coming from Chicago to Springfield to notify Lincoln that he had won the Republican nomination for president, the Lincolns had a long, loud argument over the serving of liquor. She was determined to provide brandy and champagne; Lincoln objected to any liquor being offered, knowing that several members of the group favored temperance. Mary screamed and cursed; he left the house and walked around the block. When he returned, the delegation had arrived. She so wowed them with her Southern charm, poise, and conversation that the head of the delegation, George Ashmun of Massachusetts, later said, "I shall be proud, as an American citizen, when the day brings her to grace the White House."

One of Mary's closest friends in Washington, her dressmaker Elizabeth Keckley, wrote in her memoir: "When in one of her wayward, impulsive

"Sis" Thomas, an elderly, superstitious African American, lived near Ford's Theatre and claimed that her house was haunted. She noted that ghosts appeared periodically, and she talked to them. She did not mind the spirits because she was accustomed to them, but she became terribly frightened the second week of April 1865 by a chain of bizarre occurrences: dogs howled and roosters crowed incessantly, a bird flew into the house, and a large picture of Lincoln fell off the wall. These were signs to her that someone in her neighborhood was about to meet a tragic death. The next night, Lincoln was murdered.

Edwin M. Stanton's
refusal to honor Lincoln's
request for Eckert's
services as a bodyguard
remains one of the great
mysteries of the
assassination. His refusal
has prompted some
researchers to try to link
him to the conspiracy.

moods, Mrs. Lincoln was apt to say and *do* things that wounded [the president] deeply. She often wounded him in unguarded moments." Was Keckley aware of devious acts she could not reveal? Would anyone be surprised by *anything* Mary might do when in "one of her wayward, impulsive moods"?

Police Superintendent A. C. Richards brought charges against guard John Parker in May 1865, stating "that said Parker was detailed to attend and protect the President [and] that while the President was at Ford's Theatre on the night of the 14th of April last, said Parker allowed a man to enter the President's private Box and shoot the President." Whether or not Parker was ever tried on these charges is debated among historians. The prevailing opinion is that he was, but all records of the trial have been lost or mysteriously destroyed. Not one word of any proceeding against Parker appeared in any newspaper. The charge was dropped in June without elaboration, and he continued on the police force. Historians speculate that maybe Parker had not actually been assigned to guard the president's box, but only to get him safely into and out of the theater. If one accepts that hypothesis, one must also conclude that no one was assigned to protect the president while he was enjoying the play. Considering the many threats against the president's life and Stanton's own concern for the president's safety, this hypothesis seems unsupportable. Who would place Lincoln at such great risk, unless, of course, he wanted to? One historian suggested that Lincoln may have dismissed Parker "and told him to take a seat and enjoy the play." Knowing Lincoln's concern for his own safety on April 14, that possibility seems unlikely as well.

If Parker did have a legitimate excuse—possibly illness—would officials not have been eager to enter that in the public record? He was, after all, guarding the president of the United States. But he surely wasn't physically disabled that night since he went about his other duties, even arresting an alleged prostitute and bringing her to police headquarters at 6 A.M. According to police records—the ones that were not lost—Parker could not prove his case against the prostitute, and she was released. Yet with regard to the assassination, the police superintendent obviously believed Parker had been derelict in his duties at Ford's Theatre or he would not have brought charges against him. Also, Lincoln's daytime guard William H. Crook later wrote that Parker's orders were to take his position at the rear of the box and "to stand there, fully armed, and to . . . protect the president [against] all hazards."

Meanwhile, immediately after the assassination, Stanton took charge of the investigation. While others sat sobbing, he ordered a furious dragnet in which civil liberties were ignored and dozens of people were falsely arrested—none of whom had in any way aided the assassin. Parker, however, was not among those in custody. Stanton showed no interest in him as a possible conspirator or as one whose negligence contributed to the president's death. This indifference to a logical suspect was very strange for Stanton, because during the war he consistently demanded the severest punishments for soldiers who failed to do their duties. The fact that Parker had vacated his post should have elicited Stanton's wrath. Ironically, three years later, Parker did fall asleep on his beat, and he was dishonorably dismissed. Why he was not punished and dismissed for vacating his post on April 14 is another of several unexplained mysteries surrounding the assassination. Nor was there a public outcry, no popular demand for an explanation, no questions by any of the media.

Inquiring minds should have raised the following questions regarding Mary Lincoln, Edwin M. Stanton, and John F. Parker: On what basis and on whose authority did the first lady authorize Parker's assignment to the White House? On whose recommendation was Parker's name submitted to her? Was she aware of Parker's record? If she was, why did she want such a person to guard her husband? If she was not familiar with Parker, what prompted her to approve him without knowing more about him? Did she know him at all? Was she related to him, or did she think she was related to him? (Her mother's family name was Parker.) Did she authorize Parker to leave his post to watch the play?

Was Stanton aware of Parker's assignment to the White House? If he was not, should he have been? If he was, why didn't he object to it? Considering the secretary's concern for the president's safety, shouldn't his department have investigated anyone proposed for assignment to protect the president? Considering the innocent people arrested after the assassination, why didn't Stanton order Parker's arrest or at least investigate his apparent misconduct? Was it not possible that Parker was part of Booth's conspiracy? Didn't that possibility deserve investigation? Regarding Parker's superiors, did Stanton consider that one of them might have issued orders allowing Parker to leave his post? Was he aware of Mary Lincoln's endorsement of Parker? Was that a factor in his decision not to arrest Parker? Did the secretary in any way try to influence any pending charges against Parker? If so, why? Was he trying to protect Mary Lincoln? Did Stanton know Parker or have any contact with him before April 14? Did any of his staff know Parker?

Did Parker have any communication with Mary Lincoln, John Wilkes Booth, Stanton, or anyone from the War Department on or before April 14,

Fourteen persons turned down the Lincolns' invitation to join them on the fateful night of April 14, 1865. Excuses ranged from prior engagements to sudden illness. Even the president's son Robert declined. Just back from Appomattox Court House, the young man wanted nothing more than to sleep. The only two persons who accepted the Lincolns' offer were Maj. Henry R. Rathbone and his fiancée, Clara Harris, the daughter of New York Sen. Ira Harris. After Booth shot Lincoln, Rathbone grappled with him and sustained serious wounds in his neck and head. He recovered, and the couple was married two years later. They had three children. Rathbone, however, suffered from depression, severe mood swings, and chronic indigestion. In 1882 he was appointed U.S. consul general to Germany. A year later, two days before Christmas, he went berserk, possibly reliving the struggle in Ford's Theatre. He shot and stabbed his wife to death, tried unsuccessfully to kill his children, then stabbed himself. He spent the rest of his life in an insane asylum in Germany. Back in Washington, former neighbors and others refrained from walking in front of the Rathbones' former residence at 8 Jackson Place. They swore they heard the sounds of a man crying and feared the major's deranged spirit had crossed the ocean and haunted the house.

1865? Did he know Booth? Did Booth bribe him to leave his post? Who dictated Parker's duties for that night? What specifically were his instructions? Why did he leave his post? Did it not occur to Parker that by doing so he was jeopardizing the president's life?

Did Stanton or any other governmental official in any way hinder or interfere with chief A. C. Richards's prosecution of Parker? Why wasn't Parker placed in solitary confinement? Was there a hearing? If so, why are there no records of it? If not, why not? Why, in fact, are there no government records on the investigation of Parker? Who acquitted Parker and on what basis?

Such questions apparently were never asked, and the participants never commented on them. No one seemed to want to set the record straight. Historians generally have erected a protective shield around Stanton and offered excuses for his questionable activities and judgments. In reality, no one knows the truth—the definitive answers to the above questions. There was an information blackout the likes of which would be envied by later politicians who have been pursued relentlessly by an inquisitive, cantankerous press on matters of far less significance.

After Lincoln's unsuccessful request for Eckert to protect him at Ford's Theatre, he and William H. Crook were returning to the White House. The president said: "It has been advertised that we will be there, and I cannot disappoint the people. Otherwise, I would not go, I do not want to go." For one who loved the theater and went as often as he could, does not this statement further indicate Lincoln's concern for his own life that night?

Crook's duty ended at four o'clock. Parker was due at that time to begin his four-to-midnight shift as the president's guard, but he was three hours late—three hours unaccounted for. Crook waited for Parker and briefed him on the plans for the evening. Crook asked him if he was armed. Parker said he was, supposedly a .38 Colt revolver. Since there would be no room in the carriage for Parker, Crook suggested he leave the White House fifteen minutes ahead of time and wait for the Lincolns at Ford's.

As Crook prepared to go off duty, he again begged Lincoln to avoid the theater, but the president would not hear of it. "Then let me stay on duty and accompany you," Crook insisted.

"No, Crook," Lincoln said kindly but firmly, "you have had a long, hard day's work already, and you must go home to sleep and rest. I cannot afford to have you get tired out and exhausted."

As Crook was leaving, Lincoln neglected for the first time to say good night to him. Instead, he turned to him and said, "Good-bye, Crook."

It wasn't until Saturday morning that Crook learned of Lincoln's demise. He wondered if Parker had also been killed. For years afterward Crook cringed at Parker's negligence and pondered why it had not been divulged. "So far as I know," he wrote, "it was not even investigated by the police department. Yet, had he [Parker] done his duty, President Lincoln would not have been murdered by Booth."

Crook reasoned that a single guard at the box entrance would have struggled with Booth and disarmed the assassin. Further, if both Eckert and Rathbone had accompanied the Lincolns, Booth would have been out-manned and outgunned. "It makes me feel rather bitter," wrote Crook, "when I remember that the president had said, just hours before, that he knew he could trust all his guards."

6

A
SOCKDOLOGIZING
MOMENT

I T SOUNDED LIKE A foolhardy plan with no chance of success. How could one man with a single-shot derringer, a bullet, and a knife walk nonchalantly through a crowded theater, pass unobstructed through two doors into the State Box, stand behind the president without being seen by the three other occupants in the box, kill the president with no one hearing the sound of the shot, leap eleven feet to the stage, take time to yell a message to the audience, and escape through a rear exit? Fulfilling this mission required far more than blind luck. It required information that could only have come from the highest sources in Washington. And it required a scenario of skillfully timed movements and activities. A failed link anywhere along the planned chain of events would have meant disaster for the perpetrators.

Booth was in and out of Ford's Theatre several times Friday afternoon, April 14. As a close acquaintance of theater owner John T. Ford, Booth could wander around at will and not raise anyone's suspicion. Booth had important work to do in the State Box, but he had to wait while carpenters removed a partition to combine boxes 7 and 8 for the presidential party. After that work was completed, the box had to be decorated with flags and bunting and a framed portrait of George Washington. Workmen were bringing in furniture, including a red upholstered Victorian rocking chair for the president as well as a sofa and two stuffed chairs. The sofa was placed at the back of the box. Lincoln's rocker was set near the rear of what was box 7, in a corner hidden from the audience.

To enter the State Box, one had to pass through a white door that opened into a small unlighted vestibule that housed the two doors for what had been boxes 7 and 8. In either a rare coincidence or a deliberate act, the locks on both of these doors were broken. Some believe that Booth broke them that afternoon. Others believe the locks had been broken for some time, and that the Fords were aware of the problem but were in no hurry to repair them—a rather strange circumstance, if true, for these were the most important boxes in the theater.

A cane chair for the president's guard was placed outside the white door. The guard was to sit in the chair with his back toward the door so he could see anyone coming toward the box.

Booth timed one of his visits to Ford's that day to catch the rehearsal of the second scene of the third act of *Our American Cousin*. He knew almost every line of the play, but he wanted to refresh his memory of this particular scene and the position of actors on stage.

At this point in the play, an English mother, who has been trying to marry her daughter off to an American presumed to be rich, discovers that the man really isn't rich. Outraged, she says to the American: "I am aware, Mr. Trenchard, that you are not used to the manners of good society, and that alone will excuse the impertinence of which you have been guilty." She

This Thomas Nast caricature appeared in *Harper's Weekly* on the day of the assassination. The artist's caption read: "All seems well with us.— A. Lincoln."

HARPER'S WEEKLY

storms offstage, leaving him alone. His rejoinder is: "Don't know the manners of good society, eh? Well, I guess I know enough to turn you inside out, old gal—you sockdologizing old man trap!"

The Trenchard line was always followed by a roar of laughter. Booth believed that moment would be the perfect time to fire his weapon. The laughter would mask the noise. He calculated the time it would occur. The curtain was supposed to rise at eight o'clock—it usually did—and this scene was a little more than two hours into the play. He estimated that the critical moment would occur between ten and ten-fifteen.

Around three-thirty Booth went to the Kirkwood House, where Vice President Johnson and now George Atzerodt resided. Booth shoved a note under Atzerodt's door and left a message at the front desk for Johnson (or his personal secretary, William A. Browning). It read: "Don't wish to disturb you. Are you at home? J. Wilkes Booth." The desk clerk's orders were to place Johnson's mail in Browning's box. When Browning saw Booth's note, he thought the message was for him, not Johnson. He had met the actor before, and he assumed Booth remembered him.

Historians have long debated this note. If Booth intended it for Johnson, some think Booth may have wanted to implicate Johnson in the conspiracy.

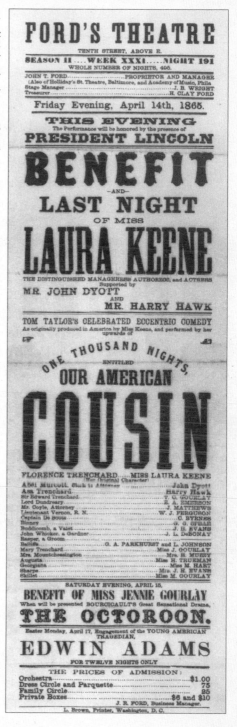

But why would Booth implicate a person slated to be murdered? Some believe that Johnson and Booth knew each other, having first met in Nashville, Tennessee, in February 1864 when Booth appeared at the newly opened Wood's Theatre there. Another claimed that while Johnson was military governor of Tennessee, he and Booth kept two sisters as mistresses and were frequently seen in each other's company. Still, why would Booth take valuable time on April 14 to deliberately leave a message for Johnson or Browning unless doing so was related to his grand scheme?

After Booth picked up his rented horse and rehearsed his departure route from the rear of Ford's, he stopped at Taltavul's Star Saloon next to the theater to have a drink with stagehands. He asked if they had to be on stage in the next hour or so, and they said the scenery was already set up and they had time to kill. Knowing he would have Ford's to himself, Booth bought the stagehands a bottle of whiskey and returned to the theater. What he did next is conjecture, since no one saw him, but he likely did not leave the preparations in the State Box to others.

Booth found a pine board that had held a music stand. Taking it upstairs to the State Box, he opened the outer white door to the vestibule fronting the doors to boxes 7 and 8 (now one box) and braced the board between the inside of the white door and the rear wall of box 7. The board being about a

A general map of Washington shows the close proximity of the principle characters involved in the plot against Lincoln. The Surratt boarding house and the National Hotel (Booth's residence) were mere blocks from the White House.

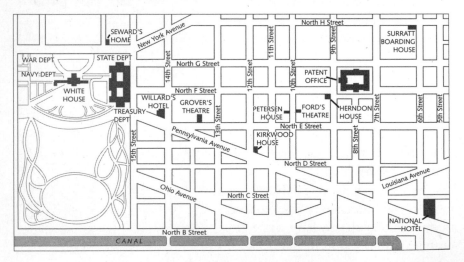

half-inch too long, he gouged some plaster from the wall to create a niche into which the board fitted perfectly. He would use the board that night to prevent anyone from rushing through the outer door into the small vestibule. For now, he put the board in a corner close to the door—out of sight but handy. He then checked both doors to the State Box to be sure they could not be locked. He either knew that the locks were broken or he broke them. He checked the layout of the furniture and studied the jump to the stage. He planned to swing over the ledge, hang on by his hands, then drop. After landing he would cross the stage, go through the Green Room (a small room where actors sat before cue time), and leave the building through a door at the rear of this room. Outside, in the alley, his horse would be in waiting, held by his friend Edman Spangler, a theater carpenter, with whom Booth had made arrangements earlier that day.

Returning to the little vestibule outside boxes 7 and 8, Booth took from his coat pocket a spiral-fluted gimlet with a wooden handle and drilled a finger-size peephole in the lower right-hand corner of the upper panel of the door closest to where the president would be sitting. He scooped up the shavings and dust and put them into his pocket. He walked back to his hotel to rest, eat, and think.

At 7:45 P.M. Booth left his room at the National Hotel dressed in black clothes, a black hat, and calf-length boots. He carried a small datebook he used as a diary, a compass, a small one-shot derringer, and a nine-inch bowie knife hidden inside his pants on the left side. Passing by the hotel clerk, Booth asked him if he were going to Ford's Theatre that evening The clerk hadn't thought about it. "There will be some fine acting there tonight," Booth promised.

At about 8 P.M. Booth met with Paine, Atzerodt, and Herold and revealed to them for the first time that the mission was to be an assassination, not a kidnapping, and not just of the president but also of Secretary of State Seward and Vice President Johnson. Booth gave each man his assignment. Horses would be available for all of them at the little stable Booth had rented near Ford's. Booth himself would kill Lincoln. Paine, the strong man, would kill Seward. Since Paine had trouble with directions, he needed a guide to Seward's house on Lafayette Square. David Herold would handle that and also help Paine escape from Washington. Herold knew the city so well he could have found his way around blindfolded. Atzerodt would kill the vice president at Kirkwood House. The attacks were to occur simultaneously, at about 10:15. After completing their assignments the conspirators

Ford's Theatre is the large building to the left. To its immediate right is Taltavul's Star Saloon where Booth drank his whiskey before entering the theater to kill Lincoln. The black bunting in the image was there during the month of mourning that followed the president's death.

LIBRARY OF CONGRESS

would leave town over the Navy Yard Bridge into southern Maryland and meet afterward on the road to Surrattsville or at Mary Surratt's leased tavern, where they would pick up the carbines and field glasses from John Lloyd.

Atzerodt cringed and whimpered. He had signed on for kidnapping, not murder. Booth yelled and cursed him. Perhaps the actor anticipated Atzerodt's reaction and wrote the earlier note to Johnson to arouse suspicion against the vice president in case Atzerodt backed out. Also, Booth must have regarded Johnson as the least important of the three men; otherwise Paine would have gotten Atzerodt's job.

Arriving at Ford's Theatre before the Lincolns, Parker the guard presumably examined the State Box. It was part of his job. Had he been thorough, he could not have missed seeing the niche in the wall, the peephole, and the plank in the corner of the vestibule. Had he seen any one of these variations from the norm, he should have been suspicious. He apparently was never asked if he had examined the box or noticed anything unusual.

The presidential carriage arrived late—at 8:25 P.M. Parker met them at the front of the theater and guided them to the State Box. At this point, the play stopped, the orchestra played "Hail to the Chief," the audience cheered the president, the presidential party took their seats, and the play continued. Parker sat down in his chair by the white door outside the State Box. Several times he became bored or restless, stood up, and peered around the edge of the wall to see the action on stage.

AUTHOR'S COLLECTION

The State Box was decorated with flags and bunting and a portrait of George Washington. When Lincoln's party arrived, the play was already in progress but halted when the orchestra played "Hail to the Chief."

Shortly before nine o'clock he committed his most irresponsible act: He got up and walked out of the theater. Noticing the president's coachman, Francis Burns, napping in the driver's seat, he nudged him and asked if he'd like to join him for some ale. Burns agreed, and they walked to Taltavul's tavern. Charles Forbes, the footman, exited from the theater and joined them. Apparently neither Forbes nor Burns had the common sense to question Parker about leaving his post or to urge him to return to the State Box.

Elsewhere in the city, Vice President Andrew Johnson, alone in his hotel suite, went to bed. Secretary of War Stanton dropped by to see Secretary of State Seward and found him in so much pain from his carriage accident that he left after a few minutes. Louis J. Weichmann and Mary Surratt finished a late dinner.

The editor of the *National Republican*, S. P. Hanscom, reached Ford's just before the end of intermission to deliver a telegram to Lincoln processed through the War Department. Near the white door to the State Box, Hanscom noticed Forbes the footman sitting against the wall. He apparently had had only a quick drink with Parker, but Parker was nowhere to be seen. Hanscom, who should have been concerned about the absence of a guard, said that he had an important telegram for the president, and Forbes casually motioned for him to go inside the State Box. Lincoln thanked Hanscom, read the message—it was of no significance— and Hanscom left and went home.

Around 9:30 P.M. Booth rode his mare to the rear of Ford's and shouted for Spangler. After Booth called out three times for the stagehand, Spangler came out and insisted he was too busy with the sets to hold the horse. Booth demanded assistance, so Spangler asked a door-boy, Joseph C. Burroughs, to substitute for him. The lad was called "Peanuts John" because he once sold peanuts in front of the theater. At first, Burroughs refused to hold the horse, saying he had to tend his door, but Spangler persuaded him and told him that if anything went wrong to lay the blame on him.

Booth then went backstage to check the progress of the play. He knew the lines well and easily calculated the time before the line that most mattered to him would be uttered. He had a moment to bolster himself with a drink, so he went to the bar at Taltavul's and asked for a bottle of whiskey and some water. It was so different from his usual order of brandy that the bartender remembered it. Further down the bar, Parker the guard and Burns the coachman were imbibing. In one of the tragic ironies in American history, the man who was supposed to be guarding Lincoln was having a drink near the man who, in less than an hour, would kill the president.

Another customer, inebriated, muttered to Booth, "You'll never be the actor your father was." Booth replied, "When I leave the stage, I will be the most famous man in America."

Moments later, at 10:07 P.M., Booth entered Ford's lobby, sprang upstairs to the dress circle, and moved down the right-hand aisle toward the white door he needed to enter to get to the little vestibule and the doors to the State

With the Lincolns at Ford's Theatre were Maj. Henry R. Rathbone, an attaché of the War Office, and his fiancée, Clara Harris, the elegant and witty daughter of Sen. Ira T. Harris of New York

Box. There was no guard, just Forbes, the unarmed footman who may have had too many drinks, and he let Booth pass after the actor apparently flashed his card.

Once inside the outer door, Booth closed it and jammed it shut with the plank, which he secured in the niche in the wall, bracing it against one of the door panels. No one could enter the vestibule and surprise him. In the darkness, Booth moved to the door of Box 7. He peeked through the hole he had drilled that afternoon, saw Lincoln's head directly in front of him, where he expected it to be, and waited for the sockdologizing line from the stage below. It came less than two minutes later.

Silently Booth opened the door to the box and slipped in, the single-shot derringer in his right hand. Lincoln was just four feet in front of him. Now was the time for the hero to emerge and change the course of history. The actor raised the little eight-ounce vest-pocket weapon, extended his arm, and pulled the trigger.

A half-inch-diameter lead ball slammed into the left side of the president's head. Lincoln slumped forward, his head pitched toward his chest. Mary Lincoln, Henry R. Rathbone, and Clara Harris were still focused on the play and did not immediately comprehend what had happened.

Rathbone, a quiet, slender man with muttonchop whiskers and a walrus mustache, was lounging on the sofa at the back of the box. He first suspected something was amiss when he saw a cloud of blue smoke and Booth forcing his way between the Lincolns, whose chairs were close together. The first lady looked confused.

Unarmed, Rathbone lunged at Booth and grappled with him. Booth freed himself, dropped the now-useless derringer, and pulled out a razor-sharp knife. He made a violent thrust toward Rathbone's heart, but the major parried it with his arm, cutting an artery, nerves, and veins. As Booth moved to the ledge for his leap to the stage, Rathbone staggered toward him. The assassin shoved him out of the way, climbed over the ledge near the picture of George Washington, and dropped to the stage.

Booth had considered everything—except for one small detail. He needed to clear the flags in front of Lincoln's box. He did not. As he dropped toward the stage, the spur of his right foot caught in the Treasury regimental flag between the two Old Glories, and he landed awkwardly on his left leg, breaking the shinbone a little above the instep, which caused him to fall on his hands. He got up and hobbled as quickly as he could across the stage and through the Green Room to the alley.

Some said that Booth faced the audience a moment and shouted the state motto of Virginia, the slogan of Brutus as he drove the assassin's knife into imperial Caesar: *Sic semper tyrannis* ("Thus be it ever to tyrants").

Standing between Booth and the door to the alley was the orchestra conductor. Booth struck him with the butt of the hunting knife and pushed him back. Outside, Peanuts John was reclining on a step, holding the mare's bridle in his hand. The assassin grabbed the bridle, kicked the boy in the chest, and mounted his steed just as an army veteran, Joseph B. Stewart, charged out of the theater yelling, "STOP! STOP!" Stewart, a big man at six and a half feet, tried to grab the horse, but Booth wheeled to avoid him, spurred his horse, and galloped away.

Booth zigzagged his hired mare through alleys and streets and, per his plan, headed east to the Navy Yard Bridge. The long wooden bridge spanned the Anacostia River separating Washington from southern Maryland—a large peninsula of little villages and people of Southern sentiment.

Throughout the war, the bridge had been closed to traffic at nine o'clock, and it was now about ten forty-five. Some historians believe that, after Lee's surrender, the curfew was quietly extended to eleven o'clock—possibly to enable peace celebrants to get home—but the change, if it existed at all, had not been publicly announced. Booth may or may not have been aware of that possibility.

As the assassin came to the bridge, a sentry halted him and referred him to Sgt. Silas Cobb, who supposedly was under orders not to let anyone pass after nine o'clock unless they tendered an official pass. Booth, with no pass, boldly identified himself by name, claiming that he lived in Maryland and had been detained in town. Cobb, unaware of the assassination—there were no telegraphic facilities at the bridge—allowed him to pass. He did so

Booth used this .44-caliber single-shot derringer to kill the president. It fired a lead ball that was nearly a half-inch in diameter.

NATIONAL PARK SERVICE

LESLIE'S

This illustration from *Frank Leslie's Illustrated Newspaper* depicts the fatal moment in the State Box when the names of Booth and Lincoln became linked forever.

either because of a relaxed curfew or because he had been told to let Booth pass. For what other reason would Booth have given his real name? By doing so, he notified the authorities of the route he was taking. On the other hand, he may have believed they would not think he was stupid enough to use his real name, and therefore, he was a decoy to throw any pursuers off his path. At least one newspaper believed the "decoy" theory. The Democratic *Easton (Pa.) Argus* expounded: "As they crossed the eastern branch [of the river] at Uniontown, Booth gave his proper name to the officer at the bridge. This, which would seem to have been foolish, was, in reality, very shrewd. The officers [later] believed that one of Booth's accomplices had given the name in order to put them out of the real Booth's track. So they made efforts elsewhere, and so Booth got a start." Still, the bottom line here is that Booth either gambled on being allowed to cross the bridge or he had official help. He was not inclined to gamble.

As Booth leaped from the State Box his spur became entangled with a decorative flag, causing him to land off balance and to break his leg.

As Booth was shooting Lincoln and slashing his knife at Rathbone, Lewis Paine was trying with all his might to fulfill his part of the mission by killing William H. Seward. Over a week earlier, the sixty-four-year-old Seward had broken his arm, fractured his jaw on both sides, and suffered a bad concussion in a carriage accident. Tending to him in his third-floor bedroom were his young daughter Fanny and George T. Robinson, a soldier temporarily assigned to nursing duty.

Paine, accompanied by David Herold as guide, approached Seward's home near the White House on the one-eyed bay horse Booth had purchased from a neighbor of Samuel A. Mudd in Maryland. At 10:10 P.M. he rang the doorbell and told a servant he was a messenger from Seward's physician with a package of medicine to be personally delivered to the secretary. When the servant hesitated to admit him, Paine pushed him aside and ran up the stairs, which were blocked by Seward's son Frederick. Paine drew a revolver, pointed it at Frederick's head, and pulled the trigger. The gun misfired. The men struggled. Paine, by far the stronger man, pistol-whipped Frederick's head, cracking his skull in two places and exposing his brain.

Finding Seward's bedroom, the ferocious giant knifed Robinson, the soldier-nurse, in the forehead, knocked Seward's daughter out of the way, and darted to the bed where Seward had lain nearly two weeks with a steel frame around his head and face. With a bowie knife, Paine stabbed savagely at Seward's throat, slicing each side of the neck and cutting his cheek so deeply that his tongue showed through. Streams of blood flooded Seward's white bandages. Had it not been for the steel frame that deflected several of the blows, Seward would have been killed instantly.

Another of Seward's sons, Maj. Augustus Seward, bolted into the room and, with Robinson, pulled Paine away from Seward. In the ensuing struggle Augustus was stabbed seven times and Robinson four. Frantically, Paine rushed down the stairs, cutting and slashing at anyone in his way, exclaiming, "I am mad! I am mad!" He escaped through the open doorway and ran into a messenger. Paine plunged the knife into the man's chest and left the grounds, leaving behind his bloodstained knife, the battered pistol, and his slouch felt hat.

The scene resembled that of a battlefield hospital, with five persons bleeding from ghastly wounds and others badly beaten. Everyone survived, but Seward's facial scars would remain for the rest of his life, and his traumatized daughter would die the following year.

Once on the stage, Booth turned to the audience and, according to eyewitnesses, shouted either "The South is avenged!" or "*Sic semper tyrannis*" ("Thus be it ever to tyrants," the state motto of Virginia).

To Paine's surprise, Herold was nowhere to be seen. The man who was to have guided him out of town had waited patiently outside while Paine attacked the house. Patience apparently turned to panic, however. With the commotion inside the house, Herold fled, leaving Paine to fend for himself.

Paine, not knowing north from south or east from west, had no idea which direction to go, so he jumped on his horse and took off, wandering aimlessly around before deciding to hide in a tree for several days. Perhaps Booth had told Herold to abandon Paine, knowing that Paine could never find his way out of the city and believing that two escapees would be harder to find than three with their noisy horses. Herold had a much better sense of direction than Paine and would have been more useful to Booth.

Some believe that Herold rode off to check on Atzerodt's attack on Johnson. When he could not find Atzerodt, his concern became one for his own safety, and he raced his horse through the streets to the Navy Yard Bridge.

Atzerodt, however, had never approached the vice president. He had asked the room clerk to point out Johnson's suite—it was behind the lobby.

A general map of Washington, D.C., shows the limited avenues of escape open to Booth and Herold after the assassination. They followed a carefully scouted route through southern Maryland, taking advantage of the network that had served Southern couriers well during the previous four years of war.

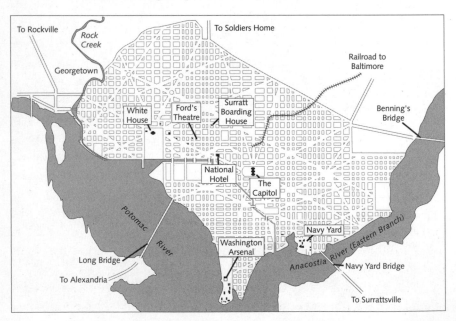

NATIONAL ARCHIVES

Booth and Herold escaped across the Navy Yard Bridge into southern Maryland even though the guards were supposedly under orders not to allow anyone to do so after nine o'clock unless they carried a special pass.

The clerk also told the would-be assassin that Johnson had just come in. Instead of going to the suite, Atzerodt went to the bar. He did not have a heart for murder. Instead, he passed the night drinking.

Soon after Booth had crossed the Navy Yard Bridge, Herold arrived and persuaded the guards to let him pass, even though, as Sgt. Silas Cobb later stated, Herold was profane and vociferous in response to questions. Interestingly, Herold introduced himself with the false name of Smith.

Not far behind Herold was John Fletcher, the foreman at the stable where Herold had rented his horse. Fletcher had seen Herold riding past the well-lighted Willard's Hotel. Convinced he was stealing the horse, Fletcher took up the chase. Herold was about a mile behind Booth, and Fletcher was about a half-mile behind Herold. At the bridge, Cobb, who was having an unusually busy night, told Fletcher he could cross but wouldn't be allowed to return that night. A good night's rest was more appealing to Fletcher, so he turned around and returned to the city.

No one else was allowed to cross the bridge that night, and Cobb was never punished for his laxness in letting Booth and Herold pass. Considering the hundreds who were arrested, Stanton's lack of interest in both Parker and Cobb was very much out of character for the war secretary.

A few moments before Booth crossed the bridge, the commercial telegraph line to Baltimore suddenly ceased to operate. It was out about three hours. Historians say the line frequently malfunctioned, but the timing was astounding. This line was the only one available to the Washington police to communicate with their counterparts in Baltimore—the home base of Booth, Arnold, and O'Laughlin. Military wires remained operational, however, giving the War Department near total command of communications as Booth fled. These circumstances raised questions about a possible conspiracy to stymie police work.

Months later the Washington telegraph manager, William H. Heiss, admitted that he had deliberately shorted out the commercial wire "to prevent panic in outlying areas and to give the military and law enforcement authorities a head start against those who might otherwise act to hinder any investigation." Since Heiss acted before Stanton knew of the assassination, he likely shorted the wires on his own initiative.

The scene back at Ford's Theatre was unimaginable bedlam. "There will never be anything like it on earth," wrote witness Helen Truman. "The shouts, groans, curses, smashing of seats, screams of women, shuffling of feet, and cries of terror created a pandemonium that . . . through the ages will stand out . . . as the hell of hells."

The president, who never regained consciousness, was carried across the street to a room at merchant William A. Petersen's boarding house. Physicians pronounced the wound fatal. Altogether, some sixteen doctors tended to Lincoln.

Stanton was preparing for bed when his wife, Ellen, shouted from downstairs: "Mr. Seward is murdered!"

"Humbug," murmured Stanton. "I left him only an hour ago." But he hurried downstairs and was questioning the messenger when others arrived announcing that Lincoln too had been assassinated. Stanton, now shaken, started to leave, but someone shouted, "You must not go out!"

The secretary of war ignored him, summoned a hack, and told the driver to go to Seward's. There he learned from a sergeant more details of the attack on Lincoln and ordered guards placed around the homes of all the cabinet officers and the vice president.

Without obtaining a description of Seward's assailant—a remarkable lapse on his part—Stanton, joined by Navy Secretary Gideon Welles, continued on to the Petersen house. After assessing the situation there, Stanton set up a communications post, made himself acting president, and issued orders and telegrams. Afraid of a broader conspiracy against other governmental leaders, including himself, he quickly found two hundred soldiers to secure

While recuperating in his home from a street accident in which he suffered a fractured jaw and a broken arm, Secretary of State William H. Seward was viciously attacked in bed by Lewis Paine. Although many in the household were left bloody after Paine's invasion, no one was killed.

the Petersen house. Unfortunately, he had failed to provide a single soldier to protect Lincoln that night. Stanton's indifference to Lincoln's protection was insensitive, irrational, and irresponsible.

Several troubling questions beg consideration. Booth had carefully planned and rehearsed his performance. He was thorough and meticulous—traits consistent with his character. He was not likely to leave anything to chance. He could not afford to. Any miscalculation at Ford's Theatre would cost him his life and, in all probability, save Lincoln's life. To be successful, there were certain things he had to know in advance. Not knowing them would not only lower his odds for success but also leave many things to chance. Booth had time to think, to plan, and to scheme, and he must have used that time wisely—and with help.

Booth entered Ford's Theatre with only two weapons—a single-shot derringer and a knife—and no one else to assist him. How did he know these simple weapons were all he would need? Had Grant accompanied Lincoln—as announced in the afternoon newspapers—the Union leaders probably would have had military protection, and Booth could not possibly have gotten past the soldiers and entered the State Box. Throughout the morning of April 14, Lincoln expected Grant to be with him that night; only near noon did Grant tell him otherwise.

Somehow Booth knew the Grants had declined the president's invitation. While Booth apparently saw the general's carriage heading toward the

Lincoln died in the Petersen house at
7:22 A.M., Saturday, April 15, 1865.

AUTHORS COLLECTION

railway station around six o'clock,
that observation alone would not
assure him that the general was leaving town. Grant might have had an
appointment near the station, or he
might have been picking up someone;
there were innumerable reasons he
would go toward the depot without
having to board a train. Booth seemingly knew that Grant would not be
with Lincoln, and he knew this early
in the day, possibly even before Lin-
coln did. Otherwise, Booth would possibly have taken Paine with him to
subdue the resistance at Ford's, or he might have aborted the mission.

Further, how did Booth know how many guards Lincoln would have,
and how did he know that John F. Parker was assigned to guard Lincoln,
that Parker would be the only guard, and that Parker would not be at his
post at the moment Booth needed to enter the State Box? If, for example,
Ward Hill Lamon or William H. Crook had been guarding the Lincolns,
Booth could not have gotten past either of them. They were too smart, too
conscientious, too loyal, and always too well armed to allow any intruder—
even a famous actor—to get close to the president. Neither was there
because Lincoln had sent Lamon to Richmond and had insisted that Crook
go home after finishing his shift at the White House. Clearly, Booth knew
that neither Crook nor Lamon would be guarding Lincoln that night.

The assassin had only one bullet, and that was for Lincoln; he could not
shoot a guard, and any alert guard with a gun could have overpowered a
person reaching for a knife. Carrying this logic further, if Booth had encountered a competent guard, he would not have had time to barricade himself in
the vestibule outside the State Box. Would he have done his carpentry work
solely on the off chance a guard would have left his post at the exact time
Booth needed access? If he counted on charming a guard by showing his
card and smiling, where was Booth's guarantee that the guard would auto-
matically allow him to pass? And if Booth required force to get in, would not

the commotion have alerted Lincoln and Rathbone? Common sense suggests that Booth did not expect resistance—he knew there would not be any—and therefore he was not prepared to overcome it.

As author Robert L. Mills pointed out, Booth would not have "gambled the whole success of his conspiracy" on the lack of any obstacle to the entrance to the State Box. Obstacles would have cost him valuable time. As it was, he only had a couple of minutes to spare.

At least one historian, Richard Bak, believes no one knows with any certainty who was responsible for Lincoln's protection that night. He acknowledges that Parker is generally thought to be the one, but Bak adds that highly capable Ward Hill Lamon would have been Lincoln's bodyguard that night had he not been on special assignment in Richmond. Obviously, Booth knew about that too and acted accordingly. However, as noted earlier, Lincoln's faithful guard William H. Crook later wrote that Parker was "acting as my substitute [and] his orders were to . . . permit no unauthorized person to pass into the box . . . and to protect the president at all hazards."

Crook, whose statements about Parker are regarded by some historians as untrustworthy, claimed that Parker admitted to him the next day that he left his post and went to another seat so he could see the play. Parker was also seen outside the theater by the coachman Burns, who was with his carriage and horses when Parker and the president's footman Forbes came up to him and asked him to have a drink with them, which he did. These statements, if true, establish Parker as the guard who left his post.

Historians who accept the story that Forbes allowed Booth to pass by just flashing his card, excuse him from any culpability, reasoning that Forbes thought Lincoln would not mind being interrupted by a famous actor. Such is too kind a view of Forbes's action. Forbes was neither reliable nor trustworthy. Years later, in 1892, he swore in an affidavit that the president was not in the carriage with the first lady, Clara Harris, and Henry R. Rathbone and that the carriage was sent back to the White House for him. Many witnesses, however, testified to the contrary. Forbes also stated he was in the State Box when Booth fired his fatal shot. That statement too is contradicted

Lincoln died on a bed once occupied by John Wilkes Booth when a friend of his was renting the room from Washington tailor William A. Petersen. Lincoln had been carried to the Petersen house from Ford's Theatre. Six years later Petersen committed suicide.

by eyewitnesses and categorically denied by Rathbone's affidavit. Given Forbes's tendency to prevaricate—and his irresponsible admission of Booth to the State Box—he should have been regarded as a possible conspirator in the assassination plot.

Since Forbes was not a guard, was not armed, and was not overly bright, Booth could conceivably have flashed his card and gotten by him. But it would have been a tremendous gamble on Booth's part to have assumed a card shown to a *competent* guard would have gained him admission to the State Box. Leaving admittance to "random chance" was unimaginable for a detailed planner like Booth. When Booth, Paine, Herold, and Atzerodt assembled that night to go about their malevolent deeds, there was no turning back for Booth. After Paine attacked Seward, the jig was up. If Booth had not attacked Lincoln at the same time, he would not have a second chance. He had to know exactly who would be at, in, or near the State Box, and he had to have known that before the final meeting with his coconspirators.

Frank A. Ford, a descendant of the owners of Ford's Theatre, raised eyebrows in 1965 with a comment that it was not Booth who prepared the wedge-blockade for the outer door. He said a workman had done it at Harry Ford's request since the locks had been broken several weeks earlier. If that was true, wouldn't the Fords have told someone in the presidential party—or at least the guard—so they could have made use of the wedge-blockade? Or, better still, why didn't they have the locks repaired since they had plenty of time to do so? Where was their concern for the president's safety? More likely, and contrary to assumptions made by historians, Booth broke the locks himself that afternoon.

Booth was not on a suicide mission. Nor was he naive. He was vain and not about to subject himself to brutal treatment. He had rehearsed for his most famous role—a performance of high drama, with an escape in the darkness and rain, and a lifetime of applause from the people of the Confederacy. He was not a madman. He was, however, a dedicated Confederate agent. And he had help.

Obviously, his assistant knew the details—perhaps one or more disgruntled persons at the White House, the War Department, the National Detective Police, or the Metropolitan Police Department, probably someone who would benefit, or who felt the country would benefit, from Lincoln's death. Among the possibilities would be the Radical Republicans who favored a harsh reconstruction policy toward the South. Lincoln stood in their way.

7

STANTON'S
SWIFT
SWORD

D URING THE VIGIL AT Lincoln's bedside in the Petersen house, Stanton put himself in charge of both the investigation and the country. Operating from the sitting room near the front of the house, he usurped the role of "president, secretary of state, commander-in-chief, comforter, and dictator," wrote one of his friends. Dr. Charles A. Leale, who attended the dying president, observed that Stanton was "in reality acting president of the United States" and praised him for his "wonderful ability and power in action." To take and record the testimonies of witnesses, Stanton sent for District of Columbia chief justice David Cartter and Cpl. James Tanner, a shorthand reporter who had lost both legs at the battle of Second Bull Run and was a boarder in the house next door. When the interviews began, Cartter administered the oath, Stanton asked the questions, and Tanner recorded the testimony.

Charles A. Dana, assistant secretary of war, later recorded:

It seemed as if Stanton thought of everything, and there was a great deal to be thought of that night. The extent of the conspiracy was, of course, unknown, and the horrible beginning which had been made naturally led us to suggest the worst. The safety of Washington must be looked after. Commanders all over the country had to be ordered to take extra precautions. The people [had to be] notified of the tragedy. The assassins [had to be] captured. The coolness and clearheadedness of Mr. Stanton under the circumstances were most remarkable.

Remarkable, indeed. Always before, the death of a friend or close relative had rattled Stanton to the point of imbalance. But now he seemed calm, cool, and decisive.

After just fifteen minutes of testimony, Tanner was convinced that Booth was the assassin, but Stanton hesitated several hours before drawing the same conclusion and ordering his pursuit. Tanner later observed: "In fifteen minutes I had testimony enough to hang Wilkes Booth, the assassin, higher than even Haman hung. . . . No one said positively that the assassin was Booth, but all thought it was he. It was evident that the horror of the crime held them back. They seemed to hate to think that one they had known . . . could be guilty of such an awful crime."

It is also likely that Stanton so intimidated the witnesses—or they were so concerned for their own safety—that they would say no more than that they believed the assassin to be Booth. The witnesses were terrified. One of the play's lead actors, Harry Hawk, recalled: "I believe to the best of my knowledge that it was John Wilkes Booth. Still, I am not positive that it was him. I only had one glance at him as he was rushing towards me with a dagger, and I turned and ran and after I ran up a flight of stairs, I turned and exclaimed: 'My God! That's John Booth!' In my own mind, I do not have any doubt but that it was Booth."

Throughout the night Stanton kept in close touch with police superintendent A. C. Richards; Gen. Christopher C. Augur, commander of the Department of Washington; and Maj. James R. O'Beirne, Washington provost marshal.

While Stanton was interviewing witnesses at the Petersen house, Richards was interrogating seventeen others at police headquarters. Through stable foreman John Fletcher, from whom the conspirators had rented horses, Herold and Atzerodt were identified. Augur questioned the

Immediately after Lincoln's death, paranoia swept through the nation's capital. Persons who expressed doubts about Jefferson Davis's involvement were strung up on lampposts. An elderly woman was thrown into the Old Capitol Prison for hanging her son's gray uniform out to rid it of its vermin. A soldier knocked down a man he saw smiling. It was treason, the soldier said, to smile at a time like this.

AUTHOR'S COLLECTION

Police Superintendent A. C. Richards was searching for Booth's known associates long before Secretary of War Edwin M. Stanton announced that Booth was the assassin.

foreman further, but not far enough. Fletcher could have told him that Booth was a friend of Herold and Atzerodt, that Booth often loaned a horse to John Surratt, and that Surratt's mother owned a tavern at Surrattsville. But these matters were not pursued at that time.

One of O'Beirne's men, detective John Lee, went to Kirkwood House to check on Vice President Johnson and scrutinize the building's security. While having a drink at the bar, a customer mentioned a suspicious-looking man who had checked into the hotel the previous day and had asked numerous questions about the vice president. Examining the hotel register, Lee saw Atzerodt's name. He searched his room and found a pistol, three boxes of cartridges, a large bowie knife, an Ontario, Canada, bankbook made out to J. Wilkes Booth, a large scale map of Virginia, and an empty envelope with the frank of Sen. John Conness, a Radical Republican from California.

Lee reported his findings to O'Beirne, who notified Stanton. He now had evidence of the Booth-Atzerodt connection and of a possible tie to Conness, but he never followed up on the latter. The Conness envelope has never been adequately explained. Did Stanton ignore it because of his close relationship with the Radical Republicans and his support of their policies? One could easily infer some kind of linkage between the Radicals and Booth's team.

Back at the Petersen house, Stanton needed more time and more testimony before blaming Booth for the assassination. He feared that the simultaneous attacks on Lincoln and Seward suggested a complex conspiracy "planned and set on foot by rebels under pretense of avenging the rebel cause," and that's what he released to the press. He was concerned about his own safety and that of other officials. Within that scenario, Booth was small game.

Stanton's first priority had to be to prevent other possible assassinations. Had Confederate explosives expert Sgt. Thomas F. "Frank" Harney been successful in his mission to blow up the White House, that's exactly what Stanton would have been dealing with. He was so very close to the truth. In the days ahead, he continued to hold that view and to insist that Lincoln's death was part of a massive conspiracy approved by Jefferson Davis. Northern newspapers followed suit and published bulletins seeking Davis and other Confederate leaders as coconspirators. So in the early morning hours of April 15, Stanton, being unsure of how widespread the plot was, focused on the necessary measures to preserve the Union.

Regardless, historians and other writers have charged Stanton with almost criminal negligence for not rapidly identifying and pursuing the assassins and informing the public. Following procedures for press releases established earlier in the war, Stanton released major announcements to the news media through Gen. John A. Dix in New York. Although the crime had been committed at about 10:15 P.M., the first dispatch was not sent until 2:15 A.M., and it did not name the assassin. It was not until 3:20 A.M.

Mary Surratt's boarding house at 541 H Street, NW (now 604 H Street, NW) was searched by city police on the night of the assassination. They were looking for John Surratt, whom Stanton had incorrectly identified as Seward's attacker. Andrew Johnson dubbed the house the "nest that hatched the eggs."

that Stanton wired Dix that the "investigation strongly indicates J. Wilkes Booth as the assassin of the president. Whether it is the same or a different person that attempted to murder Mr. Seward remains in doubt." At 4:40 A.M. Stanton clarified that there had been two assassins involved in the attacks on the president and the secretary of state.

Historian Thomas Reed Turner did not regard Stanton's delay in naming Booth as an "inordinately long amount of time" since Stanton had two crimes to investigate and many other duties to perform that night, not the least of which was preventing more bloodshed—including his own. Stanton wired Gen. Winfield Scott Hancock: "The recent murders show such an astounding wickedness that too much preparation cannot be taken."

New York World correspondent George Townsend had a different view: "The departments were absolutely paralyzed. The murderers had three good hours to escape. . . . Rumors filled the town with so many reports that the first valuable hours, which should have been used to follow hard after them, were consumed in feverish efforts to know the real extent of the conspiracy."

While Stanton's concern for uncovering the full extent of the conspiracy is commendable and understandable, he had, in fact, been outwitted by Booth. Had the assassin not broken his leg, he would have had a good chance to avoid capture.

Hundreds of arrests were made, most on flimsy or no evidence. Members of the cast of *Our American Cousin*, the Fords, the livery stable man who rented the mare to Booth, and others who had been close to Booth were hauled in and detained for inquiry. To Stanton's credit, when he heard that Laura Keene and Harry Hawk (the stars of the play) were in jail, he had them released immediately.

Booth's brother Junius and brother-in-law John Sleeper Clarke were arrested and held without charge in the Old Capitol Prison for several weeks. Other family members were closely watched, including Asia Booth Clarke, who was pregnant with twins. Brother Edwin announced he would play no more dramas in America for years, if ever again. In a letter "to the people of the United States" he declared: "I shall struggle on, in my retirement, with a heavy heart, an oppressed memory, and a wounded name—dreadful burdens—to my welcome grave." Heavy debts, however, forced him back to the stage less than a year later, and the public welcomed him, not blaming him for his brother's action. Edwin Booth had always been a strong Lincoln supporter and a strong Unionist.

Sometime around midnight Stanton initiated a manhunt for Samuel Arnold and Michael O'Laughlin—two men who were involved in Booth's plot to capture Lincoln but who had nothing to do with the assassination. Stanton also erroneously decided that Seward's attacker was John H. Surratt Jr. The war secretary was finally moving against the Baltimore kidnapping conspirators—albeit too late and for the wrong reasons and apparently before obtaining a description of Seward's assailant. Surratt and Paine bore no resemblance to each other, and no evidence connected Surratt to the attack on Seward. Regardless, through press leaks based on Stanton's information, Surratt was wrongly identified as Seward's assassin.

Many historians have long believed that Stanton's assumption of Surratt's involvement indicated that the secretary was fully aware of the earlier kidnapping efforts, even to the point of knowing the names of the conspirators. How else could he have come up with the names of Surratt, Arnold, and O'Laughlin only a few hours after the assassination? Did he name Surratt as Seward's attacker on a whim? He did not have any other basis. Doing so was reckless and shameful by any standard. Why was he so intent on pursuing Surratt, against whom he had no witnesses, while waiting until 3:20 A.M. to pursue Booth, against whom he had mounds of evidence? Further, if Surratt's name surfaced because of Stanton's knowledge of the attempt to capture Lincoln on March 17, then Booth's name should have surfaced at the same time. Why it did not remains a mystery.

With regard to Arnold and O'Laughlin, one anticonspiracy author claimed that their quick pursuit resulted from "quick thinking and quick acting" by Baltimore's provost marshal, Gen. James L. McPhail. Both men were friends of Booth, McPhail asserted in a wire to the War Department that night. Author Robert L. Mills, however, pointed out that Booth had lots of friends and pondered on what basis two friends could be singled out as conspirators. Mills concluded that McPhail had previously notified Stanton about Arnold and O'Laughlin's collusion with Booth in an earlier conspiracy, and the repetition of their names on the night of April 14 prompted the search. Such a possibility raises another question: If Stanton was aware of them earlier, why did he not take action against them? The answer most often given is that Stanton had been told of many plots against Lincoln's life, and he did not have the manpower to follow up on all of them.

Maj. James R. O'Beirne of the provost marshal's office learned from personnel at Ford's Theatre where Booth lived and dispatched detective William Eaton there at once to take charge of the rooms in the name of the War

Department. Eaton returned with a trunk that contained one important item—a mysterious letter signed only with the name "Sam" and dated March 27, 1865, just ten days after the failed attempt to capture Lincoln.

The letter clearly established "Sam's" association with Booth in the scheme: "You know full well that the G—t [Government] suspicions something is going on there; therefore, the undertaking is becoming more complicated. . . . Do not act rashly or in haste. I would prefer your first query, go and see how it will be taken in R—d [Richmond]."

Stanton was reportedly fascinated with this letter, especially the reference to Richmond. The document seemingly supported his belief in Confederate complicity.

In a wire to General Dix at 4:40 A.M., Stanton included the following passage: "It appears from a letter found in Booth's trunk that the murder was planned before the 4th of March, but fell through then because the accomplice backed out until 'Richmond could be heard from.'" March 4 was inauguration day, but there was nothing in Samuel Arnold's letter that mentions that day. Stanton's wire strongly suggests that Gen. Christopher C. Augur had told him earlier about Booth, Surratt, and Atzerodt being involved in a kidnapping plot before March 4 and that the War Department had ignored it. Further, Stanton was now calling it a "murder" plot instead of a kidnapping plot, although he undoubtedly knew the original intent of the conspirators.

Edman Spangler, a handyman at Ford's Theatre, was arrested, charged, and convicted primarily for holding Booth's horse for a few seconds. Generally regarded as harmless and good-natured, Spangler helped everyone around the theater. He often took care of Booth's horse while the actor visited friends in the theater.

Combined with the information from McPhail, the "Sam" letter led to Samuel Arnold's arrest on April 17 at Fort Monroe, where he was employed as a store clerk. In custody he made a clean breast of his connection with the proposed kidnapping but denied any involvement in or knowledge of the assassination. O'Laughlin was arrested the same day in Baltimore. Atzerodt was taken from his bed at a cousin's home near Rockville, Maryland, at four o'clock on the morning of April 20. Spangler, the hapless scene-shifter at Ford's Theatre, was also hauled in. He had held Booth's horse for a moment before securing Peanuts John Burroughs for the job.

Although Stanton did not announce Booth as the assassin until 3:20 A.M., the superintendent of the Washington City Police, A. C. Richards, entered the Surratt boarding house at about 1 A.M. Such timing indicates that before that hour he had identified Booth as the killer and was searching for his associates. In a letter to Weichmann dated April 29, 1898, Richards wrote that he went to the boarding house after learning that John H. Surratt was often seen in the company of Booth, Arnold, and O'Laughlin and that Booth had often visited the house. Surely he provided this information to Stanton, with whom he was in close touch all night, but Stanton delayed identifying Booth as the assassin for another two and a half hours.

Between 2 and 2:30 A.M., four city detectives entered the boarding house to search for Booth and Surratt. Weichmann, unaware of the earlier visit, asked why, and was informed that Booth had killed the president and Surratt had killed Seward. Weichmann threw up his hands and exclaimed, "My God, I see it all now," meaning he finally understood why Booth had held those secret meetings at the boarding house. According to Weichmann, he told the detectives that Surratt, his former seminary buddy, was in Mon-

Actor Edwin Booth, brother of John Wilkes Booth, voted for and admired the man his brother hated and killed. A month before Lincoln's death, Edwin was in Trenton, New Jersey, waiting to board a train to Washington. As the train stood on the tracks, a number of passengers chatted in the station's saloon. Then, with a toot of the whistle, the train unexpectedly began to move, and the crowd rushed onto the platform and scrambled hastily to get onboard. One man stumbled and pitched forward, off balance, toward the rolling wheels. If a hand had not at that moment shot from the crowd to stop his fall, he might have been crushed beneath the train. The potential victim was Capt. Robert Lincoln, the president's son. The hand that saved him was that of Edwin Booth.

treal—he could not have killed Seward. Mary Surratt said she had a letter to prove it. Weichmann volunteered to do all he could to assist the police. He joined them in a search of the Surrattsville area and later accompanied them to Montreal to look for Surratt.

Weichmann claimed that he felt Surratt was in great danger and hoped he would surrender and clear himself of any connection with the assassination. At the same time, Weichmann asserted that he did not then know that Surratt had been involved in earlier kidnapping plots.

In Canada the authorities ran down every clue brought to them, but they were unable to find Surratt. Ironically, they came close—very close. Surratt spied them on a Montreal street, but they did not see him.

Back in Washington on Saturday, April 29, Weichmann and the detectives reported to Gen. Henry L. Burnett in the War Department, who discharged them. Yet when Stanton discovered that Weichmann was not in custody, he shook with anger and demanded to see him the following morning. Stanton questioned the clerk about his family, his involvement with the Surratts, and how he met Booth.

Weichmann identified Samuel A. Mudd as the man who had introduced him to Booth, and he described his meeting with Booth, Mudd, and Surratt the previous winter. Stanton had no choice but to incarcerate Weichmann until the conspiracy had been thoroughly investigated. "By the time the trial is over," Weichmann vowed, "you will be the first one to recognize the fact that I shall have done my whole duty to the government."

Stanton apparently had irate words that day with the police superintendent, which resulted in the War Department's asserting jurisdiction over the investigation. The timing coincided with the dropping of all charges against John F. Parker, Lincoln's guard at Ford's Theatre.

Lewis Paine somehow had evaded capture and might have escaped had it not been for a strange coincidence. After Paine had sliced up the Seward family, he lost his way and either hid in the woods or, as Weichmann later wrote, in an empty cemetery vault. On Monday night, April 17—having had no food since Friday—he ventured out and found his way to the only family he knew in Washington, the Surratts. He arrived at the boarding house carrying a pickax around ten o'clock, just as military detectives were arresting everyone there. Because his arrival and appearance seemed suspicious, he too was arrested and later identified by the victims of his attack. Paine was placed in irons, with manacles on his hands and a heavy ball and chain on his left leg. In his jail cell he tried to butt out his brains by banging

Conspirator Lewis Paine picked the wrong time to show up the Surratt boarding house. Military detectives were in the process of arresting everyone there. Suspicious of Paine, they arrested him, too.

NATIONAL POLICE GAZETTE

his head against a wall. To prevent further behavior of this sort, Stanton ordered a padded cap to be secured on his head.

Stanton offered fifty thousand dollars for Booth's arrest and twenty-five thousand dollars each for John Surratt and David Herold, who were listed as Booth's accomplices. Stanton's poster, dated April 20, stated: "All persons harboring or secreting the said persons . . . or aiding or assisting their concealment or escape, will be treated as accomplices . . . and shall be subject to trial before a military commission and the punishment of DEATH. Let the stain of innocent blood be removed from the land by the arrest and punishment of the murderers." Additional rewards were promised by some of the states. The poster was dated two days after Paine had been identified as Seward's attacker. Stanton was still after Surratt even though he had no evidence to tie him to the assassination.

To organize the search for Booth and Herold, Stanton summoned Col. Lafayette C. Baker, the head of the National Detective Police, to Washington from New York. Baker's force would be headed by his cousin, Lt. Luther B. Baker, and Col. Everton J. Conger. Under them were twenty-five cavalrymen from a New York regiment commanded by Lt. Edward P. Doherty. Lafayette C. Baker admonished the searchers "to extort confessions and procure testimony to establish the conspiracy . . . by promises, rewards, threats, deceit, force, or any other effectual means." Similar means would be used in Washington by high officials of the War Department.

LESLIE'S

Paine was hooded with a padded cap and restrained by wrist irons and a heavy ball and chain (*not shown*). All the conspirators were treated in a similar fashion.

Numerous military units, civilians, and bounty hunters joined the search—all going their own way and all hungry for the reward money. Thus they all worked at cross purposes and did not communicate with one another. Several thousand cavalrymen were involved in the search, and the New York City chief of police joined the hunt. Large rewards elevated greed and rivalry above patriotism and hampered the operation. For example, General Augur had learned by April 21 or 22 that Booth had been treated after the assassination by Mudd, but he did not share this information with Stanton. One of Augur's men, Major O'Beirne, who was on Booth's trail, mentioned this crucial information to a telegrapher, who on his own initiative wired the War Department. Stanton responded by ordering O'Beirne "to discontinue his expedition and remain in Maryland" so that Stanton's own man, Lafayette C. Baker, could take up the chase instead.

Meanwhile, Booth's friends O'Laughlin, Arnold, Paine, Spangler, and Atzerodt were kept confined under painful conditions aboard two ironclad monitors—the *Saugus* and the *Montauk*—on the Potomac. Furthermore, Stanton ordered that the prisoners "for better security against conversations, shall have a canvas bag put over the head of each and tied about the neck, with a hole for proper breathing and eating, but not seeing." No one was allowed to see the prisoners, not even a lawyer. Still at large were Booth, Herold, Jefferson Davis, and other Confederate leaders who were thought to be behind the assassination.

The Confederate president, escaping to the south, stopped briefly at the home of Lewis E. Bates in Charlotte, North Carolina. Bates later repeated Davis's comment upon hearing of Lincoln's assassination: "If it were to be done at all, it were better that it were well done; and if the same had been done to Andy Johnson, the beast, and to Secretary Stanton, the job would then be complete."

Officially, Davis and other Southern leaders called Lincoln's assassination "the irresponsible act of a crazed desperado" and said that the South had lost a true friend. Such comments were part of a vast propaganda effort to disassociate themselves from their own agent and avoid what they perceived to be a devastating retribution if Booth's connection with them were discovered. Even without that knowledge, few observers took their statements seriously. After all, the statements came from leaders who despised Lincoln and from officials of a government that was responsible for starving prisoners of war, instituting germ warfare against civilians, sanctioning a plan to poison New York City's drinking water, and killing or enslaving black soldiers after they had surrendered.

8

MUDD

For NEARLY 140 YEARS Dr. Samuel A. Mudd has been steadfastly defended as an innocent victim of the blind vengeance surrounding Lincoln's assassination. His name conjures up a kind and gentle country doctor unfairly convicted and imprisoned as a conspirator in that heinous crime because he obeyed his Hippocratic oath and treated a man with a broken leg—a man he claimed he did not recognize. Two U.S. presidents—Jimmy Carter and Ronald Reagan— have all but declared Mudd innocent of any wrongdoing. In 1973 the Michigan legislature even adopted a resolution claiming that Mudd was "innocent of any complicity" in Lincoln's assassination. Documentaries have publicized Mudd's plight, and pageants have honored his memory. At least one school is named after him. Yet despite the massive public relations effort to clear his name —an effort spearheaded by his descendants—the evidence of his guilt, even though much of it is circumstantial, is overwhelming.

In 1865 thirty-one-year-old Samuel A. Mudd was one of the most respected citizens in southern Maryland, a land of Secessionists and Confederate sympathizers. The tall, thin country doctor with a bald forehead and dark red hair, mustache, and whiskers was a Southerner by heritage and tradition—an aristocrat and rabid Secessionist who shared the political views of John Wilkes Booth and the Confederacy. Both Booth and Mudd despised Lincoln's policies and sought his removal. Mudd hated Northerners in general and condemned them as "parasitical, covert, stealthy, cowardly [and] law abiding so long as it bears them out in their selfish interest." Although calling himself a "Union man," he often sheltered and cared for Confederate soldiers either at his home or in hiding places in the woods nearby, according to reports from his former slaves. A man of culture, Mudd spoke French, Greek, and Latin and played the flute, piano, violin, and other instruments. He had attended St. John's College in Maryland, the University of Maryland, and Georgetown College in Washington, D.C.

Mudd was more a tobacco farmer than a practicing physician. There were other doctors in this rural area and very little demand for them. Full-time farming was far more profitable, and part-time devotion to the Confederate cause was far more satisfying. As a courier for the Confederate mail line, Mudd was intimately linked to key members of the Confederate Signal Service, an important communications network. Mudd owned as many as eleven slaves, whom he held in strict obedience through whippings and other forms of punishment. He shot one in the leg for not responding quickly to an order. He flogged another—a young woman. He also participated in the patrols that ran down fugitive slaves and sent them back to slavery.

Mudd married his childhood sweetheart, Frances Dyer, and they lived comfortably with their four children in a two-story frame farmhouse at the top of a long rise about five miles north of Bryantown, a village thirty miles south of Washington, D.C. Their comfort, however, was short-lived, drastically reduced after Lincoln's Emancipation Proclamation allowed for the enlistment of African American soldiers by the Union army. Mudd lost nearly all of his slave labor. To maintain house servants and fieldworkers, he had to pay them twice what he considered a fair wage. With less manpower, he had to reduce his total tobacco acreage, which resulted in a sharp drop in his revenue.

His neighbors fared similarly. Land values as well as the economy of Charles County tumbled with the disappearance of slaves valued at more than eight million dollars. Most people in southern Maryland, and especially in Charles County, detested the president and eagerly supported plots to remove this perceived tyrant from office. Even before the proclamation, Lincoln was about as popular as mosquitoes and horse flies on a hot summer day. In the 1860 election, of the 1,197 votes cast for president in Charles County, only 6 were for Lincoln.

LIBRARY OF CONGRESS

Dr. Samuel A. Mudd was one of the most respected citizens in southern Maryland and a Confederate agent. In the early morning hours of April 15, he examined the injured left leg of John Wilkes Booth. Finding a straight break near the ankle, Mudd set the bone and improvised a splint that would allow the assassin to continue his escape into Virginia.

John Wilkes Booth was fully aware of this sentiment in southern Maryland, which is why in the early part of 1865 he had established contacts in the region. They would assist him in escaping to Richmond after he had captured Lincoln.

A deeply religious family, the Mudds regularly attended nearby St. Peter's Catholic Church and undoubtedly worshiped there on Good Friday, April 14, 1865. As that day drew to a close, Mudd crawled wearily into bed at nine o'clock. It was the usual bedtime for the farmers of Charles County, whose workday began at sunrise. Frances joined him shortly after tucking in the children. It was not the best of nights for the young farmer. His muscles ached from strenuous work, and his head throbbed, probably triggered by worries about the South. Just five days earlier Robert E. Lee had surrendered the Army of Northern Virginia. Richmond was in Union hands. The Southern cause looked hopeless. Stressed by these events, Mudd prayed for a good night's sleep. Unfortunately for him, his prayers were not answered. The next twenty-four hours transformed him into one of the most controversial figures in American history—a victim of strange circumstances made more complex, if not bizarre, by the tangled web of deceit he chose to weave.

As the Mudds slept, the nearly full moon that rose over their farm was lost in clouds that unleashed rain showers on this cool, spring night. Meanwhile, up the road in Washington, D.C., a chaotic night of horror, terror, and madness had unfolded as Booth and Paine executed their plans. David

Herold had abandoned Paine and joined up with Booth after both had crossed the Navy Yard Bridge into southern Maryland. Eleven miles south of Washington they stopped at a Confederate safe house—Mary Surratt's tavern at Surrattsville—and retrieved a Spencer carbine, field glasses, a box of cartridges, and a quart of whiskey.

Booth took two deep swallows of the whiskey, hoping to relieve the wrenching pain in his left leg that had been broken by his jump from the presidential box to the stage at Ford's Theatre. The liquor did not help. He needed a physician. To get treatment, however, would require him to alter his escape route. He had intended to go straight to Port Tobacco, Maryland, and cross the broad bend of the Potomac into Virginia, but now he would go east—ten miles out of the way—to Samuel A. Mudd's place near Bryantown. It was, for him, a painful, seventeen-mile ride in the rain from Surrattsville. There were at least three other physicians along the route, but Booth bypassed them. He wanted Mudd. He knew him and could rely upon him.

At four o'clock that Saturday morning, the Mudds were abruptly awakened by a loud pounding on their front door. Half asleep and in his nightshirt, Mudd staggered through the dining room and parlor toward the door. What happened after that is less clear and even controversial.

According to Mudd's later testimony, the party at his door identified themselves as "two strangers riding to Washington." One of the men

Twenty-two-year-old David Herold, a former drugstore clerk, was a talented outdoorsman who knew the trails and waterways around Washington and southern Maryland. Assigned to guide Lewis Paine to the Seward home and to the rendezvous with Booth, Herold abandoned him and rode after Booth. Together the two men followed the network of Confederate agents who had operated in southern Maryland throughout the war.

explained, "My friend broke his leg and needs help. His horse stumbled, causing him to fall." Mudd opened the door and saw the boyish-looking Herold holding the reins of a horse whose rider was slumped in the saddle. The man looked pained and exhausted. Mudd and Herold assisted the injured man in dismounting and helped him into the parlor then to an upstairs bedroom. Mudd later told authorities that the younger man did most of the talking and urged him "to attend to his [friend's] leg as soon as possible, as they were anxious to get to Washington." Mudd claimed, "To examine and operate upon his leg, I had to cut his boot longitudinally in front of the instep" to remove it. He found a fractured bone about two inches above the ankle joint. He set the break and prepared a splint. "I had no proper paste-board for making splints," he said, "and went out and got an old band box [for that purpose]." The patient "continued still to suffer, and complained of [trouble breathing and] severe pain in the back, especially when being moved," so Mudd said he could stay for a while.

The country doctor described the injured man as of medium size with long black hair "inclined to curl," long whiskers, and a mustache. "He had a pretty full forehead and his skin was fair. . . . [He] appeared to be pretty well made, but he had a heavy shawl on all the time. . . . I did not see his face at all. [He] had his cloak thrown around his head." The other man, Mudd said, "looked to be about seventeen or eighteen—[like] a boy who had never yet shaved." Mudd said he was "about five feet two or three inches tall" with black hair and a dark complexion. "He seemed to be well acquainted throughout the whole country, and I asked his name; he gave it as Henson, and that of the wounded man as Tyser or Tyson."

After setting the injured man's leg, Mudd walked out to his farmyard then returned for breakfast. He invited the young man to join him at the table, which he did, but the injured man remained upstairs in bed. After breakfast, Mudd said that as he was about to leave for his farm work, "this young man asked me if I had a razor, that his friend desired to take a shave, as perhaps he would feel better." Mudd provided the razor. After the noon meal, Mudd "went to see the patient and although he kept his face partly turned away from me, I noticed that he had lost his mustache, but still retained his whiskers."

Mudd's descriptions and recollections appear self-serving. Taken at face value, they justify his contention that he did not recognize the injured stranger as Booth, and they protect the doctor from accusations of aiding and abetting Lincoln's assassin. If the patient had whiskers and no mustache, a cloak over his head, his face turned to the wall, and a fictitious name, how could Mudd have known who he was treating? That's the question he asked his inquisitors. If his story was believable, he and his family would, hopefully, avoid suspicion. But the story was too neat, too perfect, too illogical, and did not stand up to scrutiny.

It is highly unlikely that Booth wore a cloak over his head, sported a false beard, or used an alias. If Booth kept his cloak over his head, as Mudd alleged, how could the doctor have described in detail the man's forehead? And if he kept his face turned toward the wall, how could he have detected a mustache or the absence of one? Although Mudd claimed that the stranger shaved off his mustache, at least four credible witnesses later testified that Booth had a full mustache within days of leaving Mudd's house, and one of them, Thomas A. Jones, saw Booth for six consecutive days! The others were a young Confederate soldier, A. R. Bainbridge, who referred to Booth's "long dark mustache"; Richard B. Garrett, at whose family farm Booth was killed; and James A. Wardell, a War Department detective who saw the only photograph taken of Booth's body.

Near Bryantown, Maryland, Samuel and Frances Mudd lived in this farmhouse, which has been preserved to the present day. Booth and Herold bypassed at least three other doctors before knocking on the Mudds' door.

Garrett, a Baptist minister and Chatauqua lecturer in the 1880s, was a boy of eleven years old when he shared a room with Booth. Observing him asleep the next morning, Garrett said that he "remembered vividly" Booth's face, with "a heavy dark mustache [shading] a mouth as beautiful as a babe's."

What of the alias, "Tyson"? Booth had not used that alias at any other stop during his escape. Further, there was no need to use an alias with Mudd, because the two men were intimately acquainted, and Booth had passed up the homes of at least three other physicians en route to the Mudd farm. Booth and Herold did use an alias, "Boyd," at the Garrett farmhouse, because he did not know the Garretts, and they also used "Boyd" when they encountered three Confederate soldiers on the road earlier. But when they discovered the soldiers had been with Mosby's Rangers, they quickly used their real names and identified themselves as the assassins. The bottom line is that when Booth knew the sentiments of the people with whom he was dealing, he freely used his name and talked of his heroic deed. Mudd in all probability fell into that category.

Yet in Mudd's first statement to the military investigators, he said that he "never saw either of the parties before, nor can I conceive who sent them to my house." In another statement a few days later, however, Mudd said that the younger man told him they had obtained directions from a lady and a gentleman "walking somewhere near Bryantown" and that "they also met a Negro, but did not state where and that they also inquired of him the way to my place."

Continuing his statement, Mudd said that the younger stranger had requested crutches for his friend, and with the help of an old Englishman on his farm, they made a crude pair "out of a piece of plank." The stranger also wanted a carriage, alleged Mudd, to take his friend to the home of Parson Wilmer, whom he knew, near Piney Church. "I told [Herold] I had nothing of the sort, but that perhaps, he might get an old carriage from my father, and that as I was going to ride out that afternoon, [he] might go over there with me." They did so after lunch but found that the carriages were in need of repair.

Mudd said the young stranger then decided to go to Bryantown to look for a carriage or wagon. "He [Herold] started off at a pretty fair gallop and I after him. He soon got a good distance ahead of me as his horse was quite a sprightly one. . . . When he got a mile and a half beyond my father's house, he abruptly turned round and came back, meeting me as he did so. He seemed to be engaged in deep thought. As he passed me he observed, 'I believe I will get my friend to Rev. Dr. Wilmer's on horseback.'" It was later learned that Herold panicked when he saw a detachment of Union cavalrymen and chose to return to Mudd's farm. Mudd continued on to Bryantown alone, he said, to purchase various items, including calico cloth, pepper, and nails.

Mudd later admitted that he first heard about Lincoln's murder while shopping in Bryantown on Saturday, which contradicted an earlier statement that he first learned of it at church on Sunday. Yet he gave no indication that he learned the assassin's name.

One of Mudd's neighbors, John F. Hardy, later testified that he visited with the doctor and Francis R. Farrell as Mudd was returning home from Bryantown, and the men talked about the assassination. Hardy asked if anyone had heard who had killed Lincoln, and according to Farrell, Mudd told them, "A man by the name of Booth." Hardy remembered a Booth who had been in the area the past fall and asked the doctor if the assassin was the same man. According to Hardy, Mudd said he did not know, but if it was the same Booth, he was acquainted with him.

Mudd said that he returned home "between 4 & 5 o'clock" and added:

> The two men were just getting ready to [leave]. . . . The man on crutches had left the house, and he was some fifty to seventy yards from me when [the] young man came to me and [asked] the . . . nearest way to [Reverend Lemuel] Wilmer's. I told them there were two ways: one was [about five miles] by the public road leading by Beantown; the other led across the [Zekiah] swamp [and] could save a mile—it is not a public way, but by taking down a fence [they could] get through. They concluded to take this latter route, and I gave them the necessary directions. I did not see them leave my house. . . . I do not know where they went. . . . I have not seen either of them since.

Mudd reported that, as the two men left, Herold placed a roll of bills in his hand, "rather a trivial amount." Actually, the bills totaled twenty-five dollars, which was a generous payment for the time.

Most of Mudd's statements appear to be concocted. The time of his arrival back home is certainly questionable. According to neighbor John F. Hardy, Mudd was with him "very near sundown," about 6:30 P.M. If true, Mudd would have returned home around 7 P.M., not between 4 and 5 P.M. He would have been absent from home about six hours. The round trip of ten miles to and from Bryantown should not have taken more than a

couple of hours. Allowing
time for various stops and
errands, there are at least
three hours unexplained.

Author Edward Steers
Jr. suggests in *Blood on the
Moon* that Mudd's desire to
move the fugitives quickly
could have prompted him
to visit the home of another
member of the Confederate
underground, William Bur-
tles, who lived a mile and a
half south of Bryantown,
just east of the Zekiah
Swamp. Mudd would have
briefed Burtles, and Burtles
likely would have agreed to
help. Booth and Herold
would be safe with him,
and he would direct them
across the swamp to the
home of another agent,
Samuel Cox, who had been

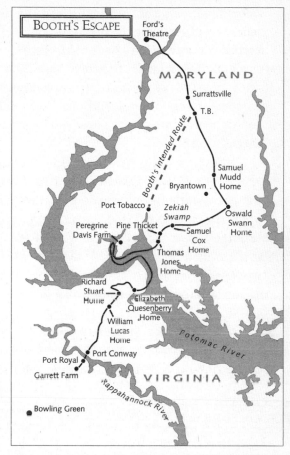

heavily involved in promoting secession in Maryland in 1861. Cox, widely
respected throughout the region, would be able to arrange for Booth and
Herold to safely cross the Potomac. Thus, when Mudd returned home at
sunset, he undoubtedly advised the fugitives to make their way to Burtles's
place by circling east around Bryantown to avoid any Union troops. Booth
and Herold would move out under the cover of darkness, not at 5 P.M., but
after 7 P.M., and Mudd would tell authorities they went in the opposite
direction toward Wilmer's place. That strategy, if it worked, would keep the
soldiers off the assassin's trail long enough for the fugitives to cross the river.
As things turned out, Booth and Herold followed this route, and they
achieved a head start of two full days over their pursuers.

After Easter services the next morning at St. Peter's, Mudd confided to
his pro-Union cousin, Dr. George Mudd, that two suspicious persons had
been to his house the previous day. One of the strangers had a broken leg,

which he set, and the men had left in the direction of Parson Wilmers's place. According to the cousin's testimony, he advised Mudd to inform the authorities in Bryantown, but Mudd was reluctant, claiming he was "fearful for my life." He added, "They may have friends in the neighborhood who might try to kill me if I talked. It would look better if you had the authorities come to me." George said that he would do so, but he waited until Monday morning to see Lt. David D. Dana of the Thirteenth New York Volunteer Cavalry.

At this time, the government did not know that Booth had broken his leg, so Dana did not make the connection between Booth and the injured stranger. Worthless information flooded Dana's headquarters, and he assumed that George Mudd's comments probably fell in that category. Nevertheless, he decided to follow up after Lt. Alexander Lovett arrived in Bryantown on Tuesday. Further discussions with George Mudd motivated Lovett and three detectives to visit Samuel A. Mudd's home later that morning and again on Friday and Saturday (April 21 and 22). During these meetings Mudd told them his well-prepared story.

On the first visit, Mudd was working in the fields when the detectives arrived, and his wife spoke with them while waiting for the doctor. She nonchalantly revealed some startling information, although surely concocted, about the injured man's departure the previous Saturday. Frances Mudd said that she noticed "when he came to the foot of the stairs, that his chin whiskers became detached." She thought it was a false whisker.

This observation was contrived to explain why the Mudds became suspicious and why the doctor expressed his concern to his cousin on Sunday. When Mudd came into the house, Lovett questioned him but did not mention the false beard. Mudd did not say anything about it, but he did say that he had not heard of the assassination until church on Sunday—a statement he changed four days later when he admitted to hearing the news on Saturday in Bryantown. During the first interview, Mudd told Lovett that the visitors stayed for "a short time," and Lovett assumed they left on Saturday morning instead of Saturday evening. When Lovett asked if the strangers carried weapons, Mudd said that he had noticed two revolvers concealed under his patient's clothing, but he did not mention the younger man's carbine.

During the next interrogation on Friday, Lovett decided to search Mudd's home. Outside, two dozen Union cavalry waited in the yard. Mudd, obviously nervous and jittery, suddenly remembered he had found the boot he had cut off the injured man and asked his wife to go upstairs and bring it down. He claimed that the boot had been accidentally shoved under the bed, and he had not discovered it until he later cleaned the room.

When Lovett examined the boot, turning it inside out, he discovered the name "J. Wilkes" inscribed along the inner top edge. He asked Mudd if he had seen the writing before. The doctor said no, but he then acknowledged that his injured guest must have been John Wilkes Booth. "He turned very pale in the face and blue about the lips," Lovett later testified at the conspirators' trial, "like a man who is frightened after recollection of something he had done."

Lovett then asked if the injured man had false whiskers. Although Frances Mudd had told Lovett earlier about an alleged false beard, Mudd replied: "I did not pay sufficient attention to his beard to determine whether it was false or natural." The Mudds had not gotten their stories straight, apparently having only agreed to say that Booth had a beard. Mudd was wallowing in verbal quicksand, and Lovett sensed it. He took him to Bryantown for further questioning by Col. Henry H. Wells.

On the road to town, Mudd volunteered some astounding information. He told Lovett he knew Booth, that he had been introduced to him the past November while attending St. Mary's Catholic Church in Bryantown, that after church Booth returned home with him and spent the night, and the next day he took Booth to a neighbor to buy a one-eyed horse known for its stamina and speed.

"I have never seen Booth since that time to my knowledge until last Saturday night," Mudd falsely stated. This remark was included in a formal statement summarizing Mudd's assertions and prepared on Saturday morning by Wells for Mudd's signature. Wells also included in the statement Mudd's comment after being shown a photograph of Booth: "I should not think that this was the man from any resemblance to the photograph, but from other causes I have every reason to believe that he is the man whose leg I dressed."

By this time Lovett and Wells had become convinced that Mudd had been cooperative only when circumstances forced him to be. He had delayed providing important information that could have been helpful in locating Booth, and he had been evasive and inconsistent. Still, they permitted Mudd to spend the weekend at home and to attend church on Sunday. It was not until Monday morning (April 24) that they arrested him and took him to Washington.

As they departed, Frances Mudd wept. An officer turned in the saddle toward her. "Don't grieve and fret," he said. "I'll see that your husband soon returns to you."

He was wrong. Mudd was placed in the Old Capitol Prison in Washington, D.C., and he and seven other "coconspirators" were tried before a military tribunal of nine senior officers of the Union army.

The government's charge against the Maryland country doctor read in part: "The said Samuel A. Mudd did . . . advise, encourage, receive, entertain, harbor and conceal, aid and assist, the said John Wilkes Booth . . . with knowledge of the murderous and traitorous conspiracy aforesaid, and with intent to aid, abet, and assist . . . in the execution thereof, and in escaping justice after the murder of the said Abraham Lincoln."

All the defendants were found guilty. Four were hanged: Lewis Paine, David Herold, George Atzerodt, and Mary Surratt. Mudd and two others—Samuel Arnold and Michael O'Laughlin—were sentenced to life imprisonment. The eighth conspirator, Edman Spangler, received a six-year sentence. O'Laughlin later died of yellow fever during a prison epidemic in which Mudd was praised for his medical services. Mudd, Arnold, and Spangler served only three and a half years of their sentences.

Andrew Johnson, in the last months of his presidency, pardoned Mudd unconditionally, thanks to Frances Mudd's relentless efforts. Within two weeks similar pardons were issued to Arnold and Spangler. Mudd returned to his Maryland home, had five more children (for a total of nine), and ran unsuccessfully for the state legislature. During the winter of 1882–83 he contracted pneumonia and died on January 10 at age forty-nine. He was buried in the cemetery next to St. Mary's Catholic Church, where he and Booth first met in November 1864.

Through the years, Mudd's relatives and others have aggressively proclaimed his innocence. He was not involved in the plot to assassinate Lincoln, they correctly state, and was innocent of any complicity in the conspiracy, a statement that simply is not true. In 1865 the government did not distinguish between the two conspiracies—kidnapping and murder. It regarded the latter as an extension of the former. Guilt in one meant guilt in both. By that reasoning, any person involved only in the kidnapping plot was liable for the actions of the others in the murder plot, even if he or she played only a minor role and did not know all the details or the identities of everyone involved in it.

Further, as observed by Edward Steers Jr. in *Blood on the Moon*, the only way a person could legally withdraw from a conspiracy would be to make "a meaningful effort" to stop it from happening. These interpretations would apply to everyone tried as coconspirators in Lincoln's murder. The defense argued, without success, that if any of them had wholly withdrawn from a conspiracy that was never consummated, they could not be charged with criminal responsibility for the consequences of another and entirely different conspiracy perpetrated without their knowledge by their former colleagues.

Pleas to clear Mudd of any wrongdoing or of any complicity in the conspiracy against Lincoln have persisted into recent decades. President Jimmy Carter in 1979 unofficially suggested Mudd's innocence in a letter to one of the descendants, a grandson, Richard Mudd. Carter told him that he supported President Andrew Johnson's declarations in pardoning Mudd in 1869 and that they "substantially discredit the validity of the military commission's judgment." Furthermore, Carter declared, "I am hopeful that these conclusions will . . . restore dignity to your grandfather's name and clear the Mudd family name of any negative connotation or implied lack of honor." President Ronald Reagan went further in a 1987 letter to Richard Mudd: "Believe me, I'm truly sorry I can do nothing to help you in your long crusade. . . . In my efforts to help, I came to believe as you do that Dr. Samuel A. Mudd was indeed innocent of any wrongdoing. But . . . that 'full unconditional pardon' [from President Johnson] is what we must settle for."

Johnson's pardon did not overrule Mudd's conviction. The pardon was a presidential thank-you for the doctor's humanitarian efforts in combating the yellow fever epidemic in the prison in which Mudd was incarcerated.

Samuel Arnold, a conspirator sentenced to life imprisonment but pardoned by Andrew Johnson, decided twenty-five years later to compose a memoir to be published after his death. His plans were disrupted in 1902 when another man of the same name died, and many newspapers assumed it was the conspirator and wrote lengthy obituaries. All of them were unflattering and distressed Arnold. Desiring less critical obituaries after his own death, he released his manuscript to the *Baltimore American*, and it was published in serial form. Attempting to justify the plot to kidnap Lincoln, Arnold described it as "purely humane and patriotic." The public did not agree, and when Arnold died in 1906 his obituaries were as critical and unflattering as the earlier ones.

Col. Samuel Cox (*left*) of Charles County, Maryland, a friend of Samuel Mudd's, sheltered Booth and Herold in a pine thicket near his home. Thomas A. Jones (*right*), a Confederate Secret Service agent, cared for the two fugitives April 16–21 and arranged for their crossing of the Potomac to get to Virginia.

Mudd's descendants, however, have been unwilling to settle for the pardon and have continued their legal battle to clear Mudd of any wrongdoing.

With two American presidents all but proclaiming Mudd's innocence, one wonders if their researchers reviewed the primary source documents. After studying the facts known today, present-day historians have reached an opposite conclusion from that of Presidents Carter and Reagan.

Clearly, Mudd's story was layered with fabrications. He deserved the sentence he received and was fortunate to have escaped the gallows. Consider the following:

1. Mudd lied when he claimed that he had only one meeting with Booth before the actor showed up at his doorstep with a broken leg. There actually had been three meetings, and Mudd had arranged two of them and was responsible for two key figures being added to Booth's team of conspirators. When Booth met with some Confederate operatives in Canada in October 1864 to discuss plans for capturing Lincoln, Booth was given letters of introduction to both Mudd and Dr. William Queen, another influential Confederate sympathizer in Charles County, Maryland. Two of Booth's coconspirators—Samuel Arnold and George Atzerodt—both provided this information in separate statements and interviews. Arnold, in fact, told

authorities about the letters on April 17, a full day before investigators first interviewed Mudd or even knew of him. Thus Mudd would have been implicated even if Booth had not sought his medical services.

To successfully carry out the capture of Lincoln, Booth needed contacts throughout southern Maryland—especially Charles County—to facilitate an escape to Richmond. Mudd and Queen were his initial contacts. Booth presented himself to Queen on Saturday, November 12, 1864, secured additional names, and spent the night with him. Queen then arranged for his son-in-law, John Thompson, to introduce Booth to Mudd on Sunday at St. Mary's Catholic Church, a little country church near Bryantown. St. Mary's was not Mudd's church—he attended St. Peter's, which was closer to his home—so he obviously went to Queen's church for the express purpose of meeting Booth. Mudd acknowledged this meeting in his statement to authorities but insisted he and Booth met only to discuss the purchase of land and horses and "the political sentiments of the people." St. Mary's, however, served as a gathering place for leaders of the Confederate underground.

Mudd also lied when he said that Booth had been an overnight guest in his home and had purchased a horse during that weekend trip. Those events occurred during a second secret meeting between Booth and Mudd in Bryantown during the weekend of December 17–19. As before, Booth stayed with Queen on the first night and attended mass at St. Mary's. After church Booth then conferred with Mudd at the Bryantown tavern, where Mudd had arranged for him to meet another important contact—Thomas Harbin, a Confederate Secret Service operative. Mudd was well acquainted with Harbin, who was the former postmaster at Bryantown. Harbin later said that Booth sought the answer to one question: Was he prepared to assist in capturing Lincoln? Harbin was willing to do so, apparently with the approval of his superiors in Richmond. It was that night, not November 12, when Booth stayed at Mudd's home, and the following morning when Mudd took Booth to see George Gardiner, from whom Booth purchased the one-eyed horse that he rode back to Washington—the horse later used by Lewis Paine on the night he attacked Seward. Mudd successfully concealed for years this incriminating second meeting since knowledge of his role in introducing Booth and Harbin probably would have resulted in a trip to the gallows.

Booth and Mudd conferred for a third time a few days later in Washington. The purpose of that meeting was for Mudd to introduce Booth to Confederate courier John H. Surratt Jr. The details of that meeting were revealed in Louis J. Weichmann's testimony at the trial of the conspirators and confirmed five years later in a lecture by Surratt. Of relevance here are three facts: Mudd introduced Surratt to Booth; Mudd and Booth talked privately in the hallway before Surratt joined them; and as a result of this meeting, Surratt signed on with Booth and gave full attention to the abduction scheme.

So, thanks to Mudd, Booth was assisted by two men who proved to be his most competent conspirators—Thomas Harbin and John Surratt. Harbin and Surratt were, in fact, responsible for enlisting their friend, river pilot George Atzerodt, as a member of Booth's team. Surratt was also responsible for recruiting another close friend, Southern Maryland trail authority David Herold, and to a large extent for bringing strongman Lewis Paine into the fold. Thus Mudd was directly or indirectly the source of five conspirators who assisted Booth: Harbin, Surratt, Atzerodt, Herold, and Paine. Without question, Mudd was waist-deep in the conspiratorial cesspool before he treated Booth's broken leg.

2. Having met Booth three times, and having had him as a guest in his home, it is impossible that Mudd did not recognize Booth while treating him on April 15. Why would Booth have resorted to false whiskers and an alias when he knew that Mudd's political feelings paralleled his, and that Mudd in fact had helped him put his team together? At no other time during his twelve days on the run did Booth wear a disguise. No false whiskers were ever found on his body, at any of his stops, or anywhere along his route. David Herold, who was with Booth constantly, made no reference to a beard or any other disguise in a long statement he gave after being imprisoned. Nor did anyone else. After leaving Mudd's home, Booth identified himself to at least six other contacts. It was only at the Garrett farm, where he was killed, that he apparently used and stuck with an alias throughout his visit—the alias of John William Boyd, to match the initials tattooed on his hand. But even then, Booth was not disguised. Booth, in fact, had given his real name at the Navy Yard Bridge as he fled from Washington, and he had told the proprietor at the Surratt tavern that he had killed Lincoln. He also told others who he was and what he had done. Undoubtedly, Mudd knew who his guest was, and when Mudd found out that Booth had killed Lincoln, he had to concoct a story to save his own life.

3. Mudd helped Booth to escape on April 15, fully aware of who he was and the crime he had committed. As noted earlier, Mudd told authorities that the "strangers" intended to head west for Parson Wilmer's place near Piney Church and that he had advised them on two ways to get there.

Mudd lied again, hoping the troops would take that route. Mudd had steered Booth and Herold to a secret route in the opposite direction and toward the homes of leaders in the Confederate underground—William Burtles and Samuel Cox.

Following Mudd's directions, Booth and Herold made a wide swing around Bryantown to the east. All went well for about five miles, but then they became lost. Noticing the light in a cabin, they gambled and walked toward it. The cabin was owned by Oswald Swann, a free black tobacco farmer—one of a few in the area. Booth and Herold approached Swann, who was on the front porch, and offered him two dollars to guide them to Burtles's house. Swann agreed to do so. Fortunately for Booth and Herold, Swann had been a guide to hunters and trappers in and around Zekiah Swamp and could negotiate the area at night.

As they headed for Burtles, Booth changed his mind and asked Swann if he knew where Cox lived. Cox once had a hundred slaves. Yes, Swann was familiar with Cox's hellish world. Coaxed by Booth's offer of another ten dollars to lead them to Cox, Swann continued across the great swamp—a five- to ten-mile-wide malarial expanse of quicksands, marshes, and dense growths occupied by snakes, lizards, and muskrats. After a perilous six-hour ride, they arrived at Cox's home around one o'clock in the morning on Easter Sunday, April 16. Swann observed a whispered conversation between Booth and Cox, after which Cox loudly ordered the fugitives to leave. It was a ploy to prevent Swann from incriminating Cox. But from a distance, Swann glanced back and later said he saw "those two men returning to Cox's house."

Cox fed them, allowed them to rest, and talked with them for nearly five hours. Booth surely mentioned that Mudd had directed them to his house. Mudd was well acquainted with Cox and had participated in Cox's local militia. Cox, however, was afraid of repercussions if he allowed Booth and Herold to stay with him. It would be too risky, but he would assist them until they could cross the Potomac into Virginia. He advised them to hide in a dense thicket of pines about a mile from the house, then he fetched Thomas A. Jones, one of the Confederacy's chief signal agents, to watch over them and make the necessary arrangements.

The forty-four-year-old Jones had been prepared to assist in the earlier plan to capture Lincoln. His farm was on a high bluff above the Potomac. The position enabled him to watch for Federal gunboats and to signal when the way was clear for Confederate couriers, such as John Surratt, to cross the river and pick up packages and letters from a hollow stump on Jones's farm. This system enabled the Confederate cabinet in Richmond to have Washington newspapers from the previous day on their desks each morning. Couriers from Richmond simply delivered Confederate mail to U.S. post offices at Bryantown or Surrattsville, and the Union postal service distributed it to any point in the United States and Canada. Jones's signal system enabled the procedure to function smoothly and worked in tandem with the Confederate signal station on the Virginia shore. It was operated by Jones's brother-in-law, Confederate operative Thomas Harbin—one of the men Mudd had introduced to Booth. Thus Cox's choice of Thomas Jones to aid Booth was carefully thought out.

The fugitives shivered in the damp, cool thicket, and Jones noted that Booth's leg "had become terribly swollen and infected, all black and painful to the touch." Jones provided food, blankets, and newspapers to the fugitives from Easter Sunday through the following Friday, April 21.

To Booth's surprise and disappointment, the newspapers condemned him. They called him a fool, a cutthroat, a thug, and "a weak tool of Confederate desperado-rulers." Booth pulled out his notebook and began to write. He would attempt to earn public approval by justifying his deed. Obviously writing for posterity, he scrawled his first entry: "For six months we had worked to capture. But our cause, being almost lost, something decisive & great must be done. But its failure was owing to others, who did not strike for their country with a heart. I struck boldly and not as the papers say. . . . Our country owed all her trouble to him, and God simply made me the instrument of his punishment."

Jones later wrote that Booth "frankly admitted" to him that he had killed Lincoln. Booth was consistent in revealing his identity to those he trusted, and Jones would not let him down. On Tuesday, while Jones was in Port Tobacco picking up news of the search for Booth, a detective approached him at a bar and said he was authorized to pay one hundred thousand dollars to anyone "who can tell me where Booth is." Jones told the man, "That is a large sum of money and ought to get him if money can do it." Jones himself was practically penniless; he was never paid the twenty-three hundred dollars due him from the Confederate government for his work as a signal agent, and he had lost three thousand dollars in Confederate bonds. But he later wrote that the thought of betraying Booth never entered his mind: "Money won by such vile means would have been accursed, and [Booth's] face . . . would have haunted me to my grave. . . . But, thank God, . . . I still possessed . . . Honor."

It was not until Friday evening that Jones determined it was safe to cross the Potomac. Returning on horseback to the hideout around ten o'clock, Jones put Booth on the horse and asked Herold to lead it as he walked ahead to be sure the way was clear. Jones guided them three miles to an inlet where he kept a flatbottomed fishing boat. Lighting a candle, Jones pointed out on Booth's compass the course to steer.

"Keep to that," he said, "and it will bring you into Machodoc Creek. Mrs. Quesenberry lives near the mouth of this creek. If you tell her you come from me, I think she will take care of you."

As Jones prepared to shove the boat into the stream, Booth exclaimed, "Wait a minute, old fellow!" He wanted to pay Jones generously for taking care of them, but Jones would only accept eighteen dollars, the value of the boat. Touched by Jones's devotion, Booth, in a voice choked with emotion, said, "God bless you, my dear friend, for all you have done for me. Good-bye, old fellow."

The fugitives rowed into the river. Fighting the strong flood tide most of the nearly three miles across the river, they eventually approached the Virginia shore. Suddenly a large shadow loomed directly in their path. It was a Yankee ship anchored at their intended destination. Herold quickly turned upriver and rowed for some six miles until, exhausted, he pulled the skiff into Nanjemoy Creek. They were back in Maryland. When Herold got his bearings, he realized they were near one of his favorite hunting grounds. He knew the territory. They made their way to a farm owned by one of Herold's friends, Peregrine Davis. It was operated by Davis's son-in law, John J. Hughes, who gave them food and allowed them to hide on the property until they could cross the river. They did so on Saturday night. Herold later said they "passed within 300 yards of a gunboat, and landed at Mathias Point [Virginia]" about a mile upriver from Machodoc Creek, their intended target.

Herold, who proved skillful at finding their contacts, located the Quesenberry home around 1 P.M. Thirty-nine-year-old Elizabeth Quesenberry was a key figure in the Confederate underground. When Herold told her that Jones had sent them, she welcomed them, fed them, and notified Harbin, who arrived at about 3 P.M.

Harbin recognized Booth instantly, thanks to Mudd's earlier introduction—an introduction that now reaped huge dividends for Booth and

Herold. Without Harbin they would have been stranded. Booth asked for horses to ride to the summer home of Richard Stuart, another Confederate recommended by Mudd. Harbin called on one of his operatives, William Bryant, to bring horses and guide the men on the fifteen-mile journey inland.

They arrived at Stuart's home around 8 P.M. Stuart was a Virginia planter who had smuggled drugs for the Confederacy. He was the richest man in King George County and a relative of Robert E. Lee. For his own security and that of his family, however, Stuart did not want anything to do with the two strangers, or at least that's what he later told federal authorities. Stuart had been under surveillance and arrest; he had to be cautious. When Booth and Herold asked for lodging, he said no, claiming that his house was full of guests. They asked him to treat Booth's swollen and blackened leg, and he supposedly refused. They asked for help in getting to Fredericksburg and Mosby's Rangers; Mosby's unit was the only one between the Potomac and James Rivers that could keep Booth out of Union hands.

Stuart later told authorities that he declined to help them or to find out anything about them, even after Herold explained that Mudd had recommended him. "Nobody was authorized to recommend anybody to me," Stuart supposedly said, again protecting himself. He said he was "suspicious" and thought they might have been connected with "the vile acts of assassination in Washington." Stuart did make one concession to Booth and Herold: He allowed them to come into his kitchen where "they ate in the fashion of a tramp given a handout." Stuart then ordered Bryant to take them off his property and to a nearby cabin occupied by a free black, William Lucas, and his wife and six children.

There Booth pulled a gun on Lucas's sick wife. "Get out of bed," he demanded. "We're sleeping here tonight." Booth forced the entire Lucas family to sleep outside. The next morning Booth "persuaded" Lucas's twenty-one-year-old son Charley, with a twenty-dollar bill, to take them, hidden under straw, in a mule-drawn wagon to Port Conway—the safest place to cross the Rappahannock River.

Whether by coincidence or Confederate intelligence, Booth and Herold connected almost immediately with three soldiers from Mosby's Rangers, and they accompanied the fugitives on the ferry across the river and eventually to the farm of Richard Garrett, where the Union dragnet closed in on them.

Interestingly, after Lucas dropped off Booth and Herold, Booth gave him a sarcastic note to deliver to Stuart. Either Stuart had treated Booth and

Herold harshly, as he told authorities, or the note was a cover for Stuart to use if needed: "I hate to blame you for your want of hospitality, [but] I was sick and tired, with a broken leg [and] in need of medical advice. I would not have turned a dog away from my door in such a condition." Then Booth thanked Stuart for the food he begrudgingly gave them and added, "because of the manner in which it was bestowed I feel bound to pay for it. . . . Be kind enough to accept the enclosed $5.00." Booth made his point even stronger by crossing out the $5.00 and writing in $2.50.

Stuart, Bryant, and Elizabeth Quesenberry were arrested in early May and shortly released. In formal statements the two men affirmed that Booth and Herold went to Stuart's home on Mudd's recommendation. These statements convinced the government that Mudd had lied about their intentions to go to Parson Wilmer's and about not knowing which direction they actually went. Mudd had further aided Booth's escape by directing him to the home of Samuel Cox, and he, in turn, had provided assistance by involving Thomas Jones. Cox and Jones served a few weeks in prison then were freed.

One of the great mysteries associated with the assassination is Stanton's leniency toward Mudd's friends and associates—Stuart, Bryant, Quesenberry, Jones, and Cox (all of whom aided and abetted Booth's escape)—as compared with Stanton's torturous treatment of Arnold and O'Laughlin (who had nothing to do with the assassination) and Spangler (who held Booth's horse for a few seconds, probably not knowing why). Arnold, O'Laughlin, and Spangler were shackled to balls and chains, hooded so they could not see, handcuffed in a way that kept their hands apart, and secluded so that they could not communicate with lawyers or friends or receive any news from the outside world—for a period of six weeks—before they were finally tried, found guilty, and hauled off to a prison from hell, out of reach of family and friends. Stanton's judgment and sense of justice were incomprehensible.

4. Samuel Cox Jr., son of the colonel who sent Thomas Jones to assist Booth and Herold, added revealing annotations in a book published by Jones in 1893 about his services to the fugitives. According to Cox—who had no reason to lie nearly thirty years after the assassination—Mudd confided to him what really happened on that Saturday afternoon, April 15, 1865, during his trip to Bryantown and his return to the farm at the time Booth and Herold were supposedly preparing to leave.

Cox said that when he and Mudd were canvassing Charles County together in 1877 as candidates for the Maryland state legislature, Mudd said that he had gone to Bryantown to mail contraband letters he had in his possession and "was surprised to find the village surrounded by soldiers" and "horrified [when he was] stopped by a sentry . . . [and told that] the president had been shot the night before, and, upon asking who had shot him the fellow had answered Booth." Then, wrote Cox, Mudd told him "his first impulse was to surrender Booth, that he had imposed upon him . . . and received medical assistance which would be certain to [cause] him [Mudd] serious trouble, but [instead] he determined to go back and upbraid him for his treachery, which he did." Booth, Cox wrote, appealed "in the name of his mother whom he professed to love so devotedly. . . . He acted and spoke so tragically that he [Mudd] told them they must leave his house, which they did, and after getting in with Oswald Swann they were piloted to Rich Hill [the home of Samuel Cox]."

Cox's statement provides more evidence that Booth did not wear a disguise and that Mudd knew who he was treating and where they were going. It is doubtful, however, that Mudd upbraided Booth "for his treachery."

Additional, but perhaps less reliable, confirmation that Mudd knew Booth when he treated him came from Capt. George W. Dutton, who commanded the military guard that accompanied Mudd, Arnold, O'Laughlin, and Spangler to a remote federal prison in the Dry Tortugas, seventy miles off of Key West, Florida. After Captain Dutton's return from the trip, he filed an affidavit with the judge advocate general, Joseph Holt, claiming that Mudd stated to him en route to the prison that "he knew Booth when he came to his house with Herold on the morning after the assassination of the president."

Mudd, upon learning of Dutton's statement, filed an affidavit denying the allegation. It is difficult to imagine Mudd's confiding such information to a military official who was taking him to a desolate prison. It is less difficult to imagine Dutton's making up the statement to score points with the judge advocate general and the secretary of war, who were under severe criticism for spearheading the effort to condemn the country doctor who, in the minds of many, had simply performed a humanitarian duty in treating an injured man.

5. Conspirator George Atzerodt left further evidence implicating Mudd in the conspiracy. Atzerodt, who had been assigned by Booth to kill Vice President Johnson, had lost his courage, gotten drunk, and wandered around the city, eventually making his way to a cousin's home in Germantown, Maryland, twenty-five miles northwest of Washington. He was

arrested on April 20, tried with the seven other coconspirators, and hanged on July 7 with David Herold, Mary Surratt, and Lewis Paine. While imprisoned, he was interviewed by the provost marshal of Baltimore, James L. McPhail, and one of his detectives, John L. Smith, Atzerodt's brother-in-law. They transcribed the statement and turned it over to Capt. William E. Doster, Atzerodt's defense counsel appointed by the War Department. For whatever reason, the statement never reached other authorities and was not used in the trial. It remained lost until being discovered among Doster's personal papers more than a hundred years later, in 1978. Succinctly, Atzerodt's statement confirmed Mudd's involvement in the kidnapping conspiracy: "I am certain Dr. Mudd knew all about it, as Booth sent liquors and provisions [to Mudd] for the trip with the president to Richmond, about two weeks before the murder." Mudd was to store these supplies, according to Atzerodt, for Booth and his accomplices to retrieve after capturing Lincoln. It may be presumed that, since Mudd's farm was not on the escape route, he was the middle man to transfer the supplies to another location. Atzerodt also affirmed the role of Thomas Harbin, the Confederate agent whom Mudd introduced to Booth: "Harbin was to meet us on the road and help in the kidnapping." While that role was never needed, Harbin came through for Booth and Herold after they crossed the Potomac into Virginia. Again, Mudd, having recruited Harbin, made that possible.

6. If Mudd had told the military authorities in Bryantown on Saturday that Booth and Herold were at his home—which he was obligated to do under the law—he probably would never have been tried as a conspirator. But he told no one that day. He faced a dilemma. Aside from whatever loyalties he felt for Booth, he knew that if he reported Booth and Herold to the authorities, they would have raced to his home, and a battle might have ensued, with his wife and children in the thick of it. His neighbors would have treated him as an outcast, and his prior participation in the kidnapping plot might have been exposed. No, his best course, he undoubtedly felt, was to cooperate with the fugitives and to get them out of his house and safely on their way to Virginia. It was in Mudd's best interest for Booth to get as far away from him as possible and to never be caught. Thus Mudd gave the fugitives precise instructions on how to avoid the troops as well as the names of Confederate sympathizers who would probably be helpful— William Burtles, Samuel Cox, Elizabeth Quesenberry, and Richard Stuart. Mudd was clearly an accessory to the crimes against Lincoln—first, before the fact, to the kidnap conspiracy, then after the fact, by aiding Booth and

Herold to escape. Mudd knew this, and that explains why he waited until Sunday morning to inform his cousin about the two strangers and asked *him* to notify the authorities, which he delayed doing until Monday morning, thereby giving Booth and Herold forty hours to reach Cox's plantation.

Newspaper reporter George Alfred Townsend interviewed several people of southern Maryland for an article in the *New York Tribune* in 1883. Among them was Frederick Stone. His perspective may be close to the truth: "The court very nearly hanged Dr. Mudd [a change of one vote out of nine would have sent him to the gallows]. His prevarications were painful; he had given his whole case away by not trusting even his counsel, neighbors, or kin. It was a terrible thing to extricate him from the coils he had woven about himself."

Perhaps Mudd's role in the conspiracy was best summed up by a member of the military commission that tried the coconspirators. Gen. Thomas Harris said: "Mudd's expression of countenance [at the trial] was that of a hypocrite. He had the bump of secretiveness largely developed, and it would have taken months of acquaintanceship to have removed the unfavorable impression made by the first scanning of the man. He had the appearance of a natural born liar and deceiver."

9

THE
INVISIBLE
MOSBY

BOOTH'S ESCAPE PLAN OBVIOUSLY took into account the presence of both Union and Confederate forces in southern Maryland and Virginia. With Lee's surrender at Appomattox Court House, the only sizable active Confederate force was Johnston's in North Carolina, and so large areas of Virginia saw few Union troops during the last two weeks of April. Confederate Col. John S. Mosby, however, and his partisan ranger command were still at large and under little Union pressure in much of eastern and northern Virginia. Nor was Mosby inclined to surrender as long as Johnston's army continued to fight. He later called Lee's surrender "the bitterest hour of my life."

Mosby, thirty-two years old in 1865, was intelligent and thoughtful; some called him a walking dictionary of the classics. He had studied at the University of Virginia and was admitted to the bar in 1858. After setting up a law practice in Bristol, a small town in southwestern Virginia, he married Pauline Clarke of Kentucky. When Virginia seceded he joined the First Virginia Cavalry and later fought at First Manassas. Shortly after that he became a scout for Jeb Stuart and won the general's respect by suggesting that the cavalry execute a long-range reconnaissance around the Union army, which was closing in on the Confederate capital of Richmond in the summer of 1862. The result was Stuart's first of several rides around a Federal army, which did much to enhance his reputation as a hero to the South. Mosby continued to serve under Stuart through four campaigns.

While in northern Virginia on December 30, 1862, Stuart rewarded Mosby by permitting him to organize and operate a small nine-man unit of partisan rangers. They were to launch raids to impede and disrupt Union operations. Mosby was soon appointed captain of the rangers by Jefferson Davis and authorized to seek recruits. During the next two years he was promoted to major then colonel.

Partisan rangers are light troops who operate in cooperation with a main army but apart from it. For Mosby such "irregular warfare" meant protecting the main army's encampment, severing the enemy's lines of communication and supply, and using every opportunity to harass Yankees. In his memoirs he stated that his purpose was "to weaken the armies invading Virginia by harassing their rear. . . . Every soldier withdrawn from the front to guard the rear of an army is so much taken from its fighting strength." Mosby's tactics, in fact, forced Union commanders to divert at least fifteen thousand troops from front-line positions to guard the rear and protect supply trains, bridges, and communications. Mosby also conducted missions for the Richmond government and engaged in clandestine operations.

These responsibilities were a tall order for this slender lawyer of medium height who weighed no more than 128 pounds and had slightly stooped shoulders. His most intimidating features, however, were his piercing deep blue eyes. With an order and a certain look from Mosby, his men listened and obeyed without question. He demanded discipline, and part of this was a prohibition of alcohol from his unit. The memory of his first encounter with a drunken man—his schoolmaster—as a seven-year-old had so disgusted him that he rarely took a strong drink the rest of his life.

Until Stuart's death on May 12, 1864, Mosby had maintained a loose association with him. After that date, Mosby reported directly to Gen. Robert E. Lee and provided him with captured mules, sabers, and carbines. Mosby's men were mounted, armed, and equipped entirely with whatever they could take from the enemy, except for the gray jackets they wore.

Mosby handpicked his men. More than a thousand served under him, but there were seldom more than three hundred together at any time. They were quartered in farms in Fauquier and Loudoun Counties in northern Virginia and came together at preestablished times and places or in response to couriers. Once assembled, they executed lightning hit-and-run raids, usually in small groups. They avoided well-traveled routes and sneaked along

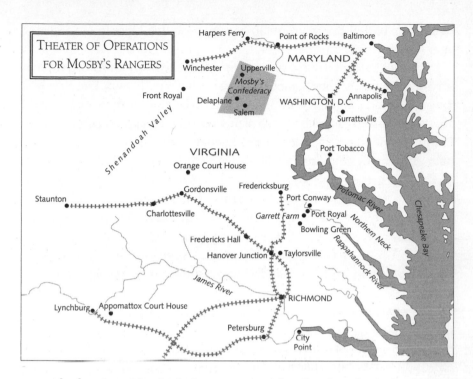

unmarked paths with which they were very familiar, but the Federals were not. These raids and Mosby's elusiveness earned him the nickname the "Gray Ghost." His rangers so dominated a region of northern Virginia that it became known as "Mosby's Confederacy." Much of his success came from the loyal support of the people of the area, who were eager to assist the rangers and devised various methods to warn and alert them to Union movements.

Mosby established a headquarters near Delaplane, about twenty-five miles equidistant from Harpers Ferry to the north and Winchester to the northwest, at the northern end of the Shenandoah Valley. Washington, D.C., was only fifty miles to the east.

Mosby had two ways to communicate with Lee and with Richmond. One required him to travel seventy-five miles south to Gordonsville (near Charlottesville), where rail and telegraph service were available. When Booth fled Washington, he hoped to head in that same direction. Mosby's other option was a string of signal stations that ran down the mountains to a point near Charlottesville, where messages could be transferred by telegraph. Later this latter system was extended to link Mosby with a portion of his command operating in the Northern Neck, that part of Virginia between the Potomac and Rappahannock Rivers. Adjacent to southern Maryland, it was a vital part of Booth's route to convey a captive Lincoln or to escape after shooting Lincoln.

Officially, Mosby's Rangers were known as the Forty-third Battalion of Virginia Cavalry, the most famous cavalry battalion of the war. The *New York Times* declared that Mosby conducted "a succession of startling personal adventures unsurpassed by those of any partisan chief on record." One of Philip H. Sheridan's captains in the Shenandoah Valley added, "A more harassing enemy could not well be imagined." Over a period of two years Mosby's Rangers conducted more than a hundred raids or skirmishes; seized thousands of soldiers, horses, and arms; derailed trains; and frequently escaped barely scathed by the encounters. "Hurrah for Mosby!" exclaimed the usually reserved Robert E. Lee. "I wish I had a hundred like him." In his memoirs, Ulysses S. Grant wrote: "There were probably but few men in the South who could have commanded successfully a separate detachment in

Mosby's Rangers attacked by surprise, quickly, with Colts blazing in close combat. If the affair turned sour, the men fell back quickly and scattered. "I think we did more than any other body of men to give the Colt pistol its great reputation," Mosby observed in explaining his preference for handguns over sabers.

MUNSEY'S MAGAZINE

the rear of an opposing army, and so near the border of hostilities, as long as Mosby did without losing his entire command." Mosby was so successful that, in the North, he became the single most hated Confederate.

Mosby's brilliant tactics keyed his success. Traditionally, cavalrymen preferred sabers, but that was slowly changing during the Civil War, as cavalry tactics changed over the months of intense combat. Slashing sabers did much to demoralize infantry opponents, but they were awkward when confronting a foe on horseback. Rifled muskets were not used because they were difficult to reload in the saddle, and carbines were not yet reliable weapons, nor were they widely available in the South. Mosby's weapon of choice was the fairly new revolver, specifically .44 Army Colts. He did not requisition these weapons; he acquired them from captured Federals! Each ranger had at least two pistols and was trained to fire rapidly and accurately and reload on horseback. Fighting at close range with pistols allowed Mosby's men to win many skirmishes against superior numbers.

Just two months after becoming a partisan ranger commander, Mosby planned a daring raid that made him a legend to the South. He set out to capture Sir Percy Wyndham, a Union cavalry colonel who accused Mosby of being a horse thief. Mosby countered by noting that all the horses he had stolen had had armed riders. The two men despised each other. Wyndham's headquarters was at Fairfax Court House—fifteen miles from Washington and well behind Union lines.

On the cold, rainy night of March 8–9, 1863, Mosby and twenty-nine men snaked their way past three thousand Yankee troops and entered Fairfax Court House around 2 A.M. "We are going to mount the skies tonight or sink lower than plummet ever sounded," the Confederate commander told his men. "My fate was trembling in the balance," he later recalled. "If we should get caught, it would end my career as a partisan; everybody would say that I had tried to do what I ought to have known to be impossible."

Quietly they captured a sentry and a telegraph operator. From them Mosby learned that Wyndham was in Washington, but Gen. Edwin H. Stoughton was in the Federal camp. Mosby divided his force into squads of fours and fives: some to collect horses, others to capture guards. He took five men with him to snatch Stoughton from the two-story brick home on the public square that served as Wyndham's headquarters. Twenty-three-year-old Stoughton was the Union's youngest general at the time.

Dismounting in front of the house, Mosby knocked on the front door and announced that he had dispatches for the general. An aide opened the door, and Mosby seized him and had him lead the way to the general's room. Walking over to the bed, Mosby pulled down the blankets and shook the general.

"Is this General Stoughton?" he asked.

Stoughton, seeing men with pistols, replied, "Yes, what do you want?"

"You are my prisoner," exclaimed Mosby.

"The hell I am," the young general responded.

"You may have heard of Captain Mosby. I am Mosby. Get dressed." Mosby then picked up a piece of coal from the fireplace and wrote his name on the wall. He took his prisoner outside and joined the other rangers. Besides Stoughton, they captured two captains, thirty enlisted men, and fifty-eight horses without firing a shot or losing a man.

As the raiding party began to leave, a man shouted from an upstairs window, "Halt! The horses need rest. I will not allow them to be taken out."

No one replied. He yelled even louder: "I am commander of this post, and this must be stopped." He was Col. Robert Johnstone, commander of the cavalry brigade in Wyndham's absence.

Mosby ordered two men to take him prisoner, but the colonel's wife blocked them at the front door, fighting and scratching them. Johnstone, clad only in his nightshirt, fled by the back door. He found a hiding place beneath the outhouse in the backyard but lost his nightshirt in the process.

Not wanting to scuffle with Johnstone's wife, Mosby withdrew his men and led the contingent out of town, riding in a column of fours, pretending to be Union cavalry. The rangers returned to their camp, from which Stoughton was delivered to Libby Prison in Richmond.

Stoughton, a West Point graduate from a prominent Vermont family, was devastated. The *New York Times* called the capture "utterly disgraceful." The *Baltimore American* referred to Stoughton as "the luckless sleeper at Fairfax who was caught napping." Lincoln told reporters he did not mind losing the general, since he could create another one with the stroke of a pen, but he hated to lose the horses, because "they cost a hundred and twenty five dollars apiece!"

Johnstone drew the nickname "Outhouse Johnstone" from his men. Embarrassed, he left the service in December.

Stuart commended Mosby for his "daring enterprise and dashing heroism." Two months later, Stoughton was exchanged for a Confederate general. Stoughton's health, however, had suffered from his treatment at Libby Prison, and he died five years later.

Twenty-three-year-old Edwin Stoughton was the youngest general in the Union army on March 8, 1863. He was in the wrong place at the wrong time when Mosby and twenty-nine rangers came behind the lines in search of another Yankee commander who had called Mosby a horse thief. Stoughton and thirty-two other Federals were taken prisoner, as well as fifty-eight horses.

NATIONAL ARCHIVES

After the Stoughton episode, it was rumored but never confirmed that the planks were removed each night from some Washington bridges to prevent Mosby's sneaking into Washington to kidnap Lincoln.

During the remainder of 1863 Mosby focused on collecting intelligence and disrupting communications between Washington and Union commands north of the Rappahannock River. The rangers conducted at least fifteen raids and captured several wagon trains, including wagonloads of boots, bridles, saddles, and other cavalry gear.

On August 24, during a raid at Annandale, on the outskirts of Washington, Mosby was wounded in the side and thigh. He was taken to his parents' home in Amherst County, north of Lynchburg, to convalesce. Lt. Tom Turner took charge of the command in his absence. The rangers were not as effective in the field without Mosby as they were with him, and so his absence was always noted.

By late September 1863 Mosby was back in the saddle, and a new man had joined the rangers. This recent recruit was Lewis Thornton Powell, later known as Lewis Paine, the able assistant of John Wilkes Booth. This handsome nineteen-year-old stood nearly six feet two inches tall and weighed 175 pounds. Born in Alabama, he spent most of his youth in Georgia before moving to Florida when he was fifteen. His father was a Baptist minister, a schoolmaster, and a farmer.

U.S. ARMY MILITARY HISTORY INSTITUTE

The Stoughton Raid brought tremendous notoriety to Mosby and his men. The defenses around Washington were tightened, which included the bridges into Virginia and Maryland. With the capture of a general from a headquarters camp, much concern was expressed for the safety of Lincoln and his cabinet.

The Reverend Powell raised his son in a moral, religious environment. The boy's five sisters considered him "pious and tender-hearted" and much devoted to Sunday school and prayer meetings. They said that he was a "sweet, lovable, kind boy" who was popular and "a great favorite with the ladies." The young Powell was called "Doc" because he cared for injured animals, and he often sang while treating these animals or playing with his pets. His father, however, noted streaks of both stubbornness and determination in his son's character. A Florida newspaper editor detected "a fierce temper" but thought the whole family was "hot-headed." By the age of sixteen, Lewis had cultivated refined manners and an ability to speak well. He loved his parents and planned to follow in his father's footsteps. Contrary to later descriptions, Lewis was neither crude nor dumb.

Powell's love for the South led him into the Second Florida Infantry after Florida seceded from the Union in January 1861. Only seventeen at the time, he lied and claimed to be nineteen. His service included major engagements at Seven Pines, Gaines's Mill, Second Manassas, Antietam, Chancellorsville, Fredericksburg, and Gettysburg. Wounded at Gettysburg on July 2, 1863, when a gunshot shattered his right wrist, Powell was captured and taken to a makeshift hospital. While mending, he also served as a male nurse and assisted Maggie Branson of Baltimore, with whom he fell in love, although she was twelve years older. Both of them were transferred to a Baltimore hospital in early September, but Powell escaped a few days after his arrival. A hospital steward charged that Branson was responsible. He said that she had secured a Union uniform and a cloak for Powell as well as a cake in which she concealed a ten-dollar bill. With the money, Powell bribed his guards and fled. Branson disappeared at about the same time. The steward described Powell as "a man of unusual intelligence and one of the most unyielding of all the rebels."

After his escape, Powell's first stop was to call on Maggie Branson at her mother's Baltimore home. Spending a pleasant two hours in the parlor, he visited not only Maggie but also her younger sister, twenty-eight-year-old Mary, with whom he later became involved.

Traveling through Virginia in search of his old regiment, Powell sauntered across the lawn of an old-fashioned homestead near Warrenton and asked to stay the night. The home was the residence of John Scott Payne, a Confederate soldier home on furlough. Tired of tailing his unit, Powell lingered there a few days and became fascinated with the stories of Mosby's exploits. Sometime in October, Powell met Mosby.

Author Betty Ownsbey, Powell's biographer, believes the contact was arranged by Gen. William H. Payne, commander of a cavalry unit involved in Jeb Stuart's 1863 Pennsylvania raid. Powell was tired of extended marches and anxious to join the cavalry. Although Mosby had far more applications than he could accept, he did not hesitate to sign up Powell. Thus Powell joined Mosby's Rangers sometime in October or November 1863 and was assigned to Company B. Mosby was a good judge of men, and Powell did not let him down. John W. Munson, one of Mosby's top lieutenants, noted that Powell was "always keyed up for any new sensation [and] was a first-class fighting man."

One of Powell's first raids with Mosby occurred in November, when the rangers captured two sutler's wagons filled with ginger cakes and milk. Sutlers were civilians licensed to operate shops at military posts. Powell gained a measure of popularity with the local residents by distributing part of the bounty to them. "For some time afterwards, everybody was munching ginger cakes, and every Negro had a new tin cup," according to young Lewis Edmonds Payne, son of Dr. Albin H. Payne, with whose family Powell boarded from time to time. Powell developed a close friendship with the boy and within a year assumed his name.

Mosby's Rangers conducted three "Calico Raids" in 1864, and Powell was involved in at least one of them. The most famous of these raids occurred on July 4 in support of Jubal Early's advance toward Washington. Mosby and 250 rangers crossed the Potomac under heavy fire to Point of Rocks, Maryland, near Washington. They drove the Federals from their entrenchments and cut off rail and telegraph service between Harpers Ferry and the Federal capital for two days. In addition they plundered the stores. To celebrate, the men decorated themselves and their horses with colorful bunting, draped crinoline dresses over their shoulders, and stacked women's bonnets on their heads. They also hung boots and shoes over their horses' necks and placed bolts of calico behind their saddles.

Two days later, having sent most of his men home with their plunder, Mosby clashed head-on with a 150-man Union cavalry at Mount Zion Church near Leesburg. It was a savage encounter. Mosby's coat was pierced by a saber, but he was not injured. The rangers' pistols overcame the Union sabers and left at least 50 Federals dead or wounded. Mosby took 57 prisoners and 100 horses. His losses were 1 killed and 6 wounded.

On July 9 some of Mosby's men startled a group of young men and women on a picnic a few miles outside of Washington, near Falls Church, Virginia. While the ladies and their escorts were dancing in a shady nook, twenty-five rangers, dressed in Confederate uniforms and turned-up hats, suddenly rode out from the trees. The women screamed, but their unarmed escorts could do nothing. "Don't be afraid," coaxed one of the rangers, as the men dismounted and danced a set with the ladies. Then they helped themselves to the picnic baskets, bowed, and rode away.

When Early returned to the Shenandoah Valley from his advance on Washington, Philip H. Sheridan assumed command of the Union forces in the Valley. Grant ordered him to destroy not only Early's small army but also to confiscate livestock, burn crops, and render the region unfit to supply anything to Lee's army. Mosby's challenge was to keep Sheridan's supply line disorganized and drive back any scouts trying to get through to the Federal commander. The campaign against Sheridan was critical to the Confederacy, and Mosby accepted the challenge with all his skill.

One of Mosby's most massive attacks and most famous successes—and one in which Lewis Powell participated—occurred in mid-August 1864. The rangers disrupted a 525-wagon Union supply train on its way to Sheridan's army at Winchester from Harpers Ferry and accompanied by more than 3,000 soldiers. With part of the 5-section wagon train parked at a small creek near Berryville to water the animals and rest the men, Mosby attacked near sunrise. He struck first with a light howitzer from a nearby hill, firing

three shots. Then 300 whooping rangers charged through a light fog and created so much confusion that unhitched horses and mules dashed wildly in
the road, upsetting many wagons, 75 of which Mosby set on fire. Mules still
hitched to their wagons ran frightened by the flames and smashed their
loads into trees and fences. The rangers captured about 200 prisoners, 500
horses and mules, 200 beef cattle, and five days' rations for 2,200 Union soldiers. In addition, Mosby confiscated a chest with $112,000 in payrolls. His
only casualties were 2 killed and 2 wounded.

Feisty Sheridan was furious when he learned what had happened. As
soon as Grant heard the news, he wired the Valley commander: "When any
of Mosby's men are caught, hang them without trial. . . . If you can possibly
spare a division of cavalry send them through Loudoun County to destroy
and carry off the crops, animals, Negroes, and all men under fifty years of

Supply wagons were susceptible to raids by Mosby's Rangers. The goods included
food, tobacco, cloth, cutlery, liquor, newspapers, and books. After seizing a large
wagon train and then losing it to Union cavalry, one of the rangers quipped that he
had hoped to open the first department store in Mosby's Confederacy.

HARPER'S WEEKLY

age capable of bearing arms. In this way you will get many of Mosby's men. All male citizens under fifty can fairly be held as prisoners of war."

In September, six of Mosby's men were captured. On orders from one of Sheridan's junior commanders, four of them were shot to death and the other two were hanged. A sign pinned to one of the bodies read: "Such is the fate of all Mosby's men." Mosby was not in the Valley at the time; he had been wounded on September 14. It was rumored that the executions had been ordered by George A. Custer—and Mosby remained convinced of Custer's guilt for the rest of his life—but it is unlikely that Custer did anything more than concur with the action. Mosby did not retaliate upon his return to action, but then another ranger was hanged in October.

On October 29 Mosby wrote to Robert E. Lee, "It is my purpose to hang an equal number of Custer's men whenever I capture them." By November 6 he had thirty prisoners. The unlucky ones were chosen by lottery, and Mosby ordered three to be hanged and four to be shot, just as his men had been executed. None of the rangers, including Mosby, were anxious to carry out the sentences. As a result, the only Federals to be executed were the three who were hanged; of the other four, two escaped and the remaining two were only wounded. Mosby pinned a note to the bodies of the dead: "These men have been hung in retaliation for an equal number of Colonel Mosby's men hung by order of General Custer, at Front Royal. Measure for measure."

Mosby did not have the appearance of a warrior. He was five feet seven (or eight) and weighed no more than 128 pounds. His most striking features, however, were his piercing blue eyes. No one who saw him ever forgot his eyes. One of his men commented, "When he spoke, [his eyes] flashed the punctuations of his sentence."

He hoped the action would prevent his men from being summarily executed in the field. It did. Federal commanders instead focused their retaliation on the residents who supported Mosby.

When one of Mosby's men killed a Union picket during a skirmish, Custer ordered the homes of five families burned. Lewis Powell was with a small group of rangers in a clash with the soldiers who were in the process of burning one of the houses; the Southerners killed eighteen Federals.

Powell sometimes went off on his own behind the lines and returned with prisoners, horses, and plunder. He once came back with a small herd of twenty army horses.

During his tenure with the rangers, Powell had two narrow escapes. On one occasion, the house in which he was staying was surrounded. To escape he blackened his face with lampblack and wandered outside. A Union soldier remarked, "That is a damn tall Negro." Powell passed without any interference. Later, several soldiers with Powell were captured and shot in Front Royal. Thanks to the speed of his mare, Powell escaped. Bullet holes reportedly were found in his uniform.

Mosby himself had a close call. While getting a shave in a Warrenton barbershop, Union troops entered the town and began to search for him. An officer even came into the barbershop and questioned Mosby, but the Confederate commander used a fictitious name, and the officer departed.

During the fall of 1864, Lt. Edward Thompson of Mosby's command asked for two volunteers. Lewis Powell and Tom Shipley responded. Their mission was to ride into Salem (now Marshall), fire on the Union pickets, and lead the pursuing bluecoats into an ambush. According to one of Mosby's commanders, John Munson,

> Powell and Shipley galloped up the road in full view of the enemy, discharged their revolvers almost in their very faces, and turning their horses, sped down the road, followed by a volley of balls. The pursuit was almost instantaneous. When the rear of the charging column of the enemy had passed on in pursuit of Powell and Shipley, Thompson wheeled his men into the road and with a terrible "yell" and a storm of bullets rushed upon the enemy [from the rear]. In the meantime Powell and Shipley turned in the road and charged the enemy from the front. The result was the capture by Thompson of almost the entire command of the enemy, who thought they were entirely surrounded.

Powell was one of eighty-three men who rode in Mosby's "Greenback Raid" on October 13, 1864. That night they derailed a Baltimore and Ohio passenger express train loaded with Union supplies and $173,000 in green-backs headed for Sheridan. The rangers emptied the cars and burned the train, but no one was killed or wounded. Mosby distributed the money to his men—$2,100 each—but kept none for himself, as was his custom. Powell and the other rangers then chipped in and purchased as a gift a thoroughbred horse Mosby had admired at a Leesburg farm. The horse, Coquette, became Mosby's favorite.

Mosby struck repeatedly at the railroad from Manassas to Front Royal, a major supply route for Union forces. The damage he caused probably pro-longed the war at least six months. He also continued his raids in the Shenandoah Valley and outside of Washington. At the end of the campaign, Mosby reported that his men had killed or captured about six hundred Union soldiers at a loss of about twenty-five of his own.

Frustrated and hampered by Mosby's successes, Sheridan assembled a hunter-killer team of a hundred men under Capt. Richard Blazer with one mission: kill or capture Mosby and his men. Mosby, accompanied by Lewis Powell and other troopers, responded by annihilating Blazer's command. After Mosby discovered Blazer's whereabouts, he set a trap by concealing one company while another feigned retreat. The Union troops charged after the withdrawing horsemen, then the retreating group wheeled to face their pursuers head-on while the other company clashed from the rear. Four rangers, including Powell, spotted Blazer and overtook him. One of Mosby's men clubbed him over the head with his pistol butt. Powell bandaged Blazer's head, and the four rangers delivered their captive to Mosby, who then assigned them to escort Blazer to Richmond's Libby Prison.

Powell was sent to Richmond for another reason. With Confederate leaders planning to capture Lincoln, they had spread the word in December that the operation needed a fearless strongman. The man chosen was Pvt. Lewis Thornton Powell of Company B, Mosby's Rangers. Given the nature of the request and the chain of command, Mosby recommended, selected, or approved Powell.

Almost eight months later, on the night before he was hanged, Powell (then known as Paine) told his religious comforter, Dr. Abram D. Gillette (pastor of Washington's First Baptist Church), that he had worked "for months before the assassination" in the Secret Service of the Confederacy and had traveled back and forth from Richmond to Washington and Balti-more with prominent men. Powell claimed that he had been encouraged "with dreams of glory and the lasting gratitude of the Southern people."

When he returned from Richmond after delivering Blazer, Powell seemed to be "a changed man." Young Lewis E. Payne observed: "He seemed more grave and thoughtful than ever. He often spoke . . . of his intention soon to go to Baltimore to meet friends he had met in Richmond. Powell said he would be gone for several months."

Powell was involved in one last raid. Near Christmastime he captured six Union stragglers (soldiers who had wandered away from their regiment to avoid combat). The stragglers had inflicted "infamous brutality to Isham Keith and his family," according to Gen. William H. Payne.

> They had sacked the house, piled the furniture and beds in the yard, and burned them while Keith was concealed in the woods. As soon as they left, Keith started in pursuit [and] found them in Warrenton, where Powell had caught them and left them in charge of someone in the town. [Keith] killed four of the prisoners. When the news was brought to Powell, he galloped to the place, stopped the massacre and was with difficulty prevented from killing Keith. Powell claimed the prisoners as his own and announced his intentions of saving their lives at the risk of his own.

Payne admired Powell and called him a "chivalrous, generous, gallant fellow, particularly fond of children." When Powell stayed at the general's home in Warrenton, Powell usually brought presents for the children. Powell also became infatuated with one of their cousins, eighteen-year-old Betty Meredith, daughter of a prosperous farmer. Before leaving Mosby's Rangers in January 1865, Powell gave her his photograph, left his diary in her care, and promised to return for her in a few months. He probably would have, had he not been hanged six months later. Powell also left a small bit of prose, reflecting his creative flair: "In battle, in the fullness of pride and strength, little recks the soldier whether the hissing bullet sings his sudden requiem or the cords of life are severed by the sharp steel."

Many scholars claim that Powell "deserted" Mosby's command. He did not. His actions after leaving Mosby were carefully orchestrated. Powell was part of an operation to accomplish what he and Mosby construed to be another mission in their war for independence.

Changing into civilian garb, Powell arrived at a Union encampment at Fairfax Court House, Virginia, on January 13, 1865. Under the alias Lewis Paine, he applied to the provost marshal for protection as a civilian refugee from Fauquier County. The provost marshal agreed and sent Paine/Powell to nearby Alexandria. There he took the oath of allegiance and was discharged from custody.

Paine/Powell went to Baltimore and established his residence at the Branson boarding house—a place frequented by others involved in the Confederate Secret Service. John Wilkes Booth or John H. Surratt quickly learned of Paine's presence. Surratt and Louis Weichmann caught a train for Baltimore on the evening of January 21. At Surratt's 1867 trial, Weichmann testified that on the morning of January 22, "Surratt took a carriage and said he had $300 in his possession, and that he was going to see some gentlemen on private business, and that he did not want me along."

A few days later Surratt went to Richmond to meet with Mosby and Secretary of State Judah P. Benjamin. The addition of Lewis Paine/Powell to Booth's action team allowed the final plans to be put in motion. The Confederate Signal Corps along the lower Potomac would be alerted, and Mosby was to provide an adequate force to convey the captured Lincoln to Richmond after Booth's team had brought him across the river. Mosby's involvement in this plan and in later efforts to kill Lincoln was uncovered in the latter part of the twentieth century. The timing and developments follow.

September 1864: After Atlanta and Mobile had fallen, Mosby met with Robert E. Lee at the general's headquarters in Petersburg. The meeting occurred a few days after Mosby had been wounded (mentioned earlier in connection with the execution of several of his men), but the ranger commander was able to get around. This was the first of three planning sessions between the two men, and it followed a meeting in Richmond attended by Lee, Jefferson Davis, Thomas Nelson Conrad, and cabinet members Judah P. Benjamin and James Seddon. Two Confederate Canadian operatives—George Sanders and Clement C. Clay—also probably attended.

Conrad and his team shortly left from Richmond to study Lincoln's movements and investigate the prospects of capturing him. Secretary of War Seddon gave Conrad a document, declaring that "Lt. Col. Mosby and Lieutenant Cawood are hereby directed to aid and facilitate the movements of Captain Conrad." At Lee's meeting with Mosby, the general probably informed him of Conrad's mission and his assignment to support him.

During the same month Mosby organized a new company, Company F, with Walter Bowie as one of the lieutenants. In a move out of character with Mosby's normal operations, he sent Bowie with twenty-five men to Maryland to capture Gov. Augustus Bradford in Annapolis and use him as a hostage to exchange for Confederate prisoners from Maryland. Probably approved by Lee, the operation was a rehearsal for Lincoln's capture. It would help to determine if a small armed unit could travel unimpeded through Maryland. Bowie and Conrad apparently met in Washington and coordinated their activities. Traveling to Annapolis, Bowie determined that the governor was too well guarded while Conrad ascertained that southern Maryland was the best route to use for moving Lincoln to Richmond. Bowie, while returning to Virginia, raided a Maryland store for new boots. The matter ended poorly for him when angry residents pursued and killed him on October 7.

December 1864–February 1865: With Richmond in a desperate plight, President Davis summoned Mosby to the Confederate capital for a meeting with him and Secretary of War Seddon on December 5. One objective of the meeting was to work out plans to increase guerrilla warfare, but more likely the discussion focused on the plot to kidnap Lincoln. At the meeting Mosby was made a full colonel; he returned to his troops with a new uniform and a scarlet-lined cape. Seddon and Mosby met again in January and early February. After the latter meeting Mosby also conferred with Lee. On February 15, a War Department clerk noted in his diary: "General Lee was in town walking about briskly, as if some great event was imminent."

Mosby was critically wounded a few days after the December meeting. While recuperating at his parents' home, he organized his command into two battalions and ordered one of them to the lower end of the Northern Neck—the kidnap route. This battalion was commanded by Col. William H. Chapman. He dispersed his four companies of about six hundred men over four counties, where they lived with local families until the second week of April. These men would become part of the sensitive covert operation for guarding and transporting Lincoln and protecting the escape routes.

Interestingly, among Chapman's recruits in the Northern Neck were three men who later played a role in Booth's escape: William S. Jett, an eighteen-year-old private in the Ninth Virginia Cavalry who had been wounded and was on detached service as a commissary agent; Absalom R. Bainbridge, a seventeen-year-old private from the Third Virginia Infantry; and Lt. Mortimer B. Ruggles, who was second in command in Conrad's spy group.

Over the ensuing weeks other Confederate troops were quietly moved into the area between the Potomac River and Richmond to provide additional support.

March 1865: After Booth failed to capture Lincoln, Mosby received instructions from Lee's adjutant, Walter H. Taylor, on March 27 to remove his command from the Northern Neck, "call it to you" and "collect your command and watch the country from the front of Gordonsville to the Blue Ridge and also the Valley." Mosby, however, received other orders from the Confederate government a few days later for another mission, which kept Chapman's men in the Northern Neck until April 9. Jett, Bainbridge, and Ruggles were part of a group that remained behind even longer, apparently to support the Thomas F. Harney mission (the plot to blow up the White House). After Lincoln's assassination, Mosby, one of his officers, or another person in the clandestine operation met with Ruggles and sent the three men to look for Booth and Herold. Ruggles soon found the fugitives at Port Conway. Other Confederate troops in the area were told to stay put and await developments—an easy arrangement since most of the men had been recruited from this region.

On or about April 1, 1865: With the evacuation of Richmond planned for April 2, and with John H. Surratt in the Rebel capital to report on the failure to kidnap Lincoln, the Confederate high command abandoned the abduction plan and authorized a covert operation to kill the top echelon of the Federal government. Jefferson Davis approved fifteen hundred dollars in gold from the Secret Service account, with two hundred dollars given to Surratt and most or all of the rest apparently going to Mosby and Harney for the White House plot. Harney was ordered to report to Mosby with fuses and detonators; Mosby was directed to get Harney in and out of Washington, where Harney was to blow up the White House while Lincoln and his cabinet were in session. Confederate planners reasoned that such action would disorganize the Union command, damage coordination between Grant and Sherman, and enhance Lee's chances of success.

Mosby was well experienced in irregular warfare and would not have flinched at the thought of killing high government officials if such action would lead to victory.

Harney's team traveled by train to Gordonsville on Saturday, April 1. The post commander, Maj. Cornelius Boyle, provided horses and a guide to escort Harney to Mosby, probably arriving in Fauquier County late on Monday, April 3. With Richmond abandoned during the night of April 2–3, Mosby could not have communicated with the Confederate government after that date. The Harney mission would go forward.

April 5–10, 1865: On Wednesday, April 5, Mosby organized a new company—Company H—and chose twenty-four-year-old George Baylor as its commander. To give the company some experience working together,

Mosby directed Baylor to "go out and see what you can do." On April 6, Baylor's men stormed into the campsite of a Union group, captured sixty-five men, and effectively "cleaned them out," said Gen. John Stevenson at Harpers Ferry.

While Baylor executed this shakedown mission, Mosby was planning Baylor's role in the Harney operation and preparing for contingencies. He had to organize military and civilian support along Harney's three possible escape routes—the most likely being through southern Maryland with its large population of Southern sympathizers. The authors of *Come Retribution* believe that Mosby placed "a small, mobile team of armed men" in each area so that the civilian underground could guide Harney's men to them. Mosby also would have maintained communication with the Confederate apparatus in Washington.

When Baylor returned, Mosby created a task force of Companies D and H to provide a diversion between the Union troops at Fairfax and Alexandria by raiding a mule train near Burke on April 10, unaware that Lee had surrendered on April 9. During the diversion, Harney and his escorts would be infiltrated into Washington. Two problems developed. There was no mule train, and Union troops at Fairfax had learned that the Confederates were in the area. A force from the Eighth Illinois Cavalry set off in pursuit. Before Harney could separate from the main body, the Federals engaged the rear guard in a running fight and captured him as well as several other Confederates. They were taken to the Old Capitol Prison, and the skirmish was reported in the newspapers.

Booth apparently learned of Harney's capture through the Confederate underground in Washington. Lacking the skills to blow up the White House and very much aware of the Confederacy's order to attack the Union high command, he took matters into his own hands. He would use other means to eliminate key leaders. With Mosby's preparations for assisting Harney still in place, Booth decided to exploit these arrangements during his escape after killing Lincoln, Johnson, and Seward.

April 12: Two days after Baylor had returned to Mosby's headquarters, Mosby received a message from Union Gen. Winfield Scott Hancock that called on him to surrender. Hancock offered the same generous terms accorded Lee at Appomattox Court House. Mosby stalled for time. He had troops in southern Maryland and in the Northern Neck, and he was not convinced that Harney's operation was finished, even though Harney had been captured.

This 1865 image of Mosby reveals his stern and determined demeanor. In April, with Lee's surrender imminent, a battalion of Mosby's Rangers still operated in northern Virginia and were assigned to convey an ordnance expert, Frank Harney, to Washington to blow up the White House. Another battalion was engaged in the area known as the Northern Neck for the progressive missions of escorting a captive Lincoln to Richmond and aiding Harney's and Booth's escapes.

LIBRARY OF CONGRESS

Mosby replied to Hancock's offer: "I am ready to agree to a suspension of hostilities for a short time, in order to enable me to communicate with my own authorities, or until I can obtain sufficient intelligence to determine my future action. I am ready to meet any person you may designate to arrange the terms of the armistice."

Mosby then sent Capt. Robert W. Walker of Company B and a small party to Gordonsville "to learn the true state of affairs" and consider future action. This meeting also undoubtedly included senior Confederate operatives from Canada, New York, and Washington.

April 12: A Union scouting party spotted a group of thirty Confederates in St. Mary's County in southern Maryland.

April 15 (the day after the assassination): Union forces skirmished with one of Mosby's teams near Mechanicsville, Maryland, and with another team in St. Mary's County near government farms. During the latter skirmish, Booth and Herold were approaching that exact area from the direction of Samuel A. Mudd's house—only five miles separated the fugitives from a likely rescue team. Thus, as author William Tidwell points out in *April '65*, this Union force probably disrupted one of Mosby's escape plans for Harney that Booth had learned about.

April 16: News of Lincoln's assassination reached Mosby's planning group at Gordonsville and caused them to drastically revise their strategies. By the next day they learned that Booth had been with Samuel Cox in Charles County, Maryland, on April 16. They reached a major conclusion: If Booth were to be kept out of Union hands, Mosby's Rangers would have to do it. There was no other option. Mosby's motivation would have been monumental: The Gray Ghost had worked with Conrad, furnished Lewis Powell/Paine to Booth, and was instrumental in launching the Harney mission against Lincoln. Mosby's life depended on Booth's escape and/or his silence. Booth was now his objective.

April 18: Mosby met with Hancock's representative, Brig. Gen. George H. Chapman, at noon to request an extension of the truce to give him more time to communicate with his superiors. The truce was extended to noon on April 20.

April 20: Mosby and Chapman met again, but this parley was interrupted when one of Mosby's men burst into the room and exclaimed that he had seen Union cavalry in nearby woods. "The damned Yankees have got you in a trap," he warned. "There is a thousand of them hid in the woods right here."

Mosby stood and placed his hand on his revolver. "If the truce no longer protects us, we are at your mercy," he said in a low voice. "But we shall protect ourselves."

An eyewitness observed: "It was a scene difficult to describe. . . . Every partisan was well prepared for instant death and more than ready for a desperate fight. Had a single pistol been discharged by accident, or had Mosby given the word, not one Yankee officer in that room would have lived a minute."

Mosby simply turned and left. He was playing for time. He had not yet heard from Walker's meeting at Gordonsville.

April 21–26: Walker's group reported to Mosby, and Mosby decided to assemble most of his command at Salem (Marshall) to disband them. He retained a small force of about fifty rangers, however, and headed south.

Most of them remained at Fredericks Hall, a station on the Virginia Central Railroad, while Mosby continued to Taylorsville with a select group of ten to twelve men.

He arrived at Taylorsville late on April 25 or early on April 26. The town, on the Secret Line of the Confederate Signal Corps, was about twenty-five miles south of the Richard Garrett farm, where Booth and Herold were housed on the night of April 25–26. Booth had told Dr. Richard Stuart he wanted to find his way to Mosby, and Stuart probably learned of Mosby's effort to reach Booth from the local station of the Secret Line. Herold also had asked for guidance to Bowling Green, which was on the way to Taylorsville.

At Taylorsville, Mosby learned of Booth's whereabouts. The information could have come from one of his men who had crossed the Rappahannock on a ferry with Booth. Mosby's "stay-behind" men in the Northern Neck had formed a security screen around Booth and were reporting his movements and situation to their leader. The climactic moment was only hours away.

10

A BIT
OF GOSSIP

HUNTED LIKE A DOG through swamps and woods," as Booth phrased it in his diary, he and Herold had taken ten days to get to Port Conway, Virginia, on the banks of the Rappahannock River after the assassination of Lincoln. They had been aided by Samuel A. Mudd, Oswald Swann, Samuel Cox, Thomas A. Jones, Elizabeth Quesenberry, Thomas Harbin, William Bryant, Richard Stuart, and, among others, Charley Lucas, who took them to Port Conway hidden under straw in a mule-drawn wagon. Except for Mudd, none of these individuals was ever prosecuted for aiding and abetting the fugitives, despite Stanton's warning to the contrary.

Booth and Herold arrived at Port Conway at about ten o'clock on the morning of April 24. They waited for the ferry, hoping to make contact with Mosby.

The village, once a thriving tobacco port, was a near ghost town with a few residences and a small store operated by William Rollins and his recent teenage bride, Bettie. Rollins, a farmer and a fisherman, also served as a Confederate Signal Corps agent. With the ferry unattended on the other side of the three-hundred-yard stream at Port Royal, Booth and Herold were temporarily stranded. Rollins, apparently not knowing who they were, invited them to wait at his home, a run-down building near the waterfront. Booth asked Rollins if he could find someone to help them get to Orange Court House near Gordonsville, but Rollins replied that he could not on short notice. Interestingly, Gordonsville was on the route to the area toward which Mosby was traveling; the town was also a major communications post for Mosby. When Booth discovered that Rollins had a boat, he offered him ten dollars to take them across the river. Rollins agreed but said he had to set out his nets first, because the shad were running, and he would come back shortly.

While they waited for Rollins to return for them, three Confederate soldiers rode up to catch the ferry: Lt. Mortimer B. Ruggles; his seventeen-year-old cousin, Pvt. Absalom R. Bainbridge; and eighteen-year-old Pvt. William S. Jett. All served with Mosby, and so it is possible that they were detailed to find Booth and assist him. Ruggles, the son of Gen. Daniel Ruggles, had been second in command to Confederate agent Capt. Thomas N. Conrad, who had attempted to capture Lincoln the previous September.

Booth and Herold at first concealed their identities, claiming they were anxious to join up with any Confederate units still fighting. As soon as Herold heard that the men were connected with Mosby, he blurted out: "I will tell you something. We are the 'assassinators' of the president. That man sitting there is John Wilkes Booth."

Jett was so excited he requested their autographs. Ruggles, no stranger to clandestine operations, saw the broader picture. Here was the man about whom Conrad had raved. Ruggles and his companions became extremely supportive. When Herold inquired if they knew where the two men might be able to spend the night, the three rangers promised that they would find a place.

Ruggles noticed the tattoo, "J.W.B," on the back of Booth's left hand and suggested he use the alias "John William Boyd," with Herold posing as his younger brother. Shortly, the ferry from Port Royal docked at Port Conway, and Booth and Herold no longer needed Rollins's boat. The five men boarded the old scow at about one o'clock in the afternoon. Ruggles rode double with Bainbridge, Herold doubled with Jett, leaving Booth alone on Ruggles's mount.

Another ferry passenger, Enoch Wellford Mason, joined the small party. He was a Confederate courier and a cavalryman from a regiment Mosby had stationed in the area to protect the route for moving a captured Lincoln to Richmond. Interestingly, all four soldiers lived north of the Rappahannock,

AUTHOR'S COLLECTION

William Rollins of Port Conway, Virginia, and his recent bride, Bettie, provided vital information to the Federal cavalry pursuing Booth and Herold. Rollins had helped to relay messages as part of the Confederate Signal Corps, but he was not aware of who the men were who appeared at his door, asking for help across the Rappahannock, and they did not volunteer the information.

yet they were traveling south—more evidence that they may have been detailed by Mosby to find Booth.

After crossing the river and landing at Port Royal, Mason separated from the group, probably to rush to the Confederate telegraph at Milford Station, Virginia, and report Booth's movements to other units in the area.

It was now about two o'clock, and finding a place to stay was uppermost in Booth's mind. Jett suggested the home of his friend Randolph Peyton, just two blocks from the ferry slip. Peyton was not yet home from the war, and the house was occupied only by his two spinster sisters, Sarah Jane and Lucy. There are two accounts of what happened at the Peyton home. In one, Jett entered the house alone and told the ladies about two Confederate soldiers, one wounded, who wanted to spend the night. When the women looked out the window at the two men, they demurred, saying it would not be appropriate. In the other account, Booth and Herold entered the house, and Booth, pretending to be Boyd, tried to charm them. It worked only so far. Extending Southern hospitality, the sisters served the men refreshments in the parlor, but when Jett asked them to allow Booth and Herold to spend the night, they refused for reasons of propriety.

Jett then proposed the nearby farm of Richard H. Garrett. Jett knew Garrett as a loyal Southerner who would do just about anything for a Confederate soldier. So the men rode to the Garrett farm, arriving just after three o'clock. Jett assumed the role of spokesman and asked Garrett if two Confederate soldiers, one of whom was exhausted from his war wound, could stay a couple of days. Garrett quickly agreed. Jett introduced "James [or John] W. Boyd" (Booth) to him and the rest of the household: Garrett's wife; Jack and William Garrett, paroled Confederate cavalrymen; eleven-year-old Richard Baynham Garrett; two teenage daughters; and Garrett's sister-in-law, Lucinda Holloway, a schoolteacher who lived with the family and tutored the daughters. Despite Booth's appearance, Holloway especially liked him and later said that he was extremely interesting and intelligent.

Leaving Booth in the comfortable home, the three soldiers and Herold rode south toward Bowling Green, planning to return the next day.

Booth shared a room that night with Garrett's son Richard, who later became a Baptist minister. It was the best sleep Booth had had in ten days. In a Chautauqua address in the 1880s the Reverend Garrett recalled Booth's activities the following morning. After breakfast, he said, "The visitor had lounged on the grass beneath some apple trees, talking and playing with the children of the household. He showed them his pocket compass and laughed at their puzzled faces when he made the needle swing by moving his pocket knife back and forth above it."

During most of the morning and early afternoon Booth relaxed on the front porch, from which he could see rolling fields and a stretch of high road. Teenager Annie Garrett spoke with him briefly about Lincoln's death and called it "most unfortunate," but Booth replied that the assassination was the best thing that could have happened. The result, he said, was that Andrew Johnson, a drunken sot, would be president, a revolution would ensue, and this would benefit the South.

Meanwhile, after depositing Booth at the Garretts on the previous day, Herold and his three companions paused halfway to Bowling Green at a disreputable tavern, The Trap, for an hour of drinks and promiscuous socializing with the four daughters of the mother who ran the tavern. The dalliance completed, the men continued to Bowling Green and arrived just after sundown. Herold and Bainbridge spent the night with widow Elizabeth Clarke, whose son had served with Jett and Bainbridge in Mosby's Rangers. Ruggles and Jett checked in at the Star Hotel. The proprietor's daughter, Izora Gouldman, was Jett's sixteen-year-old sweetheart. This adolescent infatuation proved most lethal for Booth.

Jett and Gouldman's love story was known throughout the region and had not escaped the attention of Bettie Rollins, the Port Conway bride whose husband had allowed Booth and Herold to rest in their home while waiting for the ferry to cross the Rappahannock. Jett had an extensive acquaintance in the county because he had once served as a commissary agent for the Confederacy, collecting beef, bacon, and other supplies at government prices from farmers exempted from military service.

On April 25, Bainbridge and Ruggles returned to the Garrett farm to drop off Herold; Jett remained in Bowling Green with Izora. Booth, now feeling better, thanked the soldiers, and they rode away, toward Port Royal. Ruggles probably assumed that Booth and Herold would be safe for a while and that he should report their situation and position to the clandestine network in the area.

Thirty minutes after Bainbridge and Ruggles rode off, they returned at a brisk gait. Booth and Herold greeted them and learned that Federal cavalry was crossing the river on the ferry and that Port Royal was "full of Yankees in search of Booth." These horsemen were Stanton's crack unit—the force organized by Lafayette C. Baker and supervised by Luther B. Baker and Everton J. Conger, both hard-nosed detectives and former Union officers. The group consisted of twenty-five troopers of the Sixteenth New York Cavalry, commanded by Lt. Edward P. Doherty.

Earlier these soldiers had gone door to door in Port Conway, demanding information at gunpoint: Have you seen a lame man with a companion? When? Where? Their rough tactics frightened the locals. A free black, Dick Wilson, reported seeing two disheveled-looking men waiting for the ferry. Wilson had been assisting Rollins with his fish nets at the time, so he suggested the soldiers talk to him.

Rollins was sitting on his front steps when Doherty and Baker approached and asked if two strangers, one of them lame, had crossed the river. Rollins said that they had. When Doherty handed him some pictures, Rollins pointed to the one of Booth and said it resembled the man on crutches, except he did not have a mustache. (Thus both Rollins and Mudd agreed on the absence of a mustache, but four others remembered Booth's heavy dark mustache!) Rollins also reported that the two men had met up with three Confederate soldiers, one of whom he knew was Willie Jett. Bettie Rollins identified the other two as Ruggles and Bainbridge then added the critical information: The men might have ridden to Bowling Green because Jett's girlfriend lived there.

Desperate for any clue, the fatigued soldiers now smelled blood. They decided to head for Bowling Green and search out Jett. They asked Rollins to go with them as a guide, but his wife objected. She did not want her husband viewed by others in the company of Union soldiers. As a compromise, they pretended to arrest him. Then they began the long, tedious task of crossing the river. It was three o'clock. The ferry could only handle six men and horses at a time. It was not until six o'clock that the entire command was on the Port Royal side of the river.

At the Garrett farm the two Confederate soldiers had raced off again—in the opposite direction from which they had come. Ruggles had done his duty. A second warning to Booth came moments later from another Confederate soldier—perhaps part of a security screen from Mosby's Rangers—and he too scurried away. Booth and Herold were on their own and terrified. They would have been even more distraught had they known who these soldiers were and what they had learned from Bettie Rollins about Willie Jett and Izora Gouldman in Bowling Green.

The end of the road for John Wilkes Booth was the home of Richard Garrett, situated between Port Royal and Bowling Green, Virginia.

AUTHOR'S COLLECTION

In need of a secure hiding place, Booth and Herold grabbed their weapons and scrambled to a nearby wooded area. Within minutes, the Union cavalry galloped by the Garrett farm, leaving behind clouds of dust. When the horsemen had passed, Booth and Herold crept from the underbrush and slowly returned to the Garretts' front porch. Jack Garrett had witnessed the scene unfold and instantly became suspicious; his family was suddenly puzzled and confused.

Booth, still known to the Garretts as Boyd, explained that he had had a run-in with some Yankees "on the Maryland side" and that possibly they were looking for him. If so, they were getting too close, and he had better move on. He asked the Garretts to help him get to Orange Court House, fifty miles west, so he and Herold could link up with other Marylanders endeavoring to get beyond the Mississippi River. If not, he wondered if they would sell him two horses so that he and Herold could ride eleven miles to Guinea Station and take the train to Richmond. He offered to pay whatever Garrett wanted, but Garrett refused to sell his horses. Instead the farm owner suggested that he arrange for the travelers to borrow a neighbor's wagon in the morning.

Sometime late that afternoon another Confederate, Sgt. Allen Bowie, stopped at the farm. He may have been interested only in the young ladies there, or more probably he was part of the effort to keep track of Booth and protect him.

Stranded at the Garrett farm for another night, Booth was likely frustrated and depressed. The Garretts all sensed that something was awry. There are two versions of what transpired that evening. A 1965 article in *Civil War Times Illustrated* claims that Booth asked Garrett for permission to sleep in the barn—a former tobacco-drying shed—and that Garrett gladly agreed because he was anxious to get the strangers out of his house. At the same time, Garrett was also afraid that the men might steal his horses, so he had sons Jack and William lock the shed after Booth and Herold retired, and the two boys slept in a nearby corn crib where they could take turns watching the barn.

In the other version, recorded by Richard Bak in *The Day Lincoln Was Shot*, Garrett told the fugitives that they were no longer welcome in his home and allowed them to sleep in the shed after they pleaded with him. The farmer allegedly told his sons, "I am afraid these men will get us into trouble. You had better watch them tonight."

Sometime that day, Garrett had learned of Lincoln's assassination but not the name of the murderer. His farm was isolated, and news traveled slowly. When the Garretts shared the news with the fugitives, Booth asked about the amount of the reward. Garrett said that he had heard it was one hundred thousand dollars.

"That is not as much as I expected them to offer," the assassin replied.

Jack Garrett suggested that the killer "had better not come this way for I would like to make $100,000 just now."

Booth asked if he would betray the assassin for that.

"He had better not tempt me," Jack replied, "for I haven't a dollar in the world."

In the meantime, Stanton's men stopped at The Trap to make inquiries. Conger, Baker, and Doherty questioned the ladies, but they were uncooperative. Their business demanded discretion. Conger then claimed that the soldiers were looking for a man who had raped a young girl. This subterfuge succeeded, and the girls described the four men who had stopped there. They said one of them was a local man, Willie Jett, and the other three had been back just that afternoon.

Stanton's men concluded that Jett was still at Bowling Green and that he would know where Booth was. Despite the late hour, they decided to continue the search there. Conger and Baker later described the scene to Stanton in a joint letter: "Once more in the saddle, horses exhausted, and men weary, hungry, and sleepy, the command pushed forward and reached Bowling Green between eleven and twelve o'clock [at night]."

The bounty-hungry soldiers quietly surrounded the Star Hotel, and Baker pounded on the front door. No one responded. Walking around to the back of the hotel, Conger and Doherty saw a black man who, upon questioning, reported that Jett was asleep inside. Doherty struck the rear door with the butt of his revolver. The noise awakened the proprietor's wife, Julia Gouldman, who got up, opened the door, and escorted the two officers into a front parlor, where Baker joined them. Her husband was away, she said, and the only people in the building were her children and Willie Jett. They asked where Jett was. She said he was sharing a room upstairs with her son Jesse. Conger ran upstairs, pulled the stunned eighteen-year-old private out of bed, and hustled him downstairs for questioning.

"What do you want?" Jett asked.

"We want YOU!" said Conger, pointing a revolver at his head. "You took Booth across the river, and you know where he is. We have witnesses who

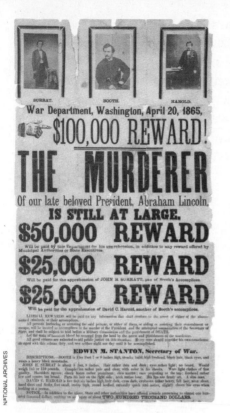

SURRAT.   BOOTH.   HAROLD.

War Department, Washington, April 20, 1865,

☞ $100,000 REWARD!

THE MURDERER

Of our late beloved President, Abraham Lincoln,

IS STILL AT LARGE.

$50,000 REWARD

Will be paid by this Department for his apprehension, in addition to any reward offered by
Municipal Authorities or State Executives.

$25,000 REWARD

Will be paid for the apprehension of JOHN H. SURRATT, one of Booth's Accomplices.

$25,000 REWARD

Will be paid for the apprehension of David C. Harold, another of Booth's accomplices.

LIBERAL REWARDS will be paid for any information that shall conduce to the arrest of either of the above-
named criminals, or their accomplices.

EDWIN M. STANTON, Secretary of War.

NOTICE.—In addition to the above, State and other authorities have offered rewards amounting to almost one
hundred thousand dollars, making in all about **TWO HUNDRED THOUSAND DOLLARS.**

NATIONAL ARCHIVES

One hundred thousand dollars would have helped any Confederate veteran to get back on his feet in style after the war. When word came to the Garrett farm of the reward, one of the farmer's sons commented about the temptation. Booth, who used an alias with the Garretts, asked if the young man would "betray" the assassin, and he replied, "He had better not tempt me." The reward poster of April 20 listed John Surratt among the wanted even though there was no evidence tying him to the assassination.

saw you with Booth, and if we find him without your help, you will be regarded as an accessory to murder."

Frightened and intimidated by the three officers who hovered around him, Jett at first denied knowing that the man was Booth but then agreed to talk if Conger would "shield [him] from complicity in the whole matter." The detective agreed on the condition that Booth was apprehended.

"They're on the road to Port Royal," Jett announced, "about three miles this side of it, at the Richard Garrett place." He would assist the search party, but like Rollins, he did not want to appear to be a willing accomplice. Conger took him as a "prisoner." Riding at Conger's side, Jett guided the weary soldiers ten miles north to the roadside entrance to Garrett's lane. They arrived about two o'clock in the morning. It was probably the day the Confederates hoped to secure Booth with Mosby and his small group. The escape might have been successful had a young bride not shared the local gossip about the teenage romance of Willie Jett and Izora Gouldman.

For his good deed, Jett was not prosecuted. His courtship with Izora, however, soon ended. He moved to Baltimore a year later, became a businessman, and married the daughter of a prominent physician. He traveled frequently to Virginia and remained friendly with his former girlfriend and her family. Contrary to some reports, few Southerners blamed him for taking the troopers to Booth's hiding place. Eventually, the man who betrayed Booth developed a brain disease that made him mentally unstable and paralyzed. He died at Williamsburg, Virginia, respected by everyone who knew him.

11

Useless . . .
Useless

Leaving William Rollins and Willie Jett under guard at the gate to the Garrett farm, the Union horsemen dismounted and quietly surrounded the house. The eerie silence was broken only by the barking of dogs. It was 2 A.M.

Detective Luther Baker pounded on the front door. After several minutes the elderly master of the house opened the door just enough to peer out, but Baker grabbed him before he could speak and dragged him outside. The Union man thrust a pistol in the farmer's face. "Where are they! Where are your two visitors!"

Startled and trembling, Garrett tried to talk about Boyd and his mysterious dash into the woods. Someone shouted: "LIAR! Where are they!" Baker called for a rope to "hang the damned old rebel" and told his men they would find Booth after they had "stretch[ed] the truth out of him."

Just as a soldier tossed a rope over the branch of a large locust tree, Jack Garrett came out from the corn crib where he had been sleeping. "WAIT!" bellowed the paroled Rebel cavalryman. "I will tell you what you want to know. . . . Don't injure Father. The men you want are in the tobacco barn."

Edward P. Doherty's company quickly encircled the shed, a building about sixty feet square. The structure was built with four-inch spaces between the planks of the vertical siding so that air could flow through the building and speed up the curing of tobacco.

Baker repeatedly struck the double door at the front of the shed with his pistol. "You men had better come out!" he shouted.

A voice from the inside demanded, "Who are you?"

"Never mind," Baker replied. "We know who you are, and you had better come out!"

Baker turned to Jack Garrett and ordered: "Unlock the door! Go in there and get their weapons and bring them out!"

"But they will shoot me," Jack complained.

"If you don't go in, I will shoot you," Baker retorted and pushed the young man into the shed. Terrified, Jack urged Booth to give up. The place was surrounded, he said.

"Damn you!" Booth responded. "You have betrayed me! Get out of here!"

"Let me out," Jack called out to Baker. "This man will kill me!"

"You can't come out," Baker protested, "unless you bring the arms."

"He won't give them to me," the young man insisted. "Let me out quick!"

Baker relented, Jack ran out, and the door was slammed shut again.

"I'll do anything for you," Jack told Baker, "except to go in there again. He is desperate, and he will shoot me."

Baker, Doherty, and Everton J. Conger discussed strategy. Doherty wanted to wait for daylight; Conger and Baker preferred immediate action. The two overruled the one.

"You've got ten minutes to come out," Baker yelled to the men in the shed, "or we will set the shed on fire!"

Booth tried to negotiate. "Captain, that's rather rough. I am nothing but a cripple, I have but one leg, and you ought to give me a chance for a fair fight." Booth had three pistols and a carbine at his side. "If you will withdraw your men thirty rods [100 yards], I will come out and we'll shoot it out. I'll fight you single-handed, but I will never surrender!"

Baker told him that their objective was to capture him, not fight him.

"Captain, I consider you a brave and honorable man," Booth replied. "I have had half a dozen opportunities to shoot you, but I did not do it."

Baker had been holding a candle at the door, which illuminated him nicely. He put it down and granted Booth five minutes before his men would torch the barn.

Coconspirator Herold had had enough. He was ready to surrender.

"You're a damned coward to desert me!" Booth shouted as he cursed him.

BOTH: LIBRARY OF CONGRESS

Boston Corbett (*left*), an eccentric religious fanatic, claimed to have shot Booth, but there is no definitive proof that he did. Lt. Edward P. Doherty (*right*) commanded the cavalry unit that traced Booth to the Garrett farm.

Herold pleaded with him to capitulate. Finally Booth told him, "Surrender if you want, but I will fight and die like a man." Then he shouted to Baker, "Captain, there is a man in here who wants to surrender mighty bad."

Baker ordered Herold to pass out his weapons first.

"Captain," Booth protested, "the arms are mine, and I shall keep them. I declare before my Maker that this man here is innocent of any crime whatever."

Conger whispered to Baker that they would have one less to fight if Herold were allowed to surrender. Baker agreed and ordered Herold to come out. The young man extended his arms through the narrow door opening, and either Doherty or Baker (their stories differ) grabbed him. Two guards bound him to a tree.

"The poor little wretch was dragged [to the tree], whining and crying like a child," recalled young Richard Garrett years later. "He kept up his whimpering until the Captain had to order him gagged." Herold pretended to be innocent of any wrongdoing; "I know nothing of this man," he claimed.

Baker gave Booth a last chance. "You have two minutes," he shouted, "before we burn the shed."

Booth knew he was trapped with no hope of escape. "All right, my brave boys," he yelled. "You may prepare a stretcher for me. Throw open your door, draw up your men in a line, and let's have a fair fight. It will be one more stain on the Old Banner."

Baker's troops were positioned on three sides of the building; he was alone at the front door with William Garrett. Conger had moved to the rear of the barn to start the fire. He twisted some hay into a rope, lit it, and tossed it into the shed through a space between the planks. The building was filled with farming implements and hay-covered furniture stored for neighbors during the war. The hay quickly ignited, and the furniture burst into flames. The light from the fire illuminated the inside of the building, making Booth clearly visible to those outside the barn.

Like some of the soldiers, William Garrett rushed forward to look inside. "It was a fearful picture," he recalled. "Framed in great waves of fire stood the crippled man leaning upon his crutches and holding his carbine in his hand. His hat had fallen off and his hair was brushed back from his white forehead. He was as beautiful as the statue of a Greek god and as calm in that awful hour."

Baker described the scene in this manner:

I opened the door quickly, and the first I saw of Booth he was leaning against the hay mow, with a crutch under each arm and a carbine resting at his hip. He was in the act of getting up from the hay. He did get up and dropped one crutch, and started toward the fire. He got within six or eight feet of the side of the barn, and peered all about as though he should like to see who fired the barn. . . . Then he seemed to give it up. . . . There was a table lying there bottom side up. He turned to throw the table on the fire, but he dropped it and turned to look around the barn. The fire was rolling over the roof. He saw the door open, and he turned and dropped the other crutch and started toward the door . . . with a kind of limping, halting jump. . . . I think he would have come out and fought the whole command. . . . I think he would have sold his life as dearly and bravely as possible.

Booth was about ten feet from the door. In one hand he held a rifle, in the other a revolver. Suddenly someone fired a shot at him. The assassin

Before Booth was shot in a shed at the Garrett farm, the structure was set on fire to force him out. One of the soldiers there, William Lightfoot, observed: "The center post, against which Booth was leaning just before he was shot, didn't burn. The next day everything was burned up but it. It stood there, all blackened but still sound, in all the ashes."

threw up his hands then fell to the floor. The soldiers and the officers were stunned.

Baker flung open the door and ran into the shed. He found the actor facedown with a revolver in his right hand. He was motionless. He had been shot below the right ear, the ball passing out the neck on the other side after severing the spinal cord. Booth was paralyzed. Seconds later Conger rushed in.

In his report, Conger said:

> I supposed he had shot himself. I went around to the front door, and found it open. Baker had gone in, and . . . stood partly bent down, looking at Booth, who lay on the floor, to all appearance dead. I stooped over, looked down at him, and said he had shot himself. Baker said, "No, he did not. . . ." He had the appearance of a man who had put a pistol to his head and shot himself, shooting a little too low; and I said again, "He shot himself." Baker said, "No, he did not." He spoke very positive about it. I thought it a little strange, rather, as if he doubted my word when he said so.

While Conger believed that Booth had committed suicide, his colleague Luther Baker pondered that Conger might have had secret orders to shoot him. Had either man examined Booth's guns, they could have determined if any of them had just been fired, but they did not do that, or if they did, they did not report it. The autopsy report prepared by the army surgeon general did not indicate the caliber of the pistol or the size of the ball but noted only that Booth had been shot by a pistol ball.

Baker and Conger dragged Booth from the flaming barn. The heat from the raging fire had become intense. "Carry him to the front porch of the house," Conger ordered two soldiers. The officers then assembled their men and asked each one if he had fired the shot. All denied it until they came to thirty-three-year-old Sgt. Boston Corbett, a slightly built cavalryman who wore long hair because he wanted to look like Jesus.

"I fired the shot," Corbett confessed.

"Why?" Conger demanded.

Corbett stood at attention, saluted, and pointed upward. "God Almighty directed me," he said. The other soldiers laughed at the remark, but Corbett continued, "I immediately took steady aim with my revolver and fired."

During the conspiracy trial Corbett significantly modified his reasoning—probably because he was coached to do so. In the hearing room he said that he fired "because . . . I thought [Booth] would do harm to our men in trying to fight his way through that den if I did not."

Corbett was a devout Methodist and an eccentric religious fanatic. Seven years earlier, after reciting passages from the Gospel of Matthew to a small gathering of prostitutes, Corbett castrated himself with a pair of scissors so that he would not succumb to sexual temptation. After his self-mutilation, he attended a prayer meeting, strolled for a while, ate a hearty dinner, then sought out a doctor for some sutures. Thus it is possible that the emotionally unbalanced trooper could have believed that God had instructed him to kill Booth.

Later Corbett also claimed to have shot Booth because the trapped man was about to fire on one of the officers. This explanation, however, was not only not corroborated but specifically denied. "It was not true," responded Jack Garrett. "Booth made no movement to fire upon anybody."

Stanton, according to many historians, had ordered Doherty's cavalry to bring Booth back alive, and Conger, according to Baker, had made this known to his men numerous times. Conger, however, gave conflicting testimony on April 27, the day after the assassin's death: "[The men] had no orders either to fire or not to fire."

Corbett and his comrades had been assigned to positions about thirty feet from the barn. If Corbett had been the killer, he would have had to move closer to the building to shoot between the planks of the siding. With the shed ablaze, he would have been seen by the other soldiers, some of whom had moved closer to see the action, but not one of them ever supported Corbett's story. Yet none ever asserted that Corbett could not have done it. The fire, the excitement, or God Almighty may have prompted Corbett to kill Booth.

Regardless, Corbett violated orders twice—to capture Booth alive and to maintain his position thirty feet from the shed—and failure to follow orders is normally a punishable offense. Thus Corbett's confession relieved Conger of responsibility. The detective needed to blame someone for violating Stanton's orders and to keep others from pointing an accusatory finger at him.

Although Corbett was arrested and brought before Stanton, his superiors defended his actions. Doherty acknowledged that Corbett had shot without orders but called him a brave and true soldier who three times had requested permission to enter the shed and bring Booth out. Stanton concluded: "The rebel is dead; the patriot lives—[and] has saved us continued excitement, delay, and expense. The patriot is released."

The secretary of war allocated Corbett a share of the reward money—$1,653.85—which was the same amount given to the other soldiers who cornered Booth at the Garrett farm. Corbett later went on the lecture circuit to discuss his bravery not only at the Garrett farm but in his earlier military service. According to his War Department file, "he distinguished himself by the ferocity of his fighting." In combat against Mosby's Rangers, he had killed seven of the enemy, rejoicing as each Rebel fell, "Amen! Glory to God!"

In later years, while serving as an assistant doorkeeper for the Kansas legislature, Corbett brandished a gun when someone mocked the opening prayer. Afterward he was committed to a mental institution from which he escaped and vanished.

Still, many Lincoln assassination scholars ask the question, Who shot Booth? Interestingly, Herold apparently was never asked if he saw the shooter. Guarded and tied to a tree, he told Baker only that he had "heard a pistol shot, looked around, and saw one corner of the barn in a light blaze."

There are at least four possible answers to the question after ruling out Luther Baker as a likely candidate. Baker was being closely observed at the time by young Richard Garrett, who confirmed Baker's report that Booth was flat on the ground when they entered the shed. For Baker to have shot Booth in a manner consistent with the direction taken by the ball, he would have had to enter the shed, hold Booth with his right arm, and fire his pistol with his left hand. And this he did not do. The remaining options are:

1. Booth shot himself. This was logistically possible. All he had to do was fire his pistol at the right side of his head and shoot low. Conger and Baker could have resolved the question by checking Booth's gun to see if it had been fired—at the very least to have determined if a chamber was empty. They testified only that Booth's three weapons were loaded. For that matter, they should have checked all the firearms on the scene to establish the truth beyond all controversy. They did not. Perhaps the oversight was intentional, perhaps because they were exhausted. Further, Booth's guns

Richard B. Garrett was eleven years old when Booth was killed at his father's farm. Many years later, as a Baptist preacher, he stressed his family's surprise and shock when they learned the identity of their guest who had given his name as John W. Boyd. Garrett failed to mention the family's financial bonanza, however. Not only did they profit by selling the bloodstained floorboards of their front porch to souvenir hunters, but they also got a new barn. Booth's brother Edwin paid for it.

LESLIE'S

After Booth was shot, detectives Luther Baker and Everton Conger dragged him from the flaming barn. In this depiction of the scene, Herold stands to the far right in the custody of other troopers. Actually, he was tied to a tree.

apparently were never checked by the War Department, a failure for which there is no excuse. Author David DeWitt noted that "the War Department, having possession of Booth's weapons, might easily have shown whether or not one chamber of the revolver was empty, [but] it does not appear that [his] pistol . . . was ever examined."

The travel of the bullet, however, supports the suicide theory. According to records of the Smithsonian Institution, the ball entered Booth's neck on the right side and, taking an oblique downward course at an angle of about twenty degrees, penetrated three vertebrae and passed out on the left side. Author Otto Eisenschiml noted in *Why Was Lincoln Murdered?* that such a wound could have been inflicted from a distance only "if Booth had been standing with his head bent sharply to the left and with his profile toward the right wall and parallel to the door." It's possible but not likely.

In a statement dated May 6, 1865, Confederate Willie Jett asserted that Booth had told him he did not intend to be taken alive: "If they don't kill me, I'll kill myself," Booth told Jett. "Those who know him best," said the *Gettysburg Compiler,* "feel confident that he has committed suicide."

2. Everton J. Conger, a close friend of Stanton's appointee, Lafayette C. Baker, shot Booth because he had been secretly ordered to do so by either Baker or Stanton. Conger, a battle-tested veteran, had served under Baker in the National Detective Police and had been handpicked by Baker to lead the chase. It was Conger who went behind the shed to set the fire. By his own sworn statement, he was by the side of the shed when the shot was fired; Corbett was on the other side, around the corner of the building. Conger's position enabled him to fire at the side of Booth's neck, but a puzzling question remains: Why would the course of the bullet have been downward? Without knowing Conger's exact position, proof of his guilt is lacking. Furthermore, as the ranking officer on the scene, Conger should have been stationed permanently near the front door where Booth would have exited, had he been able and willing to do so.

Why did Conger assume the responsibility for going to the rear of the barn and setting the fire? He easily could have delegated the task to one of the troopers. Why, in fact, was the fire needed at all? Was it to provide light so that Booth could be seen and killed, or was it simply set to smoke him out? Conger later testified that, after he set the fire, he saw Booth look at the flames to see if he could put them out, and when Booth realized he could not, he "dropped his carbine [and] came towards the front door." Hurrying to meet him at the door, Conger said that was when he heard the shot.

The part of Conger's statement that Booth "dropped his carbine [and] came towards the front door" is particularly interesting. If Booth was headed toward the door without his carbine—suggesting a high probability of surrendering—was he shot to keep him from surrendering and talking about possible Confederate connections in Washington at the highest levels of the federal government?

Luther Baker suspected that Conger fired the shot that killed Booth and later said that if Conger had done so, that fact had best not be known. Interestingly, Baker was never called as a witness in the conspiracy trial.

3. Boston Corbett fired on Booth either on his own initiative or by secret order. He later testified that he had "aimed at Booth's shoulder" and "did not want to kill him. . . . I think he stooped to pick up something just as I fired. That may probably account for his receiving the ball in the head." Three troubling facts remain, however. First, Booth was killed by a pistol ball, but according to a July 1965 article in *Civil War Times Illustrated,* Corbett was armed only with a carbine. He did not have a pistol. The article was written by Julian E. Raymond, a graduate of West Point and a retired army colonel

who spent much of his spare time over a period of fifty years studying the Lincoln murder case. Second, apparently no one checked Corbett's gun—whatever it was—to see if it had been fired. Third, the natural impulse of a shooter in this situation would be to rush into the barn and check the victim, but Corbett showed no interest in the injured man. Curiously, by Stanton's personal order, a revolver was later issued to Corbett, and the eccentric soldier thereafter gloried in being known as "the man who shot Booth." But if Corbett already had a revolver, why was he issued another one?

4. Finally, there is a possibility that one of Mosby's men shot Booth. Had one of the rangers seen that Booth had been cornered in the shed, he would have realized that rescuing Booth was no longer feasible. If Booth were questioned, he might implicate Mosby, Conrad, Mudd, Thomas Jones, and other Confederate officials as well as the whole clandestine network of which the assassin had been a part. Mosby would have hanged if Stanton had learned of any one of three connections Mosby had with the conspiracy against Lincoln: cooperating with Conrad's mission to kidnap the president, furnishing Lewis Paine for Booth's team, or supporting Harney's mission to blow up the White House. If Mosby could infiltrate twenty-nine men behind enemy lines and capture a Union general (Edwin H. Stoughton) and thirty-two men without firing a shot (which Mosby accomplished on March 8, 1863), then he or one of his men could certainly infiltrate the grounds around the Garrett shed, fire one shot, and disappear.

Among Mosby's many talents was the ability to enter a target area undetected (usually after dark), execute a lightning blow, and rapidly vanish into the countryside. He was daring and cunning. He had fast horses and some of the best scouts in the army—local men with local contacts—and they were keeping track of Booth. Mosby also used Union uniforms when he deemed it wise to do so. "He did not fight fairly," Union Col. George Gray remarked after Mosby ambushed his men twice in one night.

During the early morning hours of April 26, Mosby or one of his men, masquerading as a Union soldier, had the means and the motive to murder Booth. Surprisingly, this possibility has never been examined.

When Mosby arrived in Taylorsville late on April 25, he undoubtedly learned that Booth was at the Garrett farm and prepared to rendezvous. Through the Secret Line, Mosby's stay-behind group in the area would have known where Mosby was as well as where Booth was. Only twenty-five miles separated them, and everything was in place to bring the two men together. Once Booth was with Mosby, the small party would have rejoined

Mosby's main force near Fredericks Hall and moved to safer territory. When Union cavalry appeared at the Garretts in the early morning of April 26, that plan was no longer possible. Silencing Booth was the only option. If Mosby's men did not kill him, they were surely relieved that someone else did.

Following the money may or may not be helpful in ascertaining who shot Booth. Boston Corbett, as noted above, was rewarded when he should have been punished. Conger received the largest single amount of the bounty paid out by Stanton—fifteen thousand dollars; Luther Baker received only thirty-seven hundred dollars. His first official statement—made to Judge Advocate General Joseph Holt on the night Baker returned to Washington—disappeared and has never been found. Baker told a congressional committee he believed his testimony had been destroyed "to suppress the facts which it proved as to my having charge of the party, so that my claim to the chief share of the reward would not be so good." Baker's disappointment and resentment were, in part, self-inflicted. His cousin, Lafayette C. Baker, had placed him in command. As such, he deserved the higher compensation. Luther Baker, however, had once been a junior officer under Conger, and Conger was more experienced and more familiar with the Virginia countryside. Further, Conger did not like the idea of serving under a former subordinate. So Luther Baker relinquished command to him. It cost Baker more than eleven thousand dollars.

Interestingly, Corbett reported that he had "twice offered to my commanding officer, Lieutenant Doherty, and once to Mr. Conger, to go into the barn and take the man, saying that I was not afraid to go in and take him; it was less dangerous to go in and fight him than to stand before a crack exposed to his gunfire, where I could not see him, although he could see

Parts of Lincoln and Booth are displayed in various museums. Booth's third, fourth, and fifth vertebrae, which were removed during his autopsy, can be seen at the National Museum of Health and Medicine at the Walter Reed Army Medical Center in Washington, D.C. Another fragment is in a bottle in the Mutter Medical Museum at the College of Physicians of Philadelphia. Hair and fragments of the president's skull, as well as the bullet that killed him, also can be seen at Walter Reed. Other hair samples from Lincoln's autopsy are in the Lincoln Room Museum in the Wills House in Gettysburg, the Lincoln Museum in Fort Wayne, Indiana, and the Weldon Petz Abraham Lincoln Collection at the Plymouth Historical Society and Museum in Plymouth, Michigan.

me; but I was not sent in." The *New York Herald* agreed, stating editorially that it was difficult to understand how Booth could not be taken alive and suggested "a thorough inquest into the circumstances of the capture."

Baker, Conger, and Doherty's experienced soldiers certainly should have been able to capture a lone crippled man alive. They could have laid siege to the shed until Booth surrendered. Or they could have waited for morning and stormed the shed. Were they concerned that reinforcements might come and later demand a share of the reward bounty?

Baker and Conger, but not Doherty, seemed compelled to capture Booth immediately—or to kill him before he could talk. Otherwise, the fire would not have been necessary. Of course, their men were weary, it was late at night, and they may have feared that delays would make them less alert. Still, they could and should have captured him alive.

Beverly Tucker, a prominent Confederate leader based in Canada, wrote: "[They] have sealed the only lips that could unravel this dark and mighty mystery. Did they . . . act in this respect under instructions; and if not, why have they so promptly received the plaudit, 'Well done, good and faithful servants'? Would it have been inconvenient to any one to have taken him with the power to speak? Alas! We can never know all that died with this daring, yet misguided young man."

In the early morning hours of April 26, 1865, Booth was removed from the shed and placed on the grass near a locust tree. He was unconscious, but a splash of water revived him. Soon he was moved to the front porch of the Garrett home and put on a small straw mattress and pillows brought out by the women of the house. They placed a cloth soaked with water in his mouth and loosened his collar. Shortly, Booth opened his eyes.

"Kill me, oh, kill me," he told his captors.

Conger ordered two men to ride swiftly to Port Royal and bring back a doctor. He arrived shortly after dawn and declared the wound to be fatal. Booth's spinal cord was punctured. His breathing was labored. In his agonizing condition, Booth struggled to speak. Conger bent low and heard him whisper: "Tell my mother that I die for my country. I did what I thought was best." If Conger reported these words correctly, then there can be little doubt that the dying man was Booth. He loved his mother and would have wanted her to know his sentiments.

Later, near sunrise, Booth asked for his arms to be raised so he could see his paralyzed hands. He looked at them and moaned, very faintly, "Useless . . . useless!"

Those were his last words. He died at 7:15 A.M., about two and a half hours after he had been shot. It was twelve days since the night he shot Lincoln and within seven minutes of the same time of day that Lincoln had died. Booth was twenty-six years old.

A few hours later, in North Carolina, Confederate Gen. Joseph E. Johnston surrendered to Union Gen. William T. Sherman, and the Civil War officially ended. Johnston had commanded the last complete Confederate army in the field.

Shortly, William B. Lightfoot, an unparoled Confederate soldier from the Ninth Virginia Cavalry, came by the Garrett farm and pretended to be a curious bystander. Mosby probably sent him to learn Booth's status and to determine if he had made any incriminating statements. No one bothered Lightfoot or questioned him.

Whether from this soldier or other sources, Mosby learned of Booth's death; the assassin was no longer his responsibility or a threat to his security. Mosby's last mission ended with Booth's last breath.

Mosby disbanded his remaining rangers but waited until June 17 to surrender himself at Lynchburg. By then the conspirators' trial was nearly over, and nothing had been proven to link him with Booth. Mosby denied any complicity and, astutely, never revealed his role in the Conrad and Harney missions, in assigning Lewis Paine to the kidnap-turned-assassination plot, or in aiding Booth's escape. By keeping quiet, he not only saved his life but also enabled others to execute a convincing campaign that distanced the former Rebel government from the Lincoln conspiracies. Mosby's role

Union Gen. William T. Sherman and Confederate Gen. Joseph E. Johnston were adversaries in Georgia and the Carolinas, but their respect for each other continued throughout their lives. It was Johnston's surrender to Sherman on April 26, 1865—the same day Booth was killed—that ended the war in the East. When Sherman died of pneumonia in the winter of 1891, eighty-four-year-old Johnston served as an honorary pallbearer and stood bareheaded in a cold wind outside the church. When a friend warned him he might fall ill, Johnson replied: "If I were in Sherman's place, and he were standing here in mine, he would not put on his hat." Ten days later Johnston died of pneumonia. Both men were West Point graduates. Johnston resigned his commission in 1861 to enter Confederate service as a major general; Sherman declined a Confederate commission in 1861 to become a Union colonel.

remained unknown until the 1990s when William A. Tidwell put the puzzle together, catalogued in his books *Come Retribution* and *April '65*.

Mosby's postwar career was not without some interesting problems. His wartime successes prompted the Radical Republicans in Congress to seek revenge against him and imprison him. In a curious development, U. S. Grant interceded for his former foe, and the two men became warm friends. Mosby later stumped Virginia for Grant and helped to carry the state for him during Grant's successful 1868 campaign for the presidency. Mosby's work for Grant, however, did not sit well with Virginia Confederates, and an attempt was made on his life. Concerned for his friend's safety, Grant influenced President Rutherford B. Hayes to appoint Mosby as U.S. consul to Hong Kong. Seven years later Mosby returned to the United States to serve as an attorney for the Southern Pacific Railway in California. The brilliant Confederate commander later received federal appointments by Presidents William McKinley and Theodore Roosevelt.

While he frequently lectured in the North, Mosby refused to attend reunions of his former battalion. "They are nothing but political meetings," he explained, "where demagogues go to spout and keep alive the passions of the war. . . . I prefer healing the wounds of the war." Yet his memoirs published in 1917 reveal his true self: "No one clung longer to the Confederacy than I did, and I can say with the champion of another lost cause that if Troy could have been saved by this right hand even by the same it would have been saved."

12

A TATTOO, A SCAR, AND A BROKEN LEG

O N THE FRONT PORCH of the Garrett farmhouse, Booth's body was sewn up in a horse blanket then placed in an old market wagon and taken to Aquia Creek, where the body was carried by steamer up the Potomac to Alexandria. From there the corpse was taken by a government tugboat to the Washington Navy Yard and, under the light of flickering torches, placed on board the ironclad *Montauk*. It was 1:45 A.M., on Thursday, April 27. The body was now in the custody of Col. Lafayette C. Baker by Stanton's order. Coincidentally, four of Booth's alleged coconspirators were imprisoned aboard the same vessel—Lewis Paine, George Atzerodt, Michael O'Laughlin, and Edman Spangler.

Later that morning army surgeon general Joseph K. Barnes and Dr. Joseph J. Woodward, both of whom assisted in the Lincoln autopsy, autopsied Booth's body and determined that he had been killed by a pistol ball. They asserted "he must have endured untold anguish of body, as well as of mind, from the nature of the fracture of his leg, the small bone having cut its way through the flesh and protruded," according to a *New York Tribune* article on April 29. Barnes and Woodward removed the damaged section of the assassin's spine and delivered it to the Army Medical Museum for preservation. (It is currently displayed at the National Museum of Health and Medicine at the Walter Reed Army Medical Center in Washington, D.C.)

Except for a blue necktie, none of the dead man's clothing was preserved. Witnesses handpicked by Stanton identified the body. Excluded
were a number of individuals who had known Booth for years and had volunteered to assist in the identification.

Renowned Washington photographer Alexander Gardner was summoned to both identify the body and photograph it before the autopsy. He
was allowed to take only one exposure and make one print. The negative
and the print were then delivered to Stanton and never seen again, although
an image, likely based on the photograph, appeared in the May 13 issue of
Harper's Weekly.

Although Booth's features were badly distorted and blackened, nine or
possibly ten persons positively identified him at the autopsy, although some
did so with reservations.

John Frederick May, a doctor who had once removed a large fibroid
tumor from Booth's neck, described the scar to Dr. Barnes before looking at
it, and Barnes noted that the description matched the scar exactly. May then
requested that the body be placed in a sitting position. Looking down upon
it, May said he finally recognized Booth's features, "but never in a human
body had greater change taken place from the man whom I had seen in the
vigor of life and health than in the haggard corpse which was before me
with its yellow discolored skin, its unkempt and matted hair, and its whole
facial expression sunken and sharpened by the exposure and starvation that
it had undergone. The right lower limb was greatly contused and perfectly
black from the fracture of one of the long bones of the leg."

May then further confused the issue and raised doubts about his identification: "[The body] looks to me much older, and in appearance much
more freckled than he was. I do not recollect that he was at all freckled." He
was not. Booth was known for his famous marble-white complexion. This
discrepancy was never investigated.

Unconfirmed reports indicate that Booth's dentist, William Merrill, positively identified two fillings as his work, but his testimony is not on file.
Charles Dawson, a clerk at the National Hotel where Booth stayed, identified
the initials "J.W.B." tattooed on the back of the corpse's left hand, between his
thumb and forefinger, where Booth had clumsily marked them with India
ink when he was a boy.

The body was also identified by Seaton Munroe, a prominent Washington attorney. Munroe said he recognized Booth from the "general appearance" of the body, although Frederick May had testified that the features of

the dead man had changed greatly. Munroe noted that the body had no mustache, thereby adding to the mystery over that issue. Interestingly, detective James A. Wardell not only reported that the body had a mustache but described it as "shaggy and dirty." Wardell's written comment was based on Gardner's photograph of the body, which Wardell reported he had delivered to Col. Lafayette C. Baker at the War Department.

Altogether, three persons with whom Booth interacted during his escape testified that he had a mustache—Jones, Garrett, and Bainbridge—and three others claimed that he did not—Mudd, Rollins, and Munroe. If all of them remembered correctly, then it's possible that two different men were identified as Booth. That prospect opens a Pandora's box of mysteries about who was killed at Garrett's farm and who's buried in Booth's grave. Since nearly all historians are convinced that the answer to both questions is Booth, three witnesses must have been mistaken about the mustache.

To avoid any respect being paid to Booth's remains, Stanton ordered the body buried without ceremony in the dirt floor of a storeroom in the old penitentiary on the Washington Arsenal grounds (now Fort Leslie J. McNair) and assigned the task to the Bakers. On the afternoon of April 27, after the identification of the body, the Baker cousins took the body to the

During the early morning hours of April 27, the body of John Wilkes Booth and a bound David Herold were escorted through the Washington Navy Yard en route to the Ironclad monitor *Montauk.*

LIBRARY OF CONGRESS

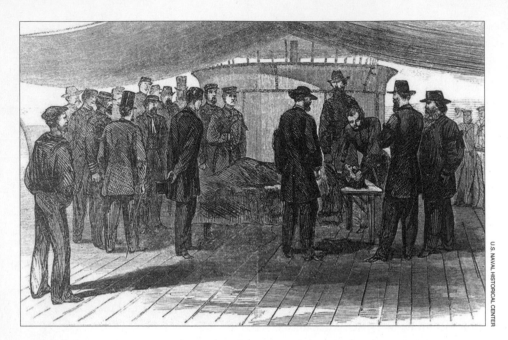

U.S. NAVAL HISTORICAL CENTER

This engraving from *Harper's Weekly* is the only image of the Booth autopsy.

Washington Arsenal, where they left it on the prison dock in a gunny sack. That night they buried it as Stanton directed.

The secret manner in which the interment was done provoked rumor, gossip, and editorials. Secrecy suggested nefarious acts. Thus the talk of the town was that Booth had neither been captured nor killed. Many asked: For what other reason could the body have been handled the way it was?

Stanton was called before a congressional committee in 1867. "There was nothing about the identity of Booth that entered your consideration in making the burial a secret?" the members asked.

"Nothing whatever," Stanton replied. "It was done simply and solely for the purpose of preventing him from being made the subject of rebel rejoicing." He did not want the corpse made "a subject of glorification by disloyal persons." No one was to decorate the grave, pray over it, or in any way honor the assassin. He knew that many Southerners praised Booth. In fact, before the autopsy, a woman sneaked aboard the *Montauk,* cut open the sack holding Booth's body, and snipped off a lock of his hair. Lafayette C. Baker discovered her and forcibly retrieved the hair. Stanton also forbade the sale of Booth's picture in Washington and closed Ford's Theatre because any entertainment was inappropriate at the place where Lincoln was shot.

Booth's body was exhumed in 1867 and reburied in a locked storeroom in a warehouse at the prison. Two years later, in February 1869, the remains were released to the Booth family. At an inquest in Washington, it was noted that the skull had become detached from the body but still had a "fine suit of hair" and that the body was in a state of severe decay. A dentist from Washington intently studied the teeth and announced, "This is Wilkes Booth, for this is some of my work." From Washington the remains were taken to John H. Weaver's undertaking establishment in Baltimore, where it was readily identified as Booth by three of his siblings and his mother as well as by John T. Ford and Henry Clay Ford of Ford's Theatre and others.

According to the *Baltimore Sun,* the detached head was passed around and scrutinized. John Ford noted the firm outline of the lower jaw that still "bore resemblance to the living man." Joseph T. Lowry, a Baltimore photographer, informed the *Boston Herald:* "There was not the slightest doubt in my mind that the face of the dead man I looked upon was that of the actor, whom I had seen many times in life. The features were the same, although considerably sunken. His dark hair, which was remarkably dark and curly, was well preserved."

Hundreds of curious bystanders assembled, and many of them were allowed to view the body in its handsome mahogany coffin. A few souvenir hunters clipped some locks of hair. Finally, the body was placed in a vault in the Booth family plot at Green Mount Cemetery in Baltimore.

Over the years many have speculated that Booth was not the one who was killed at Garrett's tobacco shed. The dominant alternate theory is that James W. Boyd, a Confederate soldier, was the man in the shed. The name is similar to Booth's alias, John William Boyd, which he used at the Garrett farm.

Historian William Hanchett noted in *The Lincoln Murder Conspiracies* that James W. Boyd was a Confederate officer released in February 1865 from the Old Capitol Prison by an order from Stanton. He had the same initials as Booth, and they were tattooed on one of his hands, but he looked nothing like Booth. He was taller, older (forty-two), and gray-haired, and he died in Tennessee on January 1, 1866, seven months after he was supposedly killed at the Garrett farm.

In addition, there have been several post-1865 Booth sightings—twenty-two in fact. None of them deserves any attention.

Only one person knew beyond any doubt who was killed in Garrett's barn: his companion, David E. Herold. To those who captured him, Herold insisted that the man in the shed was not Booth. Edward P. Doherty, the commander of the troops at the Garrett farm, reconstructed this conversation with Herold after the man in the shed had been shot:

Herold: "Who is that that has been shot in the barn?"

Doherty: "Why, you know well who it is."

Herold: "No, I do not; he told me his name was Boyd."

Doherty: "It is Booth, and you know it."

Herold: "No, I did not know it; I did not know that it was Booth."

Herold's statements were probably based on fear—fear for his own life or of immediate maltreatment from the soldiers. In the heat of that night, it would not have been prudent for him to admit that he had assisted the man who had assassinated the president. In later statements, Herold constantly referred to his companion as Booth, although he lied by denying he was with him at Mudd's house. According to Capt. Christian Rath, who was in charge of the subsequent hangings of the Lincoln conspirators, Herold related to him the details of their attempt to escape.

To provide certainty on the question of who is buried in Booth's grave, Booth's relatives filed a petition in October 1994 in the Circuit Court for Baltimore City to exhume the remains. Cemetery officials, however, refused. They were obligated, they said, to protect the sanctity of those interred unless there was overwhelming evidence that the body was not Booth's. A judge ruled that the evidence was insufficient, and his decision was upheld by the Court of Special Appeals in Annapolis. Later efforts to exhume the remains for DNA tests also were rejected.

The troopers at the Garrett farm in April 1865 claimed to know the truth. "On the boat going up to Washington with the body," recalled Sgt. Andrew Wendell, "we troopers all filed past and had a good look. Some people—and big people—said that we had the wrong man and that Booth wasn't dead. He was dead enough when we looked at him."

The soldiers, however, did not know Booth, and the search party at Garrett's farm was motivated by greed. If the dead man was not Booth, they would get nothing.

Herold's initial comments, the secret burial, and the riddles over the mustache and the freckles do generate some doubt, but this is not sufficient to outweigh one powerful argument—the body had three features that matched perfectly with Booth's medical history: a tattoo, a scar, and a broken leg.

13

THE UNLUCKIEST WOMAN

AT NOON ON THE morning of Friday, July 7, 1865, Gen. Winfield Scott Hancock stood near the gates of the Washington Arsenal and Penitentiary awaiting a messenger. As commandant of the military district, Hancock had the onerous duty of carrying out the execution of four condemned prisoners—three men and one woman. The four were to hang that day between ten in the morning and two in the afternoon for their roles in the assassination of Abraham Lincoln. The sentence, delivered to the prisoners just one day earlier, had been handed down by a military commission of nine officers—seven generals and two colonels.

Hancock, along with most of Washington, expected one of the prisoners, Mary Elizabeth Surratt, to be spared the gallows. He even arranged for a cavalry relay to be stationed between the White House and the prison so that a stay of execution from the president could be brought to him the quickest possible way. The tall, dignified general, nicknamed "Hancock the Superb" during the war, delayed the proceedings for as long as he could. By 1 P.M. his uniform was soaked with perspiration from the oppressive one-hundred-degree heat on this steamy, windless summer day. By then it was obvious that no reprieve would be coming from Andrew Johnson. The general walked into the prison yard and issued instructions for the guards to "get everything ready."

The scaffolding for the hanging had been completed by eleven that morning. Its platform was perched fifteen feet above the ground and accessible by creaky stairs at the back. Close behind it, four graves had been dug in the dry red clay. Four pine boxes originally used for packing guns had been stacked to the right of the scaffold.

Around noon Surratt was brought out of her cell and allowed to sit on a chair at the doorway. Father Jacob A. Walter, her Catholic priest, stood at her side. Solemnly she declared her innocence to him. Walter years later stated that Surratt's "exact words . . . the last confession of an innocent woman whilst she stood on the verge of eternity" were that she "was innocent of any complicity in that great crime." He asserted, "She died as innocent of that crime as a babe unborn."

Walter and another priest, Bernardin F. Wiget, a friend of the Surratts, administered last rites. They accompanied her to the gallows, one of them holding a crucifix before her. Two officers supported her. She was followed by coconspirators George Atzerodt, David Herold, and Lewis Paine. Surratt's devoted twenty-two-year-old daughter Anna watched from a second-floor window, waiting and hoping for a reprieve from the president that never came.

The prisoners mounted the thirteen steps to the gallows and were seated in chairs positioned before the dangling ropes. Umbrellas were used to shade them from the blazing sun. Gen. John F. Hartranft, governor of the military prison, read the death warrants. When he finished, the minister accompanying Lewis Paine expressed the prisoner's appreciation to the commandant and his guards for their kind treatment. During the minister's statement, Surratt groaned audibly. Hartranft then ordered the executioner to proceed.

"Her, too?" asked hangman Capt. Christian Rath.

"Yes," replied Hartranft.

A colonel then removed Surratt's bonnet and veil and fastened her hands tightly behind her back. He bound her skirts about her knees, placed the noose around her neck, and covered her face and head with a long white hood. The others were similarly bound.

The National Intelligencer reported that "Mrs. Surratt wavered a little, and . . . it was feared she would give way. . . . At one time she said to those standing by, 'Please don't let me fall.'"

Rath had prepared nooses with seven knots for the three men to ensure a quick and clean break of the neck, but he had stopped after making five knots for Surratt. He expected that she would be spared.

SURRATT HOUSE MUSEUM

Mary Elizabeth Surratt was the first woman in American history to be executed by the federal government. While there is little doubt of her involvement in the plot to kidnap Lincoln, there is much uncertainty about her role in the assassination, other than a message she sent to the proprietor of her tavern in Surrattsville to "get the shooting irons out."

With everything in place, Rath clapped his hands three times—the death signal. Four soldiers knocked the props from beneath the platform, and the four prisoners catapulted downward. Surratt died instantaneously, then Atzerodt. Paine and Herold strangled, their necks not having been broken by the fall. It took several minutes for these two to die. The four bodies were left dangling for thirty minutes before they were cut down, placed in the gun boxes, and buried beside the scaffold.

Friends of Surratt petitioned Secretary of War Stanton for possession of her body so that she might have a more dignified burial. He was not cooperative and referred the petition to Judge Advocate General Joseph Holt, who sent it back to Stanton, who returned it to Holt, who re-sent it to Stanton, who again referred it back to Holt, who finally denied the request. It was not until four years later that President Johnson honored Anna Surratt's request for her mother's remains.

Mary Elizabeth Surratt became the first woman in American history to be executed by the federal government, and her execution was one of the most controversial as well. Surratt's death resulted primarily from flimsy evidence supplied by an alcoholic and by a family friend who may have betrayed her to save himself and perhaps, more important, from the dogged determination, vindictiveness, and unforgiving actions of three men: Andrew Johnson, Edwin M. Stanton, and Joseph Holt.

At the same time, no one could reasonably protest the hangings of Atzerodt, Herold, and Paine. All of them were aware of Booth's plan to kill the president, and any of them could have stopped it by notifying the authorities. Paine had savagely attacked Secretary of State William Seward; Herold had guided Paine to Seward's home and had accompanied Booth during the twelve days he was on the run; and Atzerodt was supposed to have killed Vice President Johnson but had lost his nerve at the last moment.

With regard to Mary Surratt, the evidence against her was inconclusive, and most observers expected her sentence to be a light prison term or a pardon. While she may have been part of—or at least aware of—the conspiracy to kidnap Lincoln, there was no proof that she was part of the conspiracy to kill him. Political wangling instead plagued Surratt's situation at various times during the trial as well as during the secret deliberations of the military commission and at a critical meeting between Holt and the president.

In a peculiarity of military justice, the prosecutors (but not the defense attorneys) sat with and advised the judges in their deliberations. They participated not only in the verdicts reached but also in the determination of the sentences delivered.

The trial was held before a nine-member military commission in Washington's Old Penitentiary. The prisoners sat on the platform at the rear of the courtroom.

HARPER'S WEEKLY

Even in that environment, it was apparent that five of the nine judges were against hanging Surratt. In an 1880 article published in the *North American Review*, one of Surratt's attorneys, John Clampitt, asserted (on what he called "the most credible authority"), "It was at first proposed to acquit Mrs. Surratt, or at least to spare her life." But, he said, the judge advocate, Joseph Holt (the chief prosecutor) strongly objected. Clampitt later confirmed this information, quoting the commission's chairman, Gen. David Hunter, that the commission had voted against capital punishment for Surratt. The decision was changed, however, after Holt demanded that the testimony be reread and reinterpreted—an act Hunter supposedly condemned as a violation of "all principles of law and equity."

With a two-thirds majority required for the death penalty (six votes) and with only four of the nine judges supporting it, that should have ended the matter and saved Surratt's life. Yet Holt was determined not to let that happen. He singled Surratt out to bear the brunt of the prosecution, and in a final coup, he ensured that she would hang. According to Hunter (as related by Clampitt), Holt submitted a motion to hang Surratt and, as a compromise, to attach to the findings a recommendation for mercy. Through Holt's inducement, the commission concurred, and Hunter and four other judges (a majority of the court) signed the petition favoring life imprisonment in consideration of her age and gender—further proof of their objection to hanging her. The decisions were given to Holt to deliver to the president for final approval. To avoid public discourse, the petition was kept secret.

Such tomfoolery and political chicanery were too much for attorney and former Democratic Congressman David DeWitt. In his book *The Judicial Murder of Mary E. Surratt* (1895), he asked pointedly: "Where can we look in the history of the world for a parallel to such a spectacle?" According to DeWitt, the prosecutors probably reasoned that "with the petition in their custody and the president under their dominion," they could still hang Surratt, even though the majority of the commission was against it.

That's exactly what happened. DeWitt placed the blame on Stanton and accused him of pressuring the prosecutors and/or the commission to make an example of Surratt for aiding the conspirators. DeWitt believed that Holt, with Stanton's encouragement, emphasized that female spies for the South had been more troublesome than a hundred times as many men and should be taught their places, beginning with Mary Surratt. Another author, Guy W. Moore, gained access to documents unavailable to DeWitt but could find no direct connection between Stanton and the court's decision, only unverifiable inference.

Others have argued that the court made a distinction between those who should hang and those who should be incarcerated. Those who dealt with Booth through the day of the assassination were executed—Atzerodt, Herold, Paine, and Surratt. Those who backed away after the failed kidnapping attempt in March went to prison—Mudd, Arnold, O'Laughlin, and Spangler. Mary Surratt appeared to the court to be doing Booth's bidding within hours of the assassination. Thus she was to be hanged.

If Hunter's reported communication to Clampitt is correct, however, the court had decided that Surratt should not be executed, and that ruling would have held except for pressure from Holt and probably Stanton.

Even though the commission rendered its decision on June 30, Holt did not meet with Johnson until July 5; the delay was apparently because the president had been ill. At that meeting the judge advocate of the army reviewed the commission's deliberations. It consisted of a five-and-a-half-page summary and eighteen pages of documents containing the formal findings and sentences. The papers were held together at the top by a thin yellow ribbon. The petition on behalf of Surratt was not noted on her sentencing pages but was attached at the back, folded under the other leaves, and positioned so it was upside down and difficult to find.

Only Holt and Johnson were present at this meeting. Holt briefed the president, and Johnson signed the papers approving the sentences, but he did not sign the clemency plea. His signature condemned four of the prisoners, including Mary Surratt, to death by hanging and the other four to terms of imprisonment.

The nature of the discussion between Holt and Johnson about Mary Surratt's fate is unknown. When the petition became public knowledge two years later at the trial of Surratt's son, the news sparked public furor, and Johnson scrambled to save his political life. He emphatically denied ever seeing the petition. Holt insisted that he did. One of them lied.

Holt claimed that he "drew the president's attention specially to the recommendation in favor of Mrs. Surratt, which he read and freely commented on." Johnson asserted that it never happened. He said he was not made aware of the recommendation for leniency until some time after the hangings. Johnson later pointed out that the authorized published proceedings of the commission contained no reference to the petition for clemency. He accused Stanton and Holt of deliberately omitting it.

Johnson was right. The petition could not have been omitted without Stanton's knowledge and consent. The petition, which should have saved Surratt's life, had simply faded away for two years. Then, in 1873, when Johnson was back in politics, he again attacked Stanton and Holt. In a speech, he stated unequivocally that Mary Surratt had been executed by trickery and that Stanton (who had died in 1869) had taken his own life in remorse for this deed. He also let it be known through others that he would have commuted her sentence to life in prison if he had seen the petition. He shifted all onus from himself to Stanton and Holt.

Noted historians Benjamin Thomas and Harold Hyman concluded that Joseph Holt "willfully concealed the contents of the petition from the president" and that he did so because he wanted Mary Surratt to die. Thomas and Hyman stopped short of naming Stanton as a party to this subterfuge but acknowledged that Holt would not have deceived Stanton in a matter of such importance.

Congressman David DeWitt had no doubts about it; he was convinced that Stanton connived with the three prosecutors—Holt, Ohio Representative John A. Bingham, and Gen. Henry L. Burnett—to secure the death sentence and to keep Johnson from seeing the petition for clemency. Considering their chummy chemistry (Stanton appointed them as prosecutors; the two military men were subordinate to him; and Bingham had

SURRATT HOUSE MUSEUM

Mary Surratt's daughter, Anna, was not allowed to see President Johnson to plead for mercy for her mother. Anna later wrote that she "was spurned and treated with the utmost contempt by everyone at the White House."

worked closely with Holt during the Lincoln administration and was also Stanton's long-time friend), Stanton trusted them to keep him informed, and it seems highly unlikely that Holt or the others would have acted without Stanton's knowledge and approval.

Author Guy Moore agreed with DeWitt, Thomas, and Hyman. Moore believed that Holt was guilty of duplicity based on the physical appearance of the petition as it was presented to Johnson—by the "strange way Holt turned the sheets over."

Despite the argument over whether or not Johnson saw the clemency petition, a December 5, 1868, letter from the Reverend J. George Butler, a Washington pastor, suggests that Johnson's ensuing action would not have been affected by the petition. Butler was an eyewitness to the execution, having been on the scaffold to comfort Atzerodt. The clergyman wrote:

> The interview occurred during a social call upon the family of the President . . . a few hours after the execution. . . . Concerning Mrs. Surratt, the remarks of the President, by reason of their point and force, impressed themselves upon my memory. He said, in substance, that very strong appeals had been made for the exercise of executive clemency; that he had been importuned; that telegrams and threats had been used; but he could not be moved, for, in

Father Jacob A. Walter was not allowed to counsel and comfort Mrs. Surratt until he promised not to talk about his belief in her innocence.

his own significant language, Mrs. Surratt "kept the nest that hatched the eggs." The President further stated that no plea had been urged in her behalf, save the fact that she was a woman, and his interposition upon that ground would license female crime.

On August 19, 1873, eight years after the fact, Gen. R. D. Mussey, private secretary to President Johnson, wrote a letter to Holt, who was then seeking support for his position that Johnson saw the petition. Mussey recalled his own conversation with Johnson immediately after the president had reviewed the commission's findings with Holt:

> I asked what [the decision] was. He told me, approval of the findings and sentence of the Court. . . . I am very confident, though not absolutely assured, that it was at this interview Mr Johnson told me that the Court had recommended Mrs. Surratt to mercy on the ground of her sex (and age, I believe) But I am certain he did so inform me about that time; and that he said he thought the grounds insufficient, and that he had refused to interfere; that if she was guilty at all, her sex did not make her any the less guilty; . . . that he told me there had not been women enough hanged in the war.

Holt, after conferring with Johnson on July 5, 1865, walked to Stanton's office, where another prosecutor, Henry L. Burnett, was already with the war secretary. According to Burnett, Stanton asked what the president did, and Holt replied that he "approved the findings and sentence of the Court." Stanton, revealing his own knowledge of the secret petition, then inquired, "What did he say about the recommendation of mercy for Mrs. Surratt?" Holt replied: "He said that she must be punished with the rest. . . . He said her sex furnished no good ground for his interfering; that women and men should learn that if women committed crimes they would be punished; that if they entered into conspiracies to assassinate, they must suffer the penalty; that were this not so, hereafter conspirators and assassins would use women as their instruments; it would be mercy to womankind to let Mrs. Surratt suffer the penalty of her crime."

If Burnett connived with Stanton, Holt, and Bingham in keeping the petition secret from Johnson, then Burnett's record of this meeting may be suspect. Interestingly, shortly before Stanton's death in 1869, he secured a promise from Bingham to keep forever secret what they knew about the Mary Surratt case.

In a scalding indictment, David DeWitt wrote:

Upon their three heads [Stanton, Holt, and Bingham] should descend the full
weight of criminal turpitude involved in this most unnatural execution. . . .
They shouted into the ears of the court appeal on appeal for her head. And,
when five of their chosen [judges] sickened at the task and shrank from shed-
ding a woman's blood, they procured the death-sentence by a trick. . . . They
cheated their own court. They cheated their own president. . . . They sneaked
a woman into the arms of death by sleight-of-hand. . . . The execution of
Mary E. Surratt is the foulest blot on the history of the United States.

Even Stanton's biographers have accepted DeWitt's assertion that the petition was withheld from Johnson by trickery.

Around noon on Thursday, July 6, the president's decisions were read to
each of the prisoners. When Mary Surratt was told that she would be
hanged the next day, she was traumatized by both the sentence and the
timing. She asked to see Fathers Walter and Wiget; her daughter, Anna; and
her close friend John Brophy. As her supporters learned of her fate, they
made strenuous efforts to save her life, even though they had only one day
to do so. Probably the first person to reach the White House to plead for
mercy was Col. William P. Wood, superintendent of the Old Capitol Prison.
He believed that Mary Surratt was innocent, but his access to the Executive
Mansion was blocked by Lafayette C. Baker, chief of Stanton's National
Detective Police. Baker produced a written order over Stanton's signature
prohibiting Wood from seeing the president. Since Wood was a confidant of
Stanton, the order reflected the extent to which Stanton would go to pre-
vent anyone from trying to help Surratt.

A few years later, when Stanton was out of office and in poor health, he
rebuked Wood "for not making greater effort to save [Mrs. Surratt]" because
by doing so he "would have saved him the torments of hell," based upon a
clipping from the *Washington Gazette*.

Wood himself asserted that "some time after [her] execution . . . President Johnson assured me he sincerely regretted that he had not given Mrs.
Surratt the benefit of executive clemency, and strongly expressed his detes-
tation of what he termed the 'infamous conduct of Stanton' in keeping these
facts from him."

Surratt's priest, Jacob A. Walter, felt his first obligation on July 6 was to
comfort and counsel the condemned woman. The required pass from Stanton's War Department was delivered by a soldier who identified himself as an
Irish Catholic. During their brief conversation, Walter expressed his belief
that Surratt was innocent and that "there wasn't enough evidence against her

to hang a cat." The priest said no one could make him believe that a Catholic woman could go to communion on Holy Thursday then be involved in a murder plot on Good Friday.

The soldier reported the priest's comments to his superiors, and within the hour Stanton dispatched Gen. James A. Hardie to call on the priest. The general, a Catholic, declared the priest's pass to be invalid since Secretary Stanton had not signed it. In addition, Hardie asserted that he would not provide a valid pass unless Walter promised to say nothing more about Surratt's innocence. Father Walter was incensed.

"I'll make no such promise!" he vowed.

"Then you will not be permitted to see her," the general barked back. He added, "As yet there are no charges against *you* in the War Department!"

"The Department can hang me too if it thinks proper," the priest retorted angrily, having been forced into a position of sacrificing his civil liberties to carry out his professional obligations to a Roman Catholic.

As Hardie was about to walk away, the priest relented. He could not deny spiritual comfort to Surratt. "I cannot let Mrs. Surratt die without the sacraments," he said, "so if I must say yes, I say yes."

Hardie then gave him the authorized pass, but Stanton brought in reinforcements to keep the priest silent. He sent Gen. Winfield Scott Hancock to Walter's bishop in Baltimore. The general "advised" the bishop to "encourage"

Judge Alexander B. Wylie of the Supreme Court of the District of Columbia issued a writ of habeas corpus in an attempt to release Mrs. Surratt to civil authorities. He expected that his action would land him in prison before the day was out. Johnson suspended the writ.

AUTHOR'S COLLECTION

Assistant judge advocate John A. Bingham (*left*) promised Stanton he would keep forever secret what they knew about the Surratt case. Joseph Holt (*right*), the judge advocate general, was so determined to hang Mary Surratt that, after the commission voted against her execution, he reportedly maneuvered them into a compromise that ensured her death.

Walter to say nothing about Surratt's innocence. The bishop assured him that the priest had been "cautioned" to "observe silence."

Clearly, the restrictions placed on Jacob Walter were violations of his freedom of speech and of the separation of church and state. As head of the War Department, Stanton was responsible for this morally reprehensible directive.

Walter's carriage reached the prison gate just as Mary Surratt's daughter Anna arrived there. "Father," she screamed, "help me save her, please help me save her."

"I shall do what I can," he assured her.

Inside the prison they found Mary Surratt lying quietly on a bed of straw on the stone floor. Kneeling beside her, Anna tried to give her hope. She and Father Walter would go to the White House, Anna said, and make a personal appeal to the president.

At the White House they were joined by Pennsylvania Congressman Thomas Florence, who told them, "The president must not allow this woman to be hanged." On the second floor of the Executive Mansion, next to Johnson's office, the threesome encountered Johnson's secretary,

Gen. R. D. Mussey, and Preston King, a Radical Republican and former senator from New York.

Mussey informed the president of their presence, but he refused to see them. Three times they modified their request, and three times the president denied them. First, the priest emphasized he would detain the president for no more than five minutes. Next, the priest said he would not ask for a pardon or a commutation of the sentence, but only for a ten-day reprieve to prepare Surratt for eternity.

Finally, Anna threw herself at the general's feet and begged for his help. Moved to tears, Mussey said he would try again. He was gone for just a couple of minutes. When he returned he said the president advised them to see Judge Advocate Holt, for he had entire authority over the case. The president would agree with whatever Holt decided.

Anna and the priest rushed to Holt, but he told them: "These matters are in the hands of the president. Whatever he says will be final. Until I receive instructions from him, there is nothing I can do." Anna cried, but Walter recalled that she "received no sympathy from this cold, heartless man." They returned to the penitentiary.

The government never bothered to tell Mary Surratt's lawyers of the verdict against her. Frederick Aiken and John Clampitt learned of it around five o'clock on July 6 from the excited cry of a newsboy as they sat in their offices awaiting word of the findings. "So sudden was the shock [and] so unexpected the result . . . we hardly knew how to proceed," Clampitt recollected. They had less than twenty-four hours to act. Needing more time, they raced to the White House to see the president and request a three-day stay of execution. Preston King stopped them, saying he had been instructed not to admit anyone.

The attorneys then drove their carriage to the prison, picked up Anna, and went to Holt's office to plead for a stay of execution. Clampitt described the scene: "Upon her bended knees, bathed in tears, the forlorn girl besought him to go to the president and beg a respite for three days—three days more of life for her mother." Holt agreed to meet them at the White House.

When the daughter and the attorneys entered the Executive Mansion, Holt was waiting for them. He had already met with the president, he said, adding: "The president is immovable . . . and has no reason to change the date of the execution."

Aiken and Clampitt dropped off Anna at her mother's boarding house around 8 P.M. and told the tearful daughter they would continue their legal efforts through the night. An *Evening Star* reporter was watching the house, along with other curiosity seekers, and wrote that "she appeared heartbroken, and her cries and sobbings elicited the sympathies of all who were standing near the carriage."

Returning to their office, the attorneys wired the third member of their team, Reverdy Johnson, a distinguished Maryland senator. He advised them to seek a writ of habeas corpus based on the challenge of a military court's jurisdiction over a civilian. If granted, it would enable a judge to order Surratt's release to civil authorities, making a civil trial possible. The time was now past midnight.

At about 2 A.M. Aiken and Clampitt awakened Judge Alexander Wylie of the Supreme Court of the District of Columbia, and he issued the writ, noting, "I am about to perform an act which before tomorrow's sun may consign me to the old Capitol Prison." It was addressed to the president and General Hancock.

At 4 A.M. Clampitt handed the writ to a U.S. marshal to serve on Hancock. The general received the writ at 8:30 A.M. and delivered it to the White House. Johnson consulted informally with Stanton, Seward, Navy Secretary Gideon Welles, Interior Secretary James Harlan, and others. Welles advised commuting the sentence, but Stanton objected strenuously.

According to Harlan's recollection, Stanton said that clemency "would amount to an invitation to assassins hereafter to employ women as their instruments under the belief that if arrested and condemned they would be punished less severely then men." Stanton's comments were remarkably similar to statements made by Johnson on July 5. Taking Stanton's advice, Johnson wrote to Hancock at 10 A.M. suspending the writ and directing him to "proceed to execute the order . . . of the Military Commission."

At 11:30 A.M. Hancock and the attorney general appeared before Judge Wylie with the order suspending the writ. At that time "all hope faded for Mrs. Surratt," attorney Clampitt claimed. All legal avenues had been exhausted, but other appeals were in progress.

At the penitentiary one appeal came from a most unexpected source. Coconspirator Lewis Paine begged to talk to Capt. Christian Rath, the prison hangman. At daylight, when Rath appeared at Paine's cell, the condemned man said, "Cap'n, if I had two lives, I'd give one of 'em to save Mrs. Surratt. I know she's innocent. . . . She didn't know 'bout the conspiracy— she's innocent." Paine had made the same statement to Fathers Walter and Wiget and repeated it again to General Hartranft. Walter and Hartranft both prepared letters to the president quoting Paine, and Hartranft emphasized, "I think Paine would state the truth on this matter."

Paine had nothing to gain by lying. Still, Paine had not been present at most meetings between Mary Surratt and Booth and could not have known the extent of her involvement. Regardless, Hartranft seemed convinced. He handed both letters to Surratt's friend John S. Brophy, a professor at Gonzaga College, to deliver to the president. Hartranft provided an army conveyance and swift horses. "Drive like mad to the White House," he asserted, "and give the president [these notes]. I will delay the execution until the last moment or until I hear from you definitely and positively what the president's answer is."

When Brophy pulled up at the White House, Anna Surratt and one of her friends, Mary Wilding Queen, were already there, attempting again to meet with Johnson. Anna was weeping bitterly. She had been denied access by Preston King and another Radical Republican, Sen. James H. Lane of Kansas, along with soldiers with rifles and fixed bayonets. Apparently, the Radicals were closing ranks to ensure that Johnson did their bidding.

Perhaps haunted by their treatment of Anna Surratt, both King and Lane committed suicide within the year—Lane by shooting himself on July 1, 1866, and King by filling his pockets with lead and jumping off a ferry boat in New York Harbor on November 12, 1865.

For nearly an hour, Brophy and Anna persisted without success in their efforts to get to Johnson or to find someone to deliver the letters to him. The president's daughter, Martha Johnson Patterson, noticed Anna and offered condolences: "You break my heart, but there is not a thing I can do."

While lingering helplessly, Anna, Brophy, and Queen looked up to see a magnificent carriage arrive at the White House. Alighting from it was the widow of Stephen A. Douglas, the noted Democratic senator and presidential candidate. Shocked by the decision to hang Mary Surratt, the Widow Douglas had come to try to persuade Johnson to save her. Brophy ran up to Rose Douglas and handed her the letters he had brought for the president, and she took them and courageously pushed aside the bayonets, darted up the stairs, and walked into Johnson's office.

Johnson was unmoved, like a stubborn mule. He declared he would not interfere with the execution. As Rose Douglas came down the stairs she shook her head tearfully at Anna, and Anna begged: "Do go to him again. He won't refuse you! He can't! Do go again!" Brophy also requested that she make another appeal and that she "ask the president if he got the statement I sent him of [Louis] Weichmann's confession to me."

"I will try," Rose Douglas said, "but I feel it is of no use." The guards lowered their guns to allow her to pass, but again her petitioning was to no avail. The president would not change his mind. Anna, Brophy, and Queen drove back to the penitentiary, arriving shortly after noon.

Sixteen years later, a Philadelphia reporter asked the then former president why he had refused to see Anna Surratt. Johnson replied he did not know who it was that was calling on him, Mussey had only said it was "a crazy woman who was crying and tearing her hair!"

Regarding "Weichmann's confession," Brophy submitted an affidavit to Judge Advocate Holt that morning, swearing that Weichmann admitted to him that he gave false testimony, that Weichmann believed in Surratt's innocence, and that Weichmann would prepare a letter for President Johnson in her favor if Brophy would "keep it a profound secret and hand the letter to the president himself." An endorsement on Brophy's letter confirmed it was given to the president, but Johnson ignored it. When it was published in a Washington newspaper four days after the hangings, Weichmann denied

The three-acre yard of the Washington Old Penitentiary was the setting for the execution of the four condemned accomplices of John Wilkes Booth. On July 7, 1865, the temperature was over one hundred degrees. Four pine boxes to be used as coffins are stacked in front of the gallows.

the statements and reaffirmed his belief that Surratt was guilty. Whether truthful or not, the War Department clerk had no other choice if he wanted to avoid problems with Stanton. Johnson, meanwhile, did not respond to the letters from Hartranft or Jacob Walter.

At the prison, Anna Surratt controlled her emotions as she walked into her mother's cell and hugged her. Father Walter advised the daughter to go to another room, saying: "This is no place for you." Then Mary Surratt declared her innocence to the priest, and he believed her. She turned to Brophy and asked him "at some future time, when the passions of war are cooled, to clear her name of the crime." He promised to do so and worked to that end until his death.

Johnson's refusal to see Anna Surratt, Jacob Walter, Frederick Aiken, and John Clampitt and his rude dismissal of Rose Douglas reflect an unyielding leader so fixated on hanging Mary Surratt that he was unwilling to consider any delay or other option. His later attempts to place all blame on Stanton and Holt, compounded by his own suggestion that he would have commuted Surratt's sentence if only he had seen the petition, can only be interpreted as so much political backtracking by a weak president.

Many historians believe that the court's petition would not have changed Johnson's mind. He defended Surratt's death sentence with the irrational statement that "she kept the nest where the egg was hatched," as if a landlady should be held responsible for the crimes of her tenants or visitors. Besides, the plot was more likely hatched at the Parker House in Baltimore, where Booth met with three men from Canada on July 26, 1864, or at the St. Lawrence Hall in Montreal, where Booth and the Confederates' Canada Cabinet conferred in October 1864. Would Johnson also have hanged the managers or owners of these hotels?

Since Johnson deftly defended himself by denying that he had even seen the clemency petition, Holt and Stanton had to bear the burden of implied guilt for the rest of their lives. Such was the nature of the dirty politics surrounding Surratt's fate. This discussion, however, leaves unresolved the question of her guilt.

The specification against her read:

And in further prosecution of said conspiracy, Mary E. Surratt did . . . receive, entertain, harbor, and conceal, aid and assist the said John Wilkes Booth, David E. Herold, Lewis Paine, John H. Surratt, Michael O'Laughlin, George A. Atzerodt, and Samuel Arnold and their confederates, with the knowledge of the murderous and traitorous conspiracy aforesaid and with the intent to aid,

Mary Surratt and George Atzerodt died quickly, but Lewis Paine and David Herold did not. After reporting the news of the hangings, one newspaper editorialized, "We wish to hear their names no more."

LIBRARY OF CONGRESS

abet and assist them in the execution thereof, and in escaping from justice after the murder of the said Abraham Lincoln, in pursuance of said conspiracy in manner aforesaid.

To find her guilty, the military commission would have to determine that she knew about the conspiracy to kill Lincoln, assisted in its execution, and aided the conspirators in escaping.

Described by the *New York Times* as "fair, fat, and forty," Mary Surratt was the forty-two-year-old widow of a Confederate sympathizer. Prior to her marriage, the former Mary Jenkins had been the belle of Prince George County, Maryland. She married John Surratt when she was seventeen, and her husband purchased a place thirteen miles from Washington where he kept a small tavern and served as postmaster. Troubled by alcoholism and bad debts, Surratt died suddenly in 1862. Mary Surratt struggled for two years to keep the tavern afloat but then chose to lease it to a former policeman, John M. Lloyd, who, like her husband, drank too much.

In late November or early December 1864 Mary Surratt moved to a townhouse at 541 H Street in Washington, expecting to support herself by renting out extra rooms to boarders. She was assisted by her daughter, Anna, and by Susan Mahoney, a former slave. Her boarders often were Confederate couriers or Roman Catholics passing through Washington.

LIBRARY OF CONGRESS

Immediate interment was near the prison. Navy equipment boxes served as coffins, and a bottle with the name of the deceased was placed next to each body. The four were buried in their hoods. Souvenirs were made of the gallows and the ropes.

In fact, two of the three men hanged with her—Atzerodt and Paine—were among her houseguests. Booth himself visited there on several occasions, primarily to consult with Surratt's son John and to meet with one or more of the others, but he never stayed there.

Along with his compatriots, John Surratt used the family tavern in Surrattsville as a safe house in travels between Richmond and the North. Well acquainted in the Confederate underground in southern Maryland, John became a key member of Booth's team—the team put together for the purpose of capturing Lincoln, taking him to Richmond, and trading him for Confederates being held in Union prisons. After the failed kidnapping attempt, John Surratt and David Herold delivered various items to the tavern for later use. Included were two carbines, side arms, ammunition, a rope, and a monkey wrench. Surratt showed Lloyd where to hide the rifles (between the joists over the kitchen) and told him to be prepared to retrieve them on short notice. But while Surratt was deeply involved in the kidnapping scheme, he appears to have had no involvement in the murder plot. He was in New York at the time Lincoln was killed. The Surratt boarding house in Washington, however, became a gathering place for some of Booth's conspirators.

When John Surratt was home, he shared a room and a bed with his former schoolmate, Louis J. Weichmann, who was treated as a member of the family. Weichmann, a nondrinker with good morals, had studied for the priesthood at a Catholic seminary that John also attended, but both left abruptly in 1862—John to help his widowed mother and take his father's position as postmaster at Surrattsville (from which he was fired because of Southern sympathies), and Weichmann to enter a seminary in Philadelphia. Rejected there, Weichmann obtained a teaching position in Pikesville, Maryland, but lasted only two months. He then went to another school, which burned down shortly after his arrival. Soon he arrived in Washington to teach at St. Matthew's Institute, but he was there less than a year. In January 1864 he became a clerk in the War Department.

As Surratt's roommate, Weichmann was in a precarious position at the time of the trial of the Lincoln conspirators. He survived the inquisition by surrendering himself and convincing Stanton that he was more valuable as a witness than a defendant, and Stanton made sure he was the right kind of witness. The war secretary imprisoned him, reportedly threatened him, and viciously examined his testimony.

Edward V. Murphy, a staff member of the military commission who had attended high school with Weichmann, reported that he "saw Weichmann in manacles being escorted by an armed guard of soldiers to the War Department, [and] the next day learned that he was charged with being in the conspiracy to murder the president." If that would not intimidate Weichmann, nothing would. Stanton could very well have accused and hanged Weichmann for complicity in the plot, and Weichmann knew it. Theater owner John T. Ford, who was imprisoned with Weichmann, became convinced by his conversations with Weichmann that the War Department clerk had been coerced by Stanton into cooperating and that Stanton had, "in a threatening manner, expressed the opinion that Weichmann's hands had as much of the president's blood on them as Booth's." Tom Smart, a deputy keeper at the prison, said Weichmann was the most frightened witness he had ever seen.

Weichmann, however, swore that no threats had been made to him and that no inducements had been offered. He later wrote that he really did not mind being jailed. By "cooperating" with Stanton, Weichmann avoided prosecution and was awarded a clerkship in the Philadelphia customhouse, a post he kept for more than twenty-five years. "Physically and intellectually he was a giant," said Daniel H. L. Gleason, his colleague in the War Department, "but in bravery I should call him a dwarf." Weichmann once said, "I always look out for my self-interest."

John Surratt later claimed that Weichmann not only knew of Booth's plans to capture Lincoln but also allowed him [Surratt] to have after-hours access to governmental records. Confederate emissary Augustus Howell like-wise claimed that Weichmann had given him information from his office. He said that Weichmann had agreed to furnish Surratt "with all information that came under his notice" and that Weichmann received dispatches for Surratt from Booth. Howell could not imagine that "Booth would have trusted a matter of such great importance and risk to himself in Weichmann's hands unless he had a perfect understanding about the matter with Weichmann."

Weichmann's involvements with Booth suggest that Weichmann must have known about the kidnapping plot and probably would have been allowed into the conspiracy if he had been proficient in riding and shooting. He reportedly boasted to fellow clerks he could have made about thirty thousand dollars if he had been *willing* to participate in an enterprise in which several friends were engaged. His alleged statement would have been more accurate if he had said "allowed" instead of "willing."

Weichmann's testimony about strange activities at the boarding house linked Mary Surratt to the conspirators. He testified: "Booth called at Mrs. Surratt's frequently, generally asking for John Surratt, and in his absence for Mrs. Surratt. Their interviews were always apart from other persons. I have been in the parlor in company with Booth, when Booth has taken [John] Surratt upstairs to engage in private conversation . . . which would sometimes last two or three hours. The same thing would occur with Mrs. Surratt."

Weichmann added that around the middle of February:

A man calling himself Wood [Lewis Paine] came to Mrs. Surratt's and inquired for John Surratt. I went to the door and told him Mr. Surratt was not at home; he thereupon expressed a desire to see Mrs. Surratt, and I introduced him. . . . He acted very politely. He asked Miss [Anna] Surratt to play the piano, and he raised the piano-cover, and did every thing which indicated a person of breeding. . . . He had supper served up to him in my room; I took it to him from the kitchen. He brought no baggage. He remained till the next morning, leaving by the earliest train for Baltimore. About three weeks afterward he called again, and I again went to the door. I had forgotten his name, and asking him, he gave the name of Paine. He remained three days that time. He represented himself as a Baptist preacher.

Since the Surratts and other guests were Catholics, it seemed strange to Weichmann that "a Baptist preacher should seek hospitality at Mrs. Surratt's;

they only looked at it as odd and laughed at it. Mrs. Surratt herself remarked that he was a great-looking Baptist preacher."

Weichmann then described a strange ruckus at the house:

> I returned from my office one day at half-past four o'clock [and asked the black servant] where John had gone. He told me Massa John had left . . . with six others, on horseback, about half-past two o'clock. On going down to dinner, I found Mrs. Surratt in the passage. She was weeping bitterly, and I endeavored to console her. She said, "John is gone away; go down to dinner, and make the best of your dinner you can." After dinner, I went to my room, sat down, and commenced reading. At about half-past six o'clock Surratt came in very much excited—in fact, rushed into the room. He had a revolver in his hand. . . . I said, "John, what is the matter?" He replied, "I will shoot any one that comes into this room; my prospect is gone, my hopes are blighted; I want something to do; can you get me a clerkship?" About ten minutes later, Paine came into the room. He was also very much excited, and I noticed he had a pistol. [Shortly] Booth came into the room, and Booth was so excited that he walked around the room three or four times very frantically, and did not notice me. He had a whip in his hand. I spoke to him, and, recognizing me, he said, "I did not see you." The three then went upstairs into the back room, in the third story, and must have remained there about thirty minutes, when they left the house together.

Although not brought out at the trial, this bit of testimony described the frazzled conspirators after their failed attempt to capture Lincoln on March 17.

Continuing his testimony, Weichmann stated:

> My suspicions had been aroused . . . but were not of a fixed or definite character. I did not know what they intended to do. I made a confidant of Captain Gleason in the War Department. I told him that Booth was a secesh sympathizer, and mentioned snatches of conversations I had heard from these parties; and I asked him, "Captain, what do you think of all this?" We even talked over several things which they could do. I asked him whether they could be bearers of dispatches or blockade-runners [or involved in an attempt to] capture President Lincoln? He laughed and hooted at the idea. This happened before the horseback ride of Surratt and the six others. I remarked to the Captain, the morning after they rode, that Surratt had come back, and I mentioned to Gleason the very expressions Surratt had used, and told him that, to all appearances, what they had been after had been a failure; and that I was glad, as I thought Surratt would be brought to a sense of duty. . . . I had been a companion of Surratt for seven years. I did not [forfeit] my friendship to him in mentioning my

suspicions to Mr. Gleason; he forfeited his friendship to me by placing me in the position in which I now stand, testifying against him. I think I was more of a friend to him than he was to me. He knew that I permitted a blockade-runner at the house, without informing upon him, because I was his friend. . . . Still, when my suspicions of danger to the Government were aroused, I preferred the Government to John Surratt.

Slamming home the point that the Surratt boarding house was a home away from home for the conspirators, Weichmann said he "met the prisoner, David E. Herold, at Mrs. Surratt's on one occasion . . . and I met him at Mrs. Surratt's, in the country, in the spring of 1863."

As for Atzerodt, Weichmann said:

He first came to Mrs. Surratt's house about three weeks after I formed the acquaintance of Booth, and inquired for John Surratt or Mrs. Surratt, as he said. John Surratt was out in the country; he returned that evening; and Atzerodt, who had, I understood, been waiting to see John, left the next day. I afterward heard Miss Anna say that she didn't care about having such sticks brought to the house; that they were not company for her. . . . Since then he must have been at the house ten or fifteen times. He had interviews with John Surratt in the parlor. . . . I never saw him in the house with Booth. . . . I knew nothing of what took place between them. On the occasion of Paine's last visit to the house, Atzerodt came to see Surratt, and I saw Paine and Atzerodt together, talking in my room.

Actually, Atzerodt and Weichmann were much closer than Weichmann indicated. Fellow boarder John Holohan stated that the two men "frequently" came to the boarding house together, and that "they were as intimate as friends could be."

Anna Surratt testified that Weichmann had personally secured a room for Atzerodt at the boarding house and had held many private discussions

Mary Surratt's boarding house became a crime scene twice in the twentieth century. In 1929 federal authorities raided the building and found large stocks of paraphernalia that violated Prohibition laws. The house was raided again in the 1970s after reports of numbers racketeering there. In the 1980s the house became a Chinese restaurant. "We have heard only good things [about the place since then]," reported the *Surratt Courier* in February 1999.

with him. This alleged intimate friendship was puzzling. The two men were miles apart socially and intellectually. With Anna and probably Mary Surratt feeling antagonistic toward Atzerodt, the only apparent common source drawing them together was John Wilkes Booth.

Weichmann indirectly implicated Mary Surratt in the assassination by relating two trips she made to her tavern at Surrattsville:

> On the Tuesday previous to the Friday of the assassination, I was sent by Mrs. Surratt to the National Hotel to see Booth, for the purpose of getting his buggy. She wished me to drive her into the country on that day. Booth said that he had sold his buggy, but that he would give me ten dollars instead, that I might hire one. He gave me the ten dollars, and I drove Mrs. Surratt to Surrattsville. We remained there [about] half an hour. Mrs. Surratt stated that she went there [to see] Mr. Nothe[y], who owed her some money.

Mary Surratt did indeed see Nothey, but the military commission may have wondered why Booth would pay for a rental buggy for her. They likely assumed she had nefarious business to transact for him. Booth, however, was always generous, and it was not strange for her to ask this favor.

If the commission had any doubts about her possibly traitorous dealings with Booth, these doubts were probably erased by Weichmann's account of her second visit to Surrattsville, on the afternoon of April 14, the day of the assassination.

According to Weichmann, Mary Surratt "rapped at my room-door on that afternoon, and told me she had received a letter from Mr. Charles Calvert in regard to the money that Mr. Nothey owed her, and that she was again compelled to go to Surrattsville, and asked me to take her down." Then, said Weichmann, Booth came to the house around two o'clock, met privately with Surratt, and gave her a package later determined to contain field glasses. Shortly, Weichmann and Surratt left for Surrattsville in a rented buggy she paid for. Her tavern was their destination, and tavern manager John Lloyd was the person she wanted to see, not John Nothey. She had made no arrangements to see Nothey that day.

Tavern manager Lloyd was away on business when Surratt and Weichmann arrived, he said, and she waited for the manager in the parlor. When his wagon pulled up at five o'clock, she went out to talk to him. "Speak of the devil and his little imps appear," she said sarcastically, according to Lloyd's testimony before the military commission. Lloyd said that Surratt told him about the guns: "Mr. Lloyd, I want you to have those shooting-irons ready. There will be parties here tonight who will call for them." Then she handed him the field glasses and advised, "Hide this, for tonight [and be sure to] give them a couple bottles of whiskey."

Lloyd also stated that during Mary Surratt's trip to Surrattsville earlier that week their carriages met near the Navy Yard Bridge, and he stepped over to speak to his landlady. After a few casual remarks, he said that she told him "to get them [the weapons] out; that they would be wanted soon." Weichmann, who was sitting next to Mrs. Surratt, swore he did not hear this whispered conversation. Even Lloyd seemed unsure about the details of their dialogue. "It was a very quick and hasty conversation," he admitted. "I am confident that she named the shooting-irons on both occasions; not so positive about the first as I am about the last; I know she did on the last occasion."

Questioned several times on the subject, Lloyd rephrased his testimony but did not change the meaning. Once he declared, "I am quite positive about that, but not altogether positive." Another time, he said, "I am quite positive, but cannot be determined . . . that she said 'shooting-irons.'"

These confusing statements by a disreputable drunkard apparently created enough doubt in the minds of five of the nine judges for them to oppose the death penalty for Surratt.

Not revealed until 1977 was George Atzerodt's statement confirming Lloyd's testimony. Unknown to the prosecutors during the trial, Atzerodt stated to Maryland provost marshal James L. McPhail on May 1, "Booth told me that Mrs. Surratt went to Surrattsville to get out the guns which had been taken to that place by Herold." Had Atzerodt's statement been available to the judges, it likely would have erased all reasonable doubt any of them held about Mary Surratt's guilt.

Booth and Herold called for the carbines that night, with Herold demanding: "Lloyd, for God's sake, make haste and get those *things*." Both men knew instantly what "those things" were—a strong indication that Herold was aware that Mary Surratt had alerted Lloyd that very same day. If she did so, she probably assumed the guns were intended for Lincoln's kidnappers. That was their original purpose a month earlier, and she apparently thought Booth was going to try again. Booth had emphasized to his coconspirators and probably to Surratt that "capturing the president" was justifiable as an act of war to aid the Confederate cause. As a devout Catholic woman and a Southern sympathizer she would have condoned a kidnapping but condemned an assassination.

Lloyd's sister-in-law and Mary Surratt's brother were both at the tavern that afternoon, and both testified that Lloyd had been drinking heavily and was "pretty tight." If he had been drunk that afternoon, how could he recall what Surratt had said? The degree of his intoxication, however, may have been overstated. As Surratt and Weichmann prepared to return to Washington, they noticed their wagon had a broken coil, and Surratt asked Lloyd to fix it. He did, easily and quickly. If he had been drunk, the task would have been far more formidable.

When Lloyd was later taken to Washington for confinement, the arresting officer said that "he commenced crying and hallooing out, 'O, Mrs. Surratt, that vile woman, she has ruined me! I am to be shot! I am to be shot!'" He was not; his testimony against her was his passport to freedom.

Acting on tips from an unnamed actor and a saloon barkeeper, city police visited the Surratt boarding house twice on the night of the assassination. Superintendent A. C. Richards entered the house at about one o'clock in the morning after Surratt responded promptly to the doorbell. He was astounded to find that she had not retired for the night and was fully dressed, as if "waiting in a dark house for someone to call." He said that when he informed her of the assassination, "she expressed no surprise or regret [and] did not seem in the least affected when I said to her . . . that Booth and her son were suspected of being implicated in the crime." He said she "gave me no information in regard to Booth, his visits, or the visits of others of the assassins to her house." Her appearance and demeanor at that hour of the night made her look very suspicious, as if she were expecting news about a kidnapping or perhaps related inquiries from the police.

Then, shortly after two o'clock, four city detectives came to the house to search for Booth and her son. By this time, Surratt was asleep. Weichmann,

Lewis Paine, Booth's coconspirator who nearly killed Secretary of State William H. Seward, lost his head, literally, in a strange set of circumstances. Paine's family claimed his remains in 1871, but unknown to them, his head was missing. It had been removed by an undertaker when the body was first moved by the government in 1869, having been unclaimed at that time. The skull landed in the Army Medical Museum and was later transferred to the Smithsonian, where it was not rediscovered until 1992. After being identified, it was sent to a cemetery in Geneva, Florida, and reunited with its body. A special graveside service was conducted in November 1994.

unaware of the first visit that night, responded to the doorbell. When they demanded admission, Weichmann awakened Surratt, and she said, "For God's sake! Let them come in. I expected the house to be searched." Weichmann asked the purpose of their visit, and they said that Booth had killed the president and John Surratt had killed Seward. They demanded to know John Surratt's whereabouts. Both Mary Surratt and Weichmann said that John could not have killed Seward because he was in Canada. Actually, he was in New York at the time.

Weichmann cooperated fully with the police and even accompanied them to Montreal the following week to look for Surratt. This investigation by the city police, however, infuriated Stanton. In his mind, they had circumvented his authority. He took over the investigation, imprisoned Lloyd and Weichmann, and "convinced" them to be star witnesses.

Three days after the assassination, during the evening of Monday, April 17, at about eleven o'clock, an even more incriminating incident quickened the doom of Mary Surratt. While military detectives were searching the house and arresting everyone in it, Lewis Paine, Seward's then-unknown attacker, knocked at the door. A detective answered the door and found a tall, muscular man whose fine cashmere pants and boots were soiled with mud and dirt. He carried a pickax on his shoulder. Startled by the presence of the detectives, the stranger claimed that he had the wrong house.

"Who did you wish to see?" asked one detective.

"I came to see Mrs. Surratt," he replied.

"Well, you are right then. She lives here."

Realizing something was wrong, the stranger insisted upon leaving, but a detective pointed a pistol at him, took the pickax from him, and ordered him into an adjoining room. Responding to questions, the stranger said that he was a laborer and was supposed to dig a drain for Surratt in the morning. He said he came by at this time to find out what time he should begin work in the morning.

As was mentioned previously, Paine had been hiding in Washington since fleeing the Seward home. He appeared at the Surratt house at the worst possible time. He expected food and a safe shelter. Had his timing been better, Paine probably never would have been identified or caught.

Detectives asked Surratt: "Do you know this man? Did you hire him to come and dig a gutter for you?" According to one of the soldiers, she answered, raising her right hand, "Before God, sir, I do not know this man, and have never seen him, and I did not hire him to dig a gutter for me."

Paine had been at her home on various occasions and stood directly in front of her—an imposing man, hard to forget. But she denied knowing him. The captain commanding the arrest party stayed at her side throughout the interrogation. Later he rebutted the soldier at the trial, saying that he never heard her make that statement, but his testimony was ignored by the court.

The detectives, suspicious of Paine's statements and Surratt's denials, arrested Paine along with Surratt and the other occupants of the house—Anna Surratt and two teenage girls—seventeen-year-old Honora Fitzpatrick and fifteen-year-old Olivia Jenkins, Surratt's niece. Before being taken away, Surratt requested a minute to kneel and pray. Paine was subsequently identified as Seward's attacker.

During the trial, Surratt's family members and friends defended her denials by saying she had poor eyesight. Anna testified: "My mother's eyesight is very bad, and she had often failed to recognize her friends. She had not been able to read or sew by gaslight for some time past." Honora Fitzpatrick said that she had "often threaded a needle for her because she could not see to do it herself."

Two former boarders, however, gave conflicting testimony to that of the two girls. John Holohan's wife stated that she had never seen Surratt read or sew by candlelight, but Holohan said: "I never knew anything of Mrs. Surratt's defective eyesight."

Prosecutor John A. Bingham effectively put Paine's appearance in perspective:

> If not one word had been said, the mere act of Paine flying to her house for shelter would have borne witness against her, strong as proofs from Holy Writ. But when she . . . calls on God to witness that she had never seen him, and knew nothing of him, when, in point of fact, she had seen him for four successive days in her own house, in the same clothing which he then wore, who can resist for a moment the conclusion that these parties were alike guilty?

Numerous witnesses spoke of Surratt's "outstanding character" and described her as gentle, affectionate, charitable, and deeply religious. Even though she was a Southern sympathizer, none of the defense witnesses had ever heard her utter any political sentiment, loyal or disloyal to the Union, and not a single witness came forward to attack her character. A black servant said that she treated her servants "very well" and that she had "fed Union soldiers at her house, sometimes a good many of them, and I know that she always tried to do the best for them that she could, because I always

NATIONAL ARCHIVES

The military commission that passed judgment on the Lincoln conspirators posed with the prosecutors, with whom it deliberated: (*from left to right*) Col. Charles H. Tompkins, Maj. Gen. David Hunter, Maj. Gen. August Kautz, Brig. Gen. James Ekin, Maj. Gen. Lew Wallace, prosecutor John A. Bingham, Brig. Gen. Albion Howe, Brig. Gen. Thomas M. Harris, Judge Advocate Gen. Joseph Holt, Brig. Gen. Robert S. Foster, prosecutor Henry L. Burnett, and Col. D. R. Clendenin.

cooked for them." Weichmann himself testified: "During the whole time I have known her, her character, as far as I could judge, was exemplary and lady-like in every particular; and her conduct, in a religious and moral sense, altogether exemplary."

"That [such] a woman," argued her defense attorney, "with no motive disclosed to us that could have caused a total change in her very nature, could have participated in the crimes in question, it is almost impossible to believe."

In Weichmann's book on the assassination—written in 1898 but not published until 1975—he asserted: "I believe that both Mrs. Surratt and her son were deeply involved [in the conspiracy] and if they had done their Christian duty, they could have saved the life of Mr. Lincoln." Weichmann noted that he had been attacked many times as the chief witness against Mary Surratt, "yet anyone who will take the pains to read my testimony in 1865 will discover that there is not a line, not a word in it on which of itself there was the least possible chance to secure this woman's conviction."

Commission member Thomas M. Harris supported that conclusion in a 1901 letter to the *New York Sun:* "Had it depended on what he [Weichmann] said not a hair of her head would have been harmed." The most damaging pieces of evidence against her were Lloyd's testimony about the "shooting irons"—even though they were not used to shoot anyone—and the testimony of the arresting officers about the encounter with Lewis Paine at the boarding house.

Weichmann, however, clearly established Surratt's connection with Booth and the use of her house as "the nest where the egg was hatched"—words used by President Johnson to justify her hanging. By 1902 sixty-year-old Weichmann was a physical and mental wreck. Dying from what his physician called "extreme nervousness," Weichmann dictated a statement to his sisters: "This is to certify that every word I gave in evidence at the assassination trial was absolutely true."

Still, John Surratt, other Roman Catholics, and a large segment of the public branded Weichmann as a liar, perjurer, and traitor. Lloyd, meanwhile, maintained near the end of his life that he considered Mary Surratt innocent and a victim of circumstances. Her association with the real conspirators, he held, was the cause of her conviction.

Is it not strange that Weichmann, who regarded her as guilty, believed he said nothing that would have convicted her, and Lloyd, whose testimony was the most damaging, regarded her as innocent?

Aside from what one writer called "the judicial murder" of Mary Surratt, one other fact towers above all others and should have saved her from the gallows. Under the rules of procedure in a military court, the prosecution must present all evidence bearing on both the guilt and innocence of the accused. But it did not.

None other than Radical Republican Congressman Benjamin F. Butler brought this out on the floor of the House of Representatives in the spring of 1867. After Congressman John A. Bingham (one of the prosecutors in the trial) attacked Butler for a military failure as a general, Butler accused Bingham and his associates of hanging an innocent woman, saying that she was "convicted without sufficient evidence in my judgment."

Bingham responded, "What does the gentleman know of the evidence in the case, and what does he care?"

Butler asserted that it was Bingham's duty "to present to the commission all the evidence bearing upon the case," but he did not. He was referring to Booth's diary, which proved "that up to a certain hour Booth contemplated capture and abduction," and Mary Surratt may or may not have known that he changed his purpose to assassination. "And if Mrs. Surratt did not know of this change of purpose there is no evidence that she knew in any way of the assassination and ought not, in my judgment, to have been convicted of taking part in it."

Butler noted that other items found in Booth's pockets with the diary were put in evidence, such as his tobacco pipe, spur, and compass. "If it was good judgment on the part of the [prosecutors] to put in evidence the tobacco pipe, why was not the diary, in his own handwriting, put in evidence, and wherein he himself had detailed the particulars of the crime?"

Clearly, the prosecutors had obstructed justice by deliberately and illegally withholding material physical evidence so that they could hang or imprison legally innocent persons who had been involved only in the foiled plot to capture the president. By withholding the information in the diary, they could and did try all the conspirators for murder, not for kidnapping, even though Spangler was not involved in either plot, and Arnold and O'Laughlin had nothing to do with the assassination and could prove it.

Mary Surratt's situation remains puzzling. Butler was probably correct when he stated that she was "convicted without sufficient evidence"—a belief apparently shared by most members of the military commission. George Atzerodt's long-lost statement that she had gone to Surrattsville to tell Lloyd "to get the guns out" makes her guilty of complicity in a crime against Lincoln. The key question is: Did she know that Booth was contemplating

An apparition of Mary Elizabeth Surratt has been seen in three locations: the Surratt tavern in Surrattsville, Maryland; her boarding house in Washington; and Fort Leslie J. McNair in Washington. Fort McNair originally was the Washington Arsenal and Prison, where Surratt was incarcerated and hanged. In an officer's quarters there in 1977, a lieutenant reported that he saw "the apparition of a stout, middle aged woman, dressed in black, seemingly floating through the hallways." A major's wife also had seen a "woman in a long, dark dress floating around." She told psychic investigators it was Surratt. Others described strange sounds, unexplained voices, and the sensation of being touched by an unseen hand. Similar experiences have been reported at Surratt's boarding house, which was sold for forty-six hundred dollars, a bargain considering its historical importance. Within six weeks the purchaser was driven away because "his nervous system was shattered by what he had seen and heard." The *Boston Post* noted that other tenants came and went in "swift succession, swearing that in the dead of night Mrs. Surratt walked the hallways clad in her robe of death."

murder, not kidnapping? Either way, she must have known that something terrible was in the offing, and as Weichmann pointed out, if Mary Surratt had done her "Christian duty" and notified the right authorities, she could have saved the president's life.

Not knowing what is known today, Johnson, Holt, and Stanton appear to have stacked the deck against Surratt to secure the outcome they desperately craved. One wonders why they showed such dastardly vindictiveness toward her while sparing many others who aided Booth—men such as Thomas Jones and Samuel Cox, who had hidden Booth for six days.

Some observers believe that Stanton had a strong hatred of both Catholics and Southern women. For that reason, he regarded Mary Surratt as a model of venomous Southern women, and moreover, he decided that she should die for all the crimes committed against the Union during the war by all Southern women who had depended on their womanhood to escape justice.

As to what Mary Surratt knew about the assassination and when she knew it and what her role was—no one can say for certain. She and Booth took that secret to their graves.

14

THE
LUCKIEST
MAN

IN JULY 1865 JOHN H. SURRATT JR. was hiding out at the rectory of a Catholic priest in the small village of St. Liboire, ten miles south of Montreal. On the eve of his departure to join a hunting expedition, he was waiting at the local hotel for a train. The proprietor, not knowing who he was, handed him a newspaper and said, "Read *that* about the conspirators!"

The news devastated him. A front-page article reported that on that very day "the most hellish of deeds was . . . enacted," as Surratt phrased it in an 1870 lecture. His mother had been found guilty and hanged, all before he had any knowledge that she was in danger.

He told an audience in Rockville, Maryland, "It would be folly for me to attempt to describe my feelings." After gazing at the paper for some time, he dropped it to the floor, canceled his outing, and walked directly to his safe house. There he found a friend sitting in the parlor, and the friend turned "deadly pale" when he saw Surratt but said nothing. Earlier this friend and others had assured him that "there was no cause for anxiety; that it was only a matter of time, and it would all be well." A reliable contact from Washington had written to Surratt: "Be under no apprehension as to any serious consequences. Remain perfectly quiet, as any action on your part would only tend to make matters worse."

Surratt had followed his instructions, but now he fumed at the man in the parlor: "You doubtless thought you were acting as a friend, but you have deceived me. I may forgive you, but I cannot forget it." The friend tried to respond, but Surratt turned and walked to his room. He remained there until dark. In these moments of silence he decided to leave St. Liboire and seek asylum in a country far away from the United States.

For the rest of his life, Surratt was tormented by damnable accusations that he had deserted his mother "in the darkest hour of her need" and allowed her to die for him. Such was not the case, he insisted, but rather he had been deceived by friends. Yet his friends were undoubtedly correct: There was nothing he could have done for his mother. Had he returned to Washington, he probably would have joined her on the gallows. As it turned out, of all those charged with conspiring to kill Lincoln, John H. Surratt was the most fortunate. He was the lucky one.

Twenty-one-year-old Surratt had been Booth's right-hand man since being introduced to him by Samuel A. Mudd on December 23, 1864. Booth wanted him because he was intelligent and had valuable contacts from Canada to Richmond. Surratt later acknowledged he had "no hesitation in taking part in anything honorable" to serve his cause. To him, Booth's conspiracy to capture Lincoln was an honorable and patriotic way to help the South.

Surratt's sterling success in aiding the Confederate cause is well documented. He had been a hard-riding Secret Service courier carrying dispatches from Montreal to Richmond. He had joined up with Booth to capture Lincoln, take him to Richmond, and trade him for thousands of Confederates in Union prisons. He made available his mother's boarding house as a meeting place for Booth and his coconspirators. He recruited one of his close friends, David E. Herold, who had intimate knowledge of southern Maryland's poorly mapped roads. With Confederate agent Thomas Harbin, he purchased the boat to be used to get Lincoln across the Potomac. And he was the key link in the chain that pulled in strongman Lewis Paine to serve on Booth's team.

Surratt met with Confederate Secretary of State Judah P. Benjamin and possibly Col. John S. Mosby in Richmond in January 1865, presumably to report on Booth's team and to facilitate cooperation with other operatives along the chosen escape route. He arranged for weapons and supplies to be stored at his mother's tavern at Surrattsville. He and the other conspirators plotted to capture Lincoln on March 17, 1865, when the president was expected to be en route to a hospital for an entertainment for invalid servicemen, but the plot went awry when Lincoln changed his plans. Later

Conspirator John Surratt escaped to Canada and then to Europe. There he enlisted in the Pontifical Zouaves (the pope's guards) at the Vatican, where he expected to be forever safe.

LIBRARY OF CONGRESS

that month, Surratt met with Benjamin and other Confederate officials in Richmond on matters undoubtedly connected with the pending evacuation of the city and the need for desperate measures to save the Confederacy. He left Richmond with dispatches for Confederates in Canada at about the same time that a demolition team headed for Washington with the apparent assignment of blowing up the White House. Surratt was a critical player in a high-stakes game.

On the night of the assassination, Secretary of War Edwin M. Stanton erroneously concluded that John H. Surratt had attacked Secretary of State William H. Seward and leaked that news to the media. Further investigation revealed, however, that Surratt was nowhere near Washington on April 14. Detectives were told that he was in Montreal.

Actually, on April 14 Surratt was in Elmira, New York. He had been sent there by Gen. Edwin G. Lee to determine the feasibility of freeing Confederates from the notorious prison camp there. Lee, a cousin of Robert E. Lee, was part of the clandestine operation in Canada. Then, from Saturday night, April 15, until the following Monday morning, Surratt was in Canandaigua, New York. There he realized the danger he was in when he picked up a New York newspaper and saw that he had been accused of the attack on Seward. He was further identified as "a notorious secessionist of southern Maryland" whose "name, with that of John Wilkes Booth, will forever lead the infamous roll of assassins."

Immediately he scrambled across the border into Canada. He was in Montreal when detectives accompanied by Louis J. Weichmann arrived to search for him. Surratt later claimed to have seen Weichmann on the street but avoided the other man's notice. Mysteriously, on April 19—two days after Lewis Paine had been apprehended and identified as Seward's attacker— Stanton issued a bulletin offering a reward of twenty-five thousand dollars for Surratt, even though he had nothing to tie him to the assassination.

Surratt found refuge with friends in Montreal, then with a priest in St. Liboire, then back in Montreal, where another priest concealed him. Confederate agent Beverly Tucker, formerly the U.S. consul to Liverpool, and Edwin Lee then arranged passage for Surratt to England aboard a steamer bound for Liverpool. Using an alias, the fugitive landed at Liverpool in September 1865.

Although disguised on his arrival in England, Surratt's identity was soon discovered. "While I was in London, Liverpool, and Birmingham," he noted in his 1870 lecture, "[the U.S.] consuls at those ports knew who I was and advised our State Department of my whereabouts, but nothing was done."

On November 13, 1865, Secretary of State Seward submitted a request to the attorney general to "procure an indictment," but Stanton apparently blocked it. Congressional investigators in 1867 reported that they found no evidence of either an indictment or a demand for the English government to surrender Surratt.

Eleven days after Seward's indictment request, November 24, Stanton canceled the reward for Surratt, claiming it was unnecessary since he was out of the country and could only be arrested by governmental representa-

Beverly Tucker, a Confederate agent in Canada, was U. S. consul in Liverpool, England, before the war began. To help John Surratt escape, Tucker and fellow agent Edwin Lee arranged passage for him aboard a steamer bound from Quebec to England.

LIBRARY OF CONGRESS

tives. The vice consul at Liverpool received the following reply to his queries regarding Surratt: "Your dispatches have been received. I have to inform you that upon consultation with the Secretary of War and the Judge Advocate General, it is thought advisable that no action be taken in regard to the arrest of the supposed John Surratt at present." The communication was signed by W. Hunter, acting secretary of state.

In 1867 the *Washington Daily Morning Chronicle* asked: "Was there any reason for this lenience . . . ? The committee may well express surprise that no agent or detective was sent to England to dog the foot-steps of [Surratt] . . . and secure his capture; for all of which it appears there was ample opportunity."

Thus five months after Edwin M. Stanton and Andrew Johnson had hastily ensured the hanging of Mary Elizabeth Surratt, the same administration lacked any interest in her son, who had been far more involved with Booth. What accounts for this apathy? One explanation is that Stanton was fascinated by the idea that England had earlier connived with the former Confederacy in some enterprise to acquire cheaper cotton. Stanton considered the possibility that Surratt was the point man in the plot and believed that somehow he could uncover more information about the cotton scheme if Surratt was on the loose rather than in jail. No such international intrigue, however, was ever proven.

Moreover, the federal government's puzzling disinterest enabled Surratt to travel unmolested throughout Europe, but this was just one of many strange, remarkable happenings related to John Surratt. Using an alias, John

Gen. Rufus King, U.S. minister to the Vatican, was informed of Surratt's presence in Rome. When King wrote to Washington for guidance, neither Seward nor Stanton seemed interested in the fugitive.

Watson, Surratt enlisted in the Third Company of the Pontifical Zouaves—the pope's personal guard—at the Vatican in April 1866. He expected to be forever safe in this center of Christendom, but even with the odds heavily in his favor, he lost that gamble.

Coincidentally, a former friend of Surratt's from Maryland—Henri Beaumont de Sainte-Marie—had joined the Ninth Company of the Pontifical Zouaves. Sainte-Marie, a French-Canadian by birth, was also an acquaintance of Louis J. Weichmann, having been on the faculty with him at St. Matthew's Institute in Washington. Shortly after Surratt joined the Third Company, Sainte-Marie recognized him. "He had certain physical peculiarities that no disguise could affect," Sainte-Marie told a *New York Times* reporter, referring to Surratt's bulging forehead, goatee, and long hair.

Sainte-Marie approached Surratt and asked if he were Surratt, but the man claiming to be John Watson said that Sainte-Marie was mistaken. Later, after enjoying too much wine, Surratt admitted his identity and bragged about his involvement with Booth. Sainte-Marie, motivated by the possibility of a reward for information about the last of the Lincoln conspirators still at large, notified Vatican authorities and Gen. Rufus King, the U.S. minister in Rome. King wrote to Seward for guidance.

Although no extradition treaty existed between the Vatican and the United States, Cardinal Giacomo Antonelli assured King that "if the American government desired the surrender of the criminal there would be no difficulty." Seward, however, seemed less interested in recovering Surratt than he had been eight months earlier when Surratt was in England. He officially advised Stanton of the situation on May 17, 1866, and Stanton forwarded the unwelcome matter to Judge Advocate General Joseph Holt. Seward showed some initiative on May 28 by suggesting to Stanton that they send a special agent to Rome to demand Surratt's surrender. Stanton did not reply to his letter.

Months passed as meaningless correspondence flowed between Washington and the U.S. minister in Rome. The *Washington Daily Morning Chronicle* observed:

> [General King communicated Surratt's presence] by letter, dated August 8, 1866, to his department. Notwithstanding this, no steps were taken to identify or secure the arrest of the supposed conspirator . . . [until] the rumors of his known presence in Rome had been rife long enough for everybody to have heard them; when public speakers had declaimed it from the stand, and charged remissness, if not connivance and guilt upon the officers of the

Government of the United States. . . . The facts are bad, and the world is cen-
sorious enough to believe that bad facts have a motive behind them.

The judiciary committee of the House of Representatives, usually friendly
toward Stanton, expressed its disapproval of "the great delay in arresting a
person charged with complicity in the assassination." The committee, while
not charging improper motives upon any of the officers of the government,
reported that, in its opinion, "due diligence in the arrest of John H. Surratt
was not exercised by the executive department of the government."

Tired of waiting for a directive from American officials, the papal
authorities acted on their own. Discovering that Surratt was AWOL, they
found him at Veroli, a small town within the pope's domain, and arrested
him on November 6, 1866.

Two days later Surratt's guards awakened him at four o'clock to transfer
him to another prison. He calmly drank some coffee and put on his colorful
uniform—red fez, blue pants, red trimmings, blue jacket, and white gaiters.
Seemingly unconcerned about his fate, he was actually preparing for yet
another strange happening in his adventurous life.

The prison in which Surratt was being held was atop a small mountain.
Its gate opened onto a platform with a balustrade overlooking a steep hill-
side of rugged rocks and a deep ravine a hundred feet below.

During the early morning activities of November 8, Surratt escaped by
launching himself over the balustrade into near darkness. Miraculously,
instead of dropping a hundred feet to almost certain death, he landed
twenty-three feet down on a narrow protruding rock covered with the filth
of the barracks. He suffered only a bruised back and an injured arm.

A reporter later asked Surratt if he had landed by accident on the ledge
or if he knew beforehand of the ledge being there. "Why of course I knew of
it!" Surratt responded. "Do you think I would have been such an idiot as to
jump over a hundred-foot precipice to certain death?" For two days Surratt
had examined his surroundings and noted the ledge. Still, had he not
jumped at exactly the right place he would have missed it and died in the
ravine below.

Within minutes of his leap he was pursued by more than fifty soldiers,
but they never caught up with him. He struggled down the side of the
mountain to a little town, and from there he walked undiscovered some
twenty miles in his garish Zouave uniform to the Italian frontier, beyond
papal jurisdiction. Soon he was in the middle of a camp of Garibaldians,

who were fighting the Pontifical Zouaves to bring an end to the controversial papal political dynasty. After Surratt convinced the Garibaldians he was an American, they sheltered him for a week, gave him money, and facilitated his safe passage to Naples.

Rufus King, the American minister, was suspicious in a November 19 communiqué to Seward: "Some surprise perhaps may be expressed that Surratt was arrested by Papal authorities before any request to that effect had been made by the American government. . . . On the surface, the Pope's officers certainly show . . . perfect good faith." Four months earlier Surratt's comrade Sainte-Marie had accused the church hierarchy of far more than protecting the fugitive: "I believe [Surratt] is protected by the clergy, and that the murder is the result of a deep-laid plot, not only against the life of President Lincoln, but against the existence of the republic, as we are aware that priesthood and royalty are and always have been opposed to liberty."

From all appearances Stanton had no interest in Surratt, but neither Stanton nor Seward communicated that information to their consular officials in Italy. King continued the pursuit. He assumed that Surratt was bound for Naples and sent an agent to ask the U.S. minister there to request that Italian officials intercept Surratt. The minister, however, did not receive the papers for five days, and when he finally contacted the Italian Ministry of Foreign Affairs, he was advised that they would search for Surratt only if the Italian government received a guarantee that the fugitive would not face the death penalty for his crimes. The U.S. minister did not pursue the matter further.

King, meanwhile, dispatched his own agents to track down Surratt and advised them to search the Naples area. In fact, the Naples police had sheltered Surratt for three days in their station, but by the time King's contacts arrived, Surratt had been gone for two days. With financial assistance and other help from the British consul, Surratt—claiming Canadian citizenship and using an alias, Walters—was smuggled aboard a British steamer for Alexandria, Egypt.

Somehow the American consul at Naples learned that a person matching Surratt's description (and wearing a Zouave uniform!) was aboard the steamer. The consul wired an alarm to his counterpart, William Winthrop, on the island of Malta, where the steamer was scheduled to stop for coal.

Winthrop submitted an arrest request to Malta's British governor, but the governor was reluctant to grant the warrant. Officials informed Winthrop that no one by the name of Walters was on the ship, and that the man in the Zouave uniform was John Agostina, a native of "Candia." They also reported that the steamer had entered the port with fifteen-days' quarantine and was anchored far from shore due to a dense fog. These complications prevented Winthrop's communicating directly with the vessel, but curiously, as the ship prepared to sail, Winthrop was informed that the Zouave was Surratt and "Candia" had been a clerical error for Canada. Yet it was too late for Winthrop to do anything. Surratt was on his way to Egypt. Not to be defeated, Winthrop alerted the American consul general of Egypt.

After landing at Alexandria on November 27, 1866, Surratt might have eluded the search party charged with finding him except for one complication. The steamer's port of origin, Naples, was regarded as "a foul port" by Alexandria authorities because of an outbreak of cholera in the Italian city. All the ship's third-class passengers were placed under guard in a quarantine station for a week's observation. The American consul at Alexandria found Surratt there and arranged for him to be escorted to an even more secure place until the quarantine expired. On December 21 Surratt was put aboard a U.S. ship, the *Swatara,* and brought back to America.

For his role in finding Surratt, Sainte-Marie was later awarded ten thousand dollars by Congress, even though Stanton had withdrawn the reward.

The ship took forty-five days to cross the Atlantic—much longer than usual—but probably faster than Stanton desired. He did not want Surratt brought back at all. With Seward strangely supporting Stanton, the two federal officials encouraged further delays, keeping Surratt and the *Swatara* held up for a month at Hampton Roads, Virginia. They finally allowed the ship to dock at the Washington Navy Yard on February 19, 1867.

Indeed most of the officials involved in the investigation of the Lincoln assassination were fearful of Surratt both for what he knew and for the manner in which the conspirators had been prosecuted two years earlier. They did not know what Surratt knew or what he might reveal or who he might implicate, truthfully or falsely, and they realized they could not try him before a military commission and control the proceedings. In the spring of 1866 the Supreme Court had ruled that civilians were not to be tried by military courts except where the civil courts had ceased to function because of invasion or disorder. As a result, Surratt would be in the hands of a civil court of the District of Columbia, and officially off-limits to the War Department.

Unofficially, Stanton became very much involved. His department prepared much of the case against Surratt. Further, Stanton's close friend Edwards Pierrepont and former Congressman Albert G. Riddle were engaged by Seward to assist the local district attorney.

John Surratt was finally caught in Egypt, much to the chagrin of Stanton and Seward, and returned to the United States. The illustration from *Harper's Weekly* shows his arrival in Washington on February 19, 1867.

Navy Secretary Gideon Welles noted in his diary an interesting communication from Riddle that was read during a cabinet meeting. It "disclosed the fact that Riddle had been employed by Seward to hunt up, or *manufacture* testimony against Surratt." Welles added, "Why the State Department should busy itself in that prosecution is not clear." Author Otto Eisenschiml (*In the Shadow of Lincoln's Death*) regretted that Welles "made no effort to uncover this unsavory pot" and find "what lay simmering within."

To bend the rule of law in their favor, governmental officials arranged for the case to be heard before Judge George P. Fisher, who, according to Welles, was under the control of his associate, Judge David Cartter, "a coarse, vulgar Radical in the hands of Stanton."

While Surratt awaited trial on June 10, 1867, Radical Republicans sought to manipulate him to help them prove President Johnson's complicity in Lincoln's assassination. Congressman James M. Ashley of Ohio, one of Stanton's intimates, sent a message to the prisoner: "Give [us] the name of someone high in position [and] there is a means by which [you] can save [your] neck." But according to Surratt's sister, Anna, "John could not be induced to swear away his own soul." The government's prosecutors, however, were intent on selling their souls to the devil. They had unlimited resources and no scruples about how they would use them.

Surratt was charged as an accomplice in Lincoln's murder, which meant that the prosecution had to prove he was involved in the assassination—a major task considering that Surratt was three hundred miles from Washington when Lincoln was killed. The prosecution, with the aid of the War Department's hired witness hunters, drummed up a dozen people who swore they saw Surratt in Washington on that date. One of them even claimed that he saw Surratt in the vestibule of the presidential box at Ford's Theatre.

Henri Beaumont de Sainte-Marie was among the perjurers. He told the court that Surratt admitted to him that he left Washington "the night of the assassination, or the next morning." Yet a year earlier, Sainte-Marie had sworn under oath that "when [the assassination] took place he [Surratt] told me he was in New York."

Surratt's able attorney Joseph H. Bradley easily broke down these testimonies, drawing out so many inconsistencies that all their stories were highly suspect. Bradley, who defended Surratt without remuneration, further outmaneuvered the prosecution by showing convincingly that Surratt had been in Elmira, New York, from April 13 to 15. For the clincher, Bradley tried to acquire the register of Surratt's hotel in Elmira, which contained his signature for the dates indicated, but the register had mysteriously disappeared, and as Bradley noted, "the proprietors and servants of the hotel [were] scattered in every direction."

Clearly, the prosecutors were fully aware of Surratt's presence in Elmira and had deliberately based their case on what they knew to be fabrications. In 1865 the government had, in fact, traced Surratt's movements, and one of its own witnesses, a doctor named McMillan, had testified to a congressional committee that Surratt was in Elmira at the time of the assassination. The hotel register had apparently been confiscated by the government.

Surratt's attorneys did have the register of the Webster House in Canandaigua, where Surratt stayed from April 15 to 17, but the trial judge refused to admit it as evidence.

The government's charge that Surratt was in Washington at the time of the president's assassination was based, in part, on a white linen handkerchief marked with the name "J. H. Surratt." Prosecutors presented three witnesses—a watchman, a train conductor, and a former deputy provost marshal—all of whom testified that the handkerchief had been picked up by the watchman in the railroad station at Burlington, Vermont, on the morning of April 18, 1865, near a bench where two men had slept the night before. The prosecutors argued that if Surratt had been in Burlington on the night of April 17, he certainly could have been in Washington on April 14.

The defense countered with one of Mary Surratt's boarders, John Holohan, who claimed he had lost the handkerchief in Burlington, but he had done so on April 20, not April 18. As to why Holohan had Surratt's handkerchief, the boarder explained that he had been pressed into service by the superintendent of the Metropolitan Police Force to help identify the alleged assassins. After searching the lower counties of Maryland on April 15 and Baltimore on April 17, he requested a change of underwear. Returning to the boarding house, he pulled the needed underclothes from a freshly washed pile of laundry and accidentally picked up one of Surratt's handkerchiefs. Three days later, on April 20, he lost it at the Burlington station.

Were the government's three witnesses lying or was Holohan? Or were there two handkerchiefs? The prosecutors and the judge advocate general knew the answers to these questions from the beginning. One of Lafayette C. Baker's detectives had seized the handkerchief from the watchman at the railroad station and filed a report stating that the handkerchief was dropped in the depot on April 20. The commander at nearby St. Albans furnished confirmation of that.

Even though a Supreme Court ruling required Surratt to be tried in a civil court, Stanton's close friend Edwards Pierrepont (*left*) and former Congressman Albert G. Riddle (*right*) were engaged by Secretary of State William H. Seward to help the local district attorney.

AUTHOR'S COLLECTION

George P. Fisher was the presiding judge at John Surratt's trial in a civil court. Fisher's rulings on evidence and his charge to the jury demonstrated strong bias against Surratt.

The defense freely admitted Surratt's role in the plot to capture Lincoln but vehemently denied any part in the conspiracy to murder the president. Since the defense had firmly established that Surratt was not in Washington at the time of the assassination, it had what appeared to be a solid case. The defense also hammered home the plight of Surratt's mother in the 1865 military trial. She was portrayed as the innocent victim of political revenge and as one who had paid the highest possible price for both herself and her son. Also presented before the court was the evidence used against Mary Surratt to demonstrate how unfair her conviction and execution were. The defense questioned John M. Lloyd, whose testimony helped to send Surratt's mother to the gallows. He cast doubt on that testimony, saying he did not remember who said what to whom, because he had been intoxicated at the time, but he had been advised during the earlier trial to remember under threat of death and promises of protection and support from the government.

As the trial ran its course over two months, Surratt projected a mixed image to the public. He was a devious and dastardly accomplice of Booth who hid out while his mother was unjustly hanged, but he was nonetheless being railroaded by the government on a charge it could not prove.

The nation's newspapers followed the trial closely and maintained a lively discussion. Some of them, such as the *Springfield (Mass.) Daily Republican,* believed that Surratt would be found innocent, but others, such as the *New York World,* saw no chance for him against the heavy odds formed by an alliance of the district attorney's office with the War Department. It opined: "The accused has not the ordinary and equitable chances of an accused person in a criminal court. It is necessary to convict him in order to vindicate the government. . . . If Surratt should be acquitted, the War Department would be convicted of murder and the subornation of perjury. . . . It is not merely Surratt that is on trial; the War Department and its famous Military Commission are on trial." Twenty years later one of Stanton's confidential clerks wrote, "It is only fair to say that he [Stanton] did take an active part in the . . . trial of [Mary Surratt's] son."

Although Fisher gave highly improper instructions to the jury—supporting Surratt's guilt—the jury could not reach a verdict, with eight voting innocent and four voting guilty. With only one exception, the Northern and foreign jurors had voted for conviction and the Southern jurors for acquittal.

If Surratt had been tried two years earlier by the military commission—when the spirit of revenge was at its peak—he surely would have hanged. Instead, he was remanded to the Old Capitol Prison, from which, some months later, he was released on twenty-five thousand dollars' bail.

After tempestuous meetings in many federal offices, the government again arraigned Surratt for trial. Since the earlier prosecution had failed to convict him on a murder charge, he was instead charged with treason. The U.S. attorney for the District of Columbia secured two indictments and presented the first one to Judge Fisher on June 18, 1868. Fisher dismissed it. The District had a two-year limitation on such crimes, and the indictment was dated three years after April 14, 1865, the date of the alleged offense. The District's Supreme Court upheld the ruling. A grand jury then chose to ignore the second indictment, and John Surratt was permanently free.

In the ensuing years Surratt became a respected and exemplary citizen of Maryland. He raised tobacco, taught at the Rockville Female Academy, gave public lectures for a fee, married a second cousin of Francis Scott Key, and secured employment with, and eventually became treasurer of, the Old Bay Line, a steamship company on the Chesapeake Bay. He died of pneumonia on April 21, 1916, at the age of seventy-two—the last survivor of Booth's lost cause. A few days before his death, Surratt is said to have burned the manuscript of an autobiography, thereby destroying what might have contained revealing information about the conspiracy.

Perhaps a description most revealing of Surratt came from an acquaintance, J. Friend Lodge: "He impressed me as a man that always, under any and all circumstances, could be counted on to be in full control of himself. . . . His face, I would say, was a hard one to read. . . . There was nothing . . . to indicate what was transpiring back of those eyes."

15

Deflecting Southern Exposure

S TANTON CONCLUDED ON THE night of the assassination that the Confederate government was behind the plot to kill Lincoln, Seward, and Johnson. As noted in chapter 3, strong evidence suggested that Southern leaders were capable of such deeds when they apparently sent explosives expert Thomas F. Harney to blow up the White House. Particularly convincing to Stanton was a letter signed "Sam" in Booth's trunk. It called for checking with officials in Richmond to see how they would feel about some affair left undescribed. Substantial evidence linked Booth's earlier plan to kidnap Lincoln to Confederate agents in Canada—Rebels whose other clandestine operations included sabotaging military and transportation facilities, setting fires in New York City, robbing banks, liberating Confederate prisoners, plotting to poison water supplies, and using germ warfare to create yellow fever epidemics throughout the North. Because of these acts, Stanton felt especially vindictive against these terrorists, several of whom had once been prominent politicians in the federal government. Stanton regarded them as cowards hiding behind their privileged sanctuary in Canada.

Stanton's belief in a conspiracy born in Richmond and in Canada was evident in his actions after Lincoln's assassination. On April 15, as Lincoln lay dying at the Petersen house, Stanton ordered his assistant secretary of war, Charles A. Dana, to wire the provost marshal in Portland, Maine: "Arrest Jacob Thompson and his companions . . . who are either in Portland or on the way to Portland from Montreal en route to Europe." Thompson, of course, was the leader of the junta in Canada. He reported to Jefferson Davis and Judah P. Benjamin, the Confederacy's secretary of state. But Thompson was not in Portland. Stanton had received faulty information.

On April 15 Stanton also wired the U.S. minister to England "that these horrible crimes were committed in execution of a conspiracy deliberately planned and set on foot by rebels under pretense of avenging the South and aiding the rebel cause."

On April 25 the secretary of war announced that he had evidence that the plot had been organized in Canada and approved by Confederate leaders in Richmond.

On April 27 Stanton again wired the provost marshal in Portland that Confederate agents Jacob Thompson, George N. Sanders, and Beverly Tucker were or would be in or near Portland while trying to escape to Europe. He directed the provost marshal to search every train and vessel and to spare no attempt to capture them.

On May 2 President Johnson asked Stanton (who passed the request on to Judge Advocate General Joseph Holt) for a list of those in Canada and Richmond against whom he had proof of complicity in Lincoln's murder. Stanton brought the list to a cabinet meeting on the same day. Navy Secretary Gideon Welles recorded in his diary that "all [cabinet] members were in a degree influenced by [Stanton]," and "we had been made to believe . . . that he and Judge Advocate Holt had positive evidence that Jeff Davis, [Clement] Clay, [Jacob] Thompson, and others had conspired to assassinate Mr. Lincoln, Mr. Johnson, and most of the cabinet."

On May 2 Johnson also issued a proclamation that "the atrocious murder of the late Pres. Abraham Lincoln and the attempted assassination of Hon. W. H. Seward, Secretary of State, were incited, concerted and procured by and between Jefferson Davis, Clement C. Clay, Beverly Tucker, George Sanders, W[illiam]. C. Cleary, and other rebels and traitors." Johnson offered a reward of one hundred thousand dollars for Davis's apprehension and twenty-five thousand dollars for each of the others. All but Davis were Confederate agents in Canada.

Clay surrendered on May 11. On the same day, federal troops arrested Alexander H. Stephens, vice president of the Confederacy. Two days later

Davis was captured in southern Georgia. Davis and Clay were imprisoned at Fort Monroe, Virginia, to await trial. Stanton wanted Davis tried at once. He was opposed, however, by Chief Justice Salmon P. Chase and later by President Johnson. To Stanton's credit, when he learned that Davis had been placed in irons, he ordered the irons removed. In the meantime, Judah P. Benjamin had left the retreating presidential party and escaped to England by way of the West Indies.

On May 4 Confederate agents in Canada publicly blamed Andrew Johnson for the plot against Lincoln. George N. Sanders and Beverly Tucker wrote to Johnson: "Your proclamation is a living, burning lie, known to be such by yourself and all your surroundings . . . and all the hired perjurers in Christendom shall not deter us from exhibiting to the civilized world your hellish plot to murder our Christian President."

Thompson sent the following letter to the *New York Tribune:* "The proof, whatever it is, is a tissue of falsehoods, and its publication cannot be made without exposing its rottenness. I know that there is not half the ground to suspect me that there is to suspect President Johnson himself." Another New York paper, the *World,* advised the government: "Bring forth the proof [of the president's accusations]."

On May 10 an American official in Montreal informed Stanton that Sanders, Tucker, and Cleary were still there and asked if he wanted them arrested to await extradition. Stanton wired back, "You will be advised when action is required."

On May 12 the conspiracy trial began. It was actually two trials in one: the prosecution of Jefferson Davis and his cohorts and the prosecution of Booth's eight alleged coconspirators. Davis and his Canadian agents were not actually on trial; they were unindicted coconspirators not present in the

After Lincoln's assassination, more than ten thousand Southern leaders and aristocrats left the country. It was the biggest migration from America that the nation had ever seen. Its cause was a general amnesty proclamation that excluded "civil, diplomatic, and military leaders of the Confederacy." More than four thousand political refugees fled to Brazil. Others went to Mexico, British Honduras, and Canada. After President Johnson unconditionally pardoned all war participants except "civil and military officials of high rank" in December 1868, seventy-five hundred of the former Confederates came home. The remaining twenty-five hundred never returned.

Confederate agent George Nicholas
Sanders altered history by a successful
propaganda scheme to convince
American authorities that the
Confederacy had nothing to do with
the conspiracy against Lincoln.

LIBRARY OF CONGRESS

courtroom. The government's intent was to produce evidence proving their guilt. Instead, remarkable developments sabotaged the prosecution's case.

Stanton, Johnson, and Holt were badly deceived by unsolicited evidence they eagerly accepted as genuine. Circumstantial evidence suggests they were outsmarted by deceptive tactics masterminded by Confederate agent George N. Sanders from his Canadian base.

Sanders was a skillful manipulator and propagandist. The fifty-three-year-old Kentuckian had been associated with European democratic radicals in the 1840s and 1850s, had furnished arms to revolutionaries in the great uprisings in Europe in 1848, and had advocated assassination as a valid way to remove tyrants. "Kill Napoleon!" he reportedly advised the French people. In earlier years, he had joined movements advocating American intervention in Europe to assist revolutionary efforts to replace monarchies and dictatorships with democratic governments. He was probably the first person to recommend a Canadian covert operation to Jefferson Davis, and when Davis implemented the program in early 1864 he arranged for Sanders to be a part of it. Davis was aware of Sanders's ability to dream up political action projects to influence events, and he anticipated such results from this miracle-worker. Davis was not disappointed.

Sanders met with John Wilkes Booth in Canada in October 1864 and is believed to have influenced Booth's subsequent actions. Sanders and other Confederates with whom Booth conferred made little distinction between abduction and assassination. They regarded both as acceptable methods to deal with tyrants.

In April and May 1865 Sanders undoubtedly grasped the devastating implications for the South if Stanton succeeded in proving his charges of Confederate conspiracy in Lincoln's assassination. Counteraction was essential. Sanders had to develop a convincing program to discredit Stanton's accusations. Author William A. Tidwell called Sanders's disinformation campaign "the most important and most successful clandestine operation" undertaken by Confederate agents in Canada. In the end, Sanders outfoxed Stanton and made the Confederacy look innocent. He singlehandedly altered history for decades to come.

Stanton had relied on Holt and his Bureau of Military Justice for much of the information against the Confederate power structure. Yet as Navy Secretary Gideon Welles observed in his diary, "Holt's credulity often led him to take actions that bordered on the point of criminal negligence." Welles also noted that "Stanton has sometimes brought forward singular papers relating to conspiracies, and dark and murderous designs in which he had evident faith, and Holt had assured him in his suspicions."

Holt's hastily gathered "dark and murderous" evidence had persuaded Stanton and Johnson that Booth had been sponsored by the Richmond government and that the Confederate apparatus in Canada had played a major role. All this was probably true, but Holt had been fed bogus and intoxicating information probably brewed in Canada. He believed it unquestioningly and used it so that when the truth came out, his case against the South collapsed. As a result, generations of historians wrongly scoffed at any speculation of Confederate involvement in the assassination.

Holt's supposedly strong evidence against the Confederate government came chiefly from three witnesses who had intimate contact with Southern agents in Canada and also claimed to have personal knowledge of their relationship with Booth. These witnesses were Richard Montgomery, a Union spy who served as a Confederate courier between Canada and Richmond and allowed Union authorities to copy the dispatches he carried; James B. Merritt, a medical doctor; and Charles A. Dunham,* who used the alias Sanford Conover in dealing with Holt and Stanton. "Conover" was a self-appointed correspondent for the *New York Tribune*. These three testified during a secret session of the military commission, but part of Dunham/Conover's testimony reached the press. It created

---

*Because the record is rife with references to Dunham and to Conover, the man is referred to throughout this account by the hybrid form Dunham/Conover.

such furor that the government released the complete testimony of all three witnesses.

Dunham/Conover was the star witness. A shady character, he was a master swindler. In a career littered with bad intentions, he brilliantly concocted creative lies, adopted false identities, and wrote fictitious letters under assumed names. He practiced his craft in Canada, where George N. Sanders appears to have recognized and capitalized upon his talents. While the evidence is not conclusive, it suggests that Sanders collaborated with Dunham in a scheme to provide false information to the Union prosecutors as well as witnesses who would lie under oath, the most important being Dunham/Conover himself. Then, after the trial (and for which there is strong evidence), Sanders and his cohorts would discredit the primary witnesses against the Confederacy by proving that they were perjurers and publicize that fact skillfully. The plan would work beautifully.

Dunham/Conover told Holt exactly what Holt wanted to hear—a bizarre tale of intrigue, later proven fictitious, of Confederate agents in Canada. Posing as a Rebel in Canada, Dunham/Conover said that he had been admitted to secret meetings. He claimed to have seen Booth and John H. Surratt with Jacob Thompson and George N. Sanders. He reported that Surratt had brought dispatches from Judah P. Benjamin and a letter from Jefferson Davis that caused Thompson to exclaim: "This makes the thing allright!" According to Dunham/Conover, Thompson told him that Booth would be commissioned to kill Lincoln.

Merritt and Montgomery offered corroborating testimony. Merritt, who was likely one of Sanders's plants, said that the assassination was freely discussed among the Rebels in Montreal. He claimed that Sanders said money was available and that Davis had authorized the assassination in writing. Montgomery, who may have been telling the truth, swore that in January 1865 Thompson disclosed to him that a plot to kill Lincoln was in the works and that he was waiting for a response from Richmond. Montgomery also reported that he had seen Lewis Paine in Canada with Confederate agent Clement Clay, the former Alabama senator.

All of this information sounded incriminating until counterevidence generated by Sanders and his Confederate allies established that most of the testimony was not only highly questionable but outright lies. Stanton should have connected the dots when in early June he received a letter from W. W. Daniels, an otherwise unidentified source. Daniels confided that he had met with Sanders in Montreal in late May. Daniels said that Sanders seemed fully informed of developments in the trial and told him he had sent witnesses to Washington to testify.

In *April '65*, Tidwell reported that Dunham/Conover returned to Canada immediately after his testimony and conferred with Sanders and others in early June on the next steps to be taken. It was during this time that much of Dunham/Conover's testimony was leaked to the press and published in Canadian and American newspapers. Confederates in Canada who were not aware of the trickery denounced Dunham/Conover for making false accusations. Dunham/Conover responded (falsely, of course) that someone had used his name and told those lies. He agreed to issue a statement refuting the information.

After consulting Sanders, Dunham/Conover swore to the following, under the alias of James Watson Wallace: "I never gave any testimony whatsoever before the said court-martial at Washington City. . . . That I never went under the name of Sanford Conover. That I never had any confidential communication with Mr. George N. Sanders, Beverly Tucker, Hon. Jacob Thompson. . . . The evidence of the said Sanford Conover personating me is false, untrue and unfounded in fact."

From that point, according to Tidwell, nearly everything Dunham/Conover did was designed to destroy the government's case against the Confederacy. His testimony, indeed, had been false, and Sanders went on to expose Dunham/Conover, Merritt, and Montgomery as liars, thereby discrediting the efforts of Stanton, Holt, and Johnson to blame the Confederacy for the assassination.

Secretary of the Navy Gideon Welles maintained a diary with keen insights into the happenings in Washington during the war. His perceptions of the surreptitious maneuverings of the power brokers in the national capital and events were quite accurate.

With Dunham/Conover's sworn affidavit in hand, Confederates published a strong statement in the *Montreal Evening Telegraph* and attacked the testimonies of the three witnesses. They asserted that the depositions were "cooked to order . . . [and] couched in artfully concocted phraseology," and "all three of the witnesses . . . committed the error false witnesses so often fall into of swearing to too much and of swearing to too much alike." They promised that "other affidavits corroborative of [Dunham/Conover's] testimony will be published hereafter, and also depositions disproving the statements made by Merritt and Montgomery. The Federal prosecutors of these charges may possibly strive to avoid the effect of [Dunham/Conover's] affidavit by [alleging] that the whole affair is the result of an ingenious and deep laid conspiracy by Mr. Sanders and his confreres to deceive, mislead, and entrap." The statement was reprinted and distributed widely.

Meanwhile, countercharges against the testimonies of the three men appeared in many newspapers in the United States. Generated by Sanders, these statements claimed that Thompson and his colleagues were not in Montreal when Dunham/Conover claimed to have met with them. The *Chicago Tribune* printed a letter from Dunham/Conover to Thompson dated March 20, 1865, indicating that the two men had not met by that date, although Dunham/Conover's testimony had claimed the two men had talked in February. The letter also established that Sanders was hundreds of miles from Montreal on the date Merritt claimed to have heard him discussing the assassination. Additionally, the justice of the peace before whom Merritt supposedly swore out his affidavit reported that he did not know Merritt. Further, the Confederates claimed they knew that Montgomery was a Union spy and therefore had not taken him into their confidence.

Sanders's propaganda effort paid off. By exposing the chief Union witnesses as liars, the government's case collapsed, even though credible witnesses had indeed submitted untainted affidavits implicating the Southern president and the Confederates in Canada.

Godfrey Joseph Hyams, a former resident of Arkansas living in Canada, testified to Booth's presence in Canada at various times in 1864 and his own involvement in the plot to start a yellow fever epidemic in the United States. "This evidence," said the *New York Tribune,* "seemed to send a thrill of horror through all."

Two other men—Hosea Carter and John Deveny—also produced evidence placing Booth in Canada in the company of leading Confederates. Also, Charles A. Dana, assistant secretary of war for the Union, found a cipher in the office of Judah P. Benjamin in Richmond, and it matched the one found in Booth's trunk. Reports also came to the War Department from Richmond. Susannah Hann stated that Booth and John Surratt had been there three weeks before the fall of the Confederate capital. Hann lived with the Samuel Murray family and claimed to have heard Murray tell his wife that plans were afoot to kill Lincoln and that Jefferson Davis, Fitzhugh Lee, and Robert E. Lee had all contributed to the cause. According to the July 8, 1865, issue of the *New York Times,* conspirator Lewis Paine had told a Colonel Dodd that he believed he was acting under orders from the highest Rebel authorities.

More information came from Henry Finnegass, a former commander of a black regiment. He was a resident of Boston and reported that he had been in Montreal for eleven days in February 1865. There he claimed to have overheard a conversation between Confederate agents George N. Sanders and William C. Cleary in the St. Lawrence Hall in Montreal on February 14 or 15. Cleary was secretary to the Confederate mission and stationed in Toronto.

According to Finnegass, Cleary said, "I suppose they are getting ready for the inauguration of Lincoln next month."

Sanders replied, "Yes: if the boys only have luck, Lincoln won't trouble them much longer."

Cleary then asked, "Is everything well?"

Sanders responded: "Oh, yes! Booth is bossing the job."

Finnegass claimed that he knew both men by sight, having seen both testify at a trial in Canada. The conversation he overheard probably referred to the plan to capture Lincoln in March. Clearly, Sanders, Thompson, Cleary, and Booth were Confederates engaged in a common cause.

Since Dunham/Conover, Merritt, and Montgomery were all disgraced as witnesses, Finnegass's testimony and that of other reliable witnesses was not taken seriously. The credibility of all of the government's witnesses was marred by the fabrications of the three.

The president's cabinet then concluded that the case against Davis and the other Confederate leaders was not as strong as they had been told by Stanton and Holt. Plans were scrapped to try Davis for the assassination in a military court, and the decision was made to try him for treason in a civil court. The vote was taken exactly two weeks after the hangings. Stanton voted for the motion. That fall he revoked the rewards offered for the Confederate agents in Canada.

Stanton's continuing concern for his own safety is reflected in Gideon Welles's notes of the August 18 cabinet meeting: "Stanton is full of apprehension and stories of plots and conspiracies. . . . He read quite a long affidavit from someone . . . stating he had been in communication with C. C. Clay and others in Canada, that they wanted him to be one of a party to assassinate President Lincoln and his whole cabinet. . . . He [Stanton] still keeps up a guard around his house and never ventures out without a stout man to accompany him."

Although shaken by their mistakes at the conspirators' trial, Holt and Stanton continued to look for evidence against the Confederate government. Still susceptible to the conniving Dunham/Conover, Holt persuaded Stanton to employ Dunham/Conover as a government agent, and Stanton directed him to find more witnesses, to work quickly, and to be thorough. Almost at once Dunham/Conover announced he was aware of some "startling new information." Stanton and Holt still did not realize that Dunham/Conover was in cahoots with George N. Sanders.

Several months later—by early 1866—Dunham/Conover had produced eight men of "unimpeachable character" who he claimed had received funds from the Confederate government to dispose of Lincoln and his cabinet. These witnesses made sworn depositions for Holt's Bureau of Military Justice, and with that material in hand, Holt believed he had the proof to convict Davis. In March 1866 he assured Stanton it was time to arraign Davis and bring him to trial before a military commission. The new witnesses "were without any motive whatever to misrepresent," Holt declared, and their depositions could be "accepted as strictly true."

Stanton was hesitant, having been fooled once. He advised the president it would not be in the public interest to release the new evidence to the House of Representatives. Radical Republicans in the Congress protested; they wanted to punish Davis, but now it appeared that Johnson was trying to protect Davis.

On April 9 the House instructed its Committee on the Judiciary to inquire if there was probable cause that any person named in the president's proclamation of May 2, 1865, was guilty as charged, and if so, whether legislation should be enacted to bring any of them to trial. Holt appeared before the committee, restated his case, and said he had complete confidence in the integrity of Dunham/Conover's eight new witnesses. He urged the committee to bring the best of them to Washington so it could cross-examine them and judge their reliability. The committee authorized it, and

Holt sent Col. Levi C. Turner of his staff to New York to find Dunham/Conover and five of the witnesses and bring them to Washington.

Turner found only two of the new witnesses, William Campbell and Joseph Snevel, and they agreed to come to Turner's hotel room with Dunham/Conover. Campbell, however, was the only one to show up.

"I talked to him," Turner reported, "and he was embarrassed. He finally asserted, 'This is all false: I must make a clean breast of it; I can't stand it any longer.'" The names, identities, and statements of all eight witnesses were false—all made up by Dunham/Conover, who had even rehearsed Campbell in what he previously had said to Holt under oath.

Taken to Washington, Campbell repeated his confession to Holt, but the judge advocate general refused to acknowledge his error. The Judiciary Committee summoned both Campbell and Dunham/Conover. Campbell again confessed to lying, and Dunham/Conover, not to be put down, swore that Campbell was lying and argued that friends of Jefferson Davis had possibly bribed Campbell.

After the hearing, Holt pulled Dunham/Conover aside and said he was "utterly astounded" by Campbell's testimony. "You cannot be more so than I am," Dunham/Conover replied with a straight face. Holt told Dunham/Conover he had lost *his* credibility and the only way to restore it would be to bring his other witnesses before the committee and have them confirm their previous statements. For this purpose, an officer of the committee accompanied Dunham/Conover to New York.

Slippery as ever, Dunham/Conover eluded the officer and disappeared. Holt finally had to admit to Stanton, "Conover has been guilty of a most atrocious crime, committed under what promptings I am wholly unable to determine." Holt subsequently withdrew the depositions of the eight witnesses and told the Judiciary Committee he had been deceived.

Regardless, after reviewing the uncontested testimony from the 1865 conspiracy trial, the committee concluded in July 1866 that Davis probably "was privy" to the conspiracy and should be put on trial. A minority

When Jefferson Davis and his associates abandoned Richmond, they allegedly took with them six wagons heavy with gold. Since the gold was not with Davis when he was captured in Georgia, it was assumed stolen or hidden somewhere in the South. To this day, hopeful hunters seek clues to where the treasure, if it ever existed, may be stashed.

member of the committee, Andrew J. Rogers of New Jersey, declared that the charges against Davis were false and revealed the perjured testimony to the country. He stated, "I do not say that Judge Holt did originate the charges or organize the plot or perjurers, because I do not know that he did; I merely say that a plot based on the assassination was formed against Davis, Clay, and others, and that the plotters did, and even yet, operate through [Holt's] Bureau of Military Justice."

Rogers firmly believed that Stanton and Holt had suborned false evidence to frame Davis and, consequently, that Davis and his colleagues were victims of a governmental conspiracy. Such charges emboldened Sanders and Dunham/Conover, for in August the *New York Herald* published letters supposedly exchanged among Holt, Dunham/Conover, and Campbell—letters that proved collusion and bribery.

Holt declared his innocence to Stanton and issued a statement in pamphlet form for the press. He declared that all these occurrences were part of a plot to defame him and effect the release of Jefferson Davis. Holt was correct, but few believed him. Months later the *Herald* letters were proven to be hoaxes manufactured by Dunham/Conover.

Dunham/Conover was finally located and arrested in the fall of 1866. He was tried under his real name, Charles A. Dunham, and convicted of perjury and the suborning of perjury and sentenced to ten years in prison. Dunham/Conover maintained, however, that he had told the truth about Davis at the 1865 conspiracy trial—and Holt continued to believe him.

In the meantime, Holt persisted in pushing for a military trial for Davis. Johnson, however, had had enough. After two years in prison, Davis was released on parole on May 11, 1867. He was never brought to trial. He returned to Mississippi and wrote a two-volume history of the Confederacy, *The Rise and Fall of the Confederate Government*. For his freedom, he owed a tremendous thank-you to the covert operations of George N. Sanders and Charles Dunham (alias Sanford Conover and James Watson Wallace).

Lincoln's successor, Andrew Johnson, seemed to be haunted by superstitions or maybe even by Lincoln's ghost. He refused to board the president's yacht, the *River Queen,* and he avoided mentioning Lincoln's name in his acceptance speech the morning after the assassination. Later, when Lincoln's son Robert offered to sell various Lincoln carriages to Johnson, he declined to buy any of them and never explained why.

Thanks to the work of these two men, Clement C. Clay was also released from prison (in April 1866) and returned to his home in Alabama.

The public and many senators and congressmen had been taken in by Sanders's propaganda campaign to create a favorable opinion for the former Confederate president. Even President Johnson—who wanted all traitors hanged—told Davis's and Clay's wives that he believed their husbands to be innocent of the treason charges. He implied to Varina Davis that he would like to have released her husband earlier, but "he [Johnson] was in the hands of wildly excited people, and [he had to] show he was willing to sift the facts." He had to allow the Judiciary Committee to complete its investigation.

Dunham/Conover, meanwhile, enlivened his prison life by being as sneaky as his former employers and as shifty as he had ever been. His skills as a master deceiver appealed to Radical Republicans in Congress who, after November 1866, had given up on Jefferson Davis and transferred their energies to crucifying Andrew Johnson. Impressed by Dunham/Conover's hefty bag of dirty tricks, the Radicals attempted to use him to implicate Johnson in Lincoln's assassination. Dunham/Conover's role was to drum up fake witnesses who would swear to Johnson's involvement.

Johnson, however, learned of this scheme from Dunham/Conover's fellow prisoner William Rabe, whom Johnson subsequently pardoned. The Radicals behind the plot discovered they had been found out, and to clear themselves of suspicion, decided to betray Dunham/Conover. But Dunham/Conover had his own contacts in Congress, and they alerted him to the planned betrayal.

In July 1867 Dunham/Conover confessed the scheme to Johnson. Maintaining that Congressmen Benjamin F. Butler and James M. Ashley had led him into schemes of forgery, Dunham/Conover revealed the details of the plot and provided copies of documents incriminating the Radicals. Johnson released these documents to the press on August 10, 1867, causing much political turmoil in Washington.

It took only five days for a counterplot to develop. On August 15 the press obtained documents charging that two Democrats, Roger A. Pryor and Ben Wood, had asked Nathan Anser to swear falsely that Holt and Dunham/Conover had tried to induce him to give perjured testimony.

Some newspapers supported Holt and attacked the Democrats; others went after Holt and demanded military discipline for his offenses. The public was equally divided as to whether the plot was really one of the Radical Republicans against the president or of the president and Dunham/Conover against the Radicals. The *Chicago Tribune* summed up the mess: "It is, without exception, the most unclean thing that has ever been thrust before the eyes of the American people."

The congressional committee seeking evidence linking Johnson to the assassination pursued every possible lead, but all of them were dead ends. Even Mary Lincoln had supported their efforts. She wrote, "My own intense misery has been augmented by the [belief] that that miserable inebriate Johnson has cognizance of my husband's death." The committee, however, could find nothing to support the charge and never bothered to generate a report.

Bombastic Representative Benjamin F. Butler, a Radical Republican from Massachusetts, conceded "there was no reliable evidence at all to convince a prudent and responsible man that there was any ground for the suspicions entertained against Johnson."

Johnson never revoked his proclamation of May 2, 1865, charging Davis and his agents in Canada with having "incited, concerted, and procured" Lincoln's assassination. Three years later, however, on Christmas Day 1868, Johnson included all of the accused in a sweeping presidential pardon.

16

WITH MALICE
TOWARD
ALL

DURING THE PRESIDENCY OF Andrew Johnson it was sometimes impossible to distinguish the good guys from the bad guys. The good were often bad, and the bad were sometimes good. What the country desperately needed was Abraham Lincoln, but he was gone and there was no one like him in the halls of Washington. The monumental issue of the day was the restoration of the Union and the reconstruction of the defeated South. As it was carried out for twelve years after the war, the process proved divisive with devastating repercussions.

At the time of Lincoln's assassination the Republican Party was in disarray. The Radical Republicans (as well as the Democrats) despised Lincoln's moderate ways and were determined to thwart him. To them, he was too liberal and too forgiving. They angrily opposed his gentle peace policy toward the South and his reconstruction proposals and worried that Lincoln would undertake reconstruction without consulting them. The Radicals wanted to see the South suffer, as if it had not suffered enough already. They wanted Rebel property confiscated and the conquered South treated as a prize of war. They wanted vengeance, and they wanted suffrage for African Americans. They assumed that Andrew Johnson felt the same way.

Radical Republican Sen. Benjamin F. Wade had especially kind words for Johnson when, just after Lincoln's assassination, he and Representative Henry Dawes visited with the new president at the Kirkwood House. Wade allegedly told Johnson: "I thank God that you are here. Lincoln had too much of the milk of human kindness to deal with these damned rebels. Now they will be dealt with according to their deserts."

This feeling ran through a caucus of the Radical Republicans that day as they considered, according to Representative George W. Julian of Indiana, "a line of policy less conciliatory than that of Mr. Lincoln" whose views on reconstruction were "as distasteful as possible to Radical Republicans." Julian later wrote that "while everybody was shocked at [Lincoln's] murder, the feeling [among Radical Republicans] was nearly universal that the ascension of Johnson to the presidency would prove a godsend to the country." Sen. Zachariah Chandler of Michigan intoned that "God placed a better man in Lincoln's place."

The Radicals had rejoiced earlier that month when Johnson met with Lincoln and demanded that the Confederate leaders be executed. They were also pleased on the Monday night before the assassination when Johnson defied Lincoln's position by exclaiming in a speech that if he were president he would arrest the Rebel leaders, try them as traitors, and "hang them as traitors."

Johnson hated the slaveholding aristocracy and called them "God-forsaken and hell-deserving, money-loving, hypocritical, back-biting, Sunday-praying scoundrels." Johnson was a rugged, homespun Democrat from the mountains of East Tennessee, a land of small farmers and few slaves. As a U.S. senator in 1861 he was the only Southerner in the Senate to oppose secession and to retain his seat. The Radical Republicans placed him on the Committee on the Conduct of the War because they considered him a "safe" Democrat. He worked closely with Radical leaders Wade and Chandler and generally voted with them. In 1862 Johnson resigned from the Senate to accept Lincoln's appointment as military governor of Tennessee. In 1864 Lincoln chose him as his vice president to demonstrate that the Republicans were a Union party.

On the day Johnson took office as president, Senator Wade requested an interview. He informed the president: "I have been instructed by the Committee on the Conduct of the War to inform you that your old associates upon that committee would be pleased to wait upon you at such time as may suit your convenience. They have just returned from the city of

LIBRARY OF CONGRESS

With the war almost over, Lincoln convened Gens. Ulysses S. Grant and William T. Sherman and Adm. David D. Porter to discuss acceptable terms for ending the fighting. Sherman's effort to carry out Lincoln's wishes were repudiated by the Republican leadership in the Congress as well as by Stanton and Johnson.

Richmond, where they saw and heard many things which they deem it would be well to make known to you."

Eager for their counsel, Johnson agreed to meet with them the following day. Their purpose, however, was more devious than Wade's letter indicated. They wanted to control the reconstruction of the South, to guide Johnson's actions on that issue, and to make sure he would not initiate any measures of his own until Congress came back into session. They soon learned, however, that they had misjudged Johnson.

In speeches throughout April, Johnson continued to preach revenge and hangings—which pleased the Radicals—but shortly they learned that he shared the contemptuous hostility of Southern politicians toward African Americans, opposed suffrage for them, and was against any federal efforts to force the Southern states to guarantee equality among the races. Those views rattled the sabers of the Radicals out of their scabbards.

Meanwhile, Gen. William T. Sherman stumbled unknowingly into a hornets' nest. The hero most responsible for Lincoln's reelection by capturing

Atlanta was in April 1865 attempting to carry out Lincoln's policies by offering generous terms to secure the surrender of the last remaining sizable Confederate force in the field—the army commanded by Gen. Joseph E. Johnston in North Carolina.

In a conference with Grant, Sherman, and David Porter at Grant's City Point, Virginia, headquarters in March, Lincoln had issued several directives regarding the ending of hostilities and the beginning of the restoration of the Union. Among these was the concluding of agreements with Southern civil authorities and the promise of recognition to state governments.

Sherman was committed to carrying out the president's wishes. Thus in exchange for Johnston's offer to surrender all Confederate armies between the Potomac and the Rio Grande, Sherman agreed that the executive branch would recognize the existing state governments, guarantee the political rights of the people, and grant a general amnesty. To Sherman the agreement seemed to be consistent with Lincoln's hopes for an immediate restoration without a program of revenge. It was a peace treaty that honored Lincoln's memory, and so he expected Johnson's immediate approval of the surrender terms.

The agreement, however, landed like a bomb on Johnson's desk. Sherman had followed Lincoln's terms, but he had not kept up with Washington politics—especially in the tumultuous days that followed the assassination. He was not aware of Johnson's support of the Radicals' roaring demand for revenge; Johnson had not been a party to the City Point conference. Those ideas for reconstruction were as dead as Lincoln and his policies.

Radical Republican Sen. Benjamin Wade congratulated Lincoln's successor, Andrew Johnson, with the announcement: "I thank God that you are here. Lincoln had too much of the milk of human kindness to deal with these damned rebels. Now they will be dealt with according to their deserts."

At the cabinet meeting on April 21 to discuss the treaty, Sherman's generosity to Johnston generated horrendous outrage. Stanton fiercely denounced Sherman for negotiating political questions and claimed that the general had disobeyed Lincoln's order reserving such decisions to the president. At the same time, Stanton overlooked the fact that he had never transmitted those instructions to Sherman.

Johnson supported Stanton. U. S. Grant was instructed to deliver their response personally to Sherman and to inform him to either resume hostilities or renegotiate a purely military agreement.

Stanton and the Radicals then launched a smear attack to destroy Sherman. Stanton initiated it with a public statement of malicious lies, falsely charging Sherman with allowing Jefferson Davis to escape with millions of dollars in gold. The Radical press called Sherman a traitor and a would-be dictator. He was further accused of consorting with traitors and preparing to march his army on Washington to reestablish slavery. To quash Sherman, the Committee on the Conduct of the War ordered him to appear for questioning.

Sherman defiantly defended his agreement with Johnston. He called Stanton a "two-faced scoundrel" and bitterly exclaimed, "Had President Lincoln lived, I know he would have sustained me."

The Radicals put their own spin on the testimony. "One motive for his treaty . . was the hope of reaching the presidency," wrote Sen. Jacob Howard to Stanton, "[and] to make himself the savior of the South and the restorer of peace [in order to] ensure him their votes."

NATIONAL ARCHIVES

Gen. William T. Sherman was fiercely denounced by Stanton for negotiating political questions with Gen. Joseph E. Johnston. Stanton and the Radicals then launched a smear attack to destroy Sherman.

Andrew Johnson failed to use his power and influence as the president to persuade white Southerners that amnesty for rebellion required fairness for former slaves.

Afraid that Sherman's criticisms might damage Stanton's image, the Committee on the Conduct of the War asked Grant and George Gordon Meade to evaluate Stanton. Grant said that his work had been admirable, and Meade commented that he had shown "great ability."

Johnston finally surrendered on April 26 under less generous terms than those originally offered, but Sherman never forgave Stanton or the Radicals. The controversy confirmed Sherman's contempt for devious and dangerous politicians. Years later while responding to efforts to draw him into the presidential race in 1884, Sherman stated: "If nominated, I will not accept. If elected, I will not serve." He did succeed Grant as general in chief of the army in 1869 and is regarded by some military historians as the greatest Union commander of the war.

Johnson's problems with the Radical Republicans began while Congress was out of session during the first eight months of his term. A staunch believer in the Jeffersonian doctrine of states' rights, Johnson took the initiative. Believing with Lincoln that reconstruction was the business of the president rather than Congress, Johnson chose to reestablish state governments in the South as quickly as possible. He did so by permitting former Confederate politicians to continue in power. They were required to frame new state constitutions abolishing slavery, but they were allowed to decide for themselves how to cope with emancipation. Naturally, they were not about to recognize African American rights of citizenship. Their solution was to set up "black codes"—laws that essentially maintained discrimination and slavery under another name and made a mockery of the Emancipation Proclamation and the Thirteenth Amendment, which had abolished slavery. Mississippi and South Carolina, for example, ruled that the labor of unemployed blacks over the age of eighteen should be sold at auction by the sheriff, and Florida provided for whipping posts and pillories as punishments for blacks.

When Congress convened in December 1865, the Republican majority opposed Johnson's actions and set out to undo the damage. The Radicals demanded certain safeguards before restoring full recognition to the South. Furthermore, Congress refused to seat *any* senator or representative from the old Confederacy, regarding them as intent on keeping blacks "in their place." The Radicals bitterly hated slavery, and they despised its political representatives who had dominated Congress in the 1850s. If Radical leader Thaddeus Stevens had had his way, the South would have been "laid waste and made a desert, and repeopled by a band of free Negroes."

To guarantee the rights of former slaves, Congress passed legislation continuing and extending the Freedmen's Bureau, thus providing military protection for African Americans, and a civil rights bill establishing blacks as American citizens and decreeing equal status in law for blacks and whites. This latter bill gave African Americans the right to acquire and hold property, make contracts, teach, preach, and testify in court. It made anyone who deprived any citizen of equal rights in law subject to punishment by the federal courts. The bills were sponsored by moderate Republicans seeking party harmony and deliberately avoided the subject of suffrage. They believed that the party could stand on the accomplishments in these bills and allow suffrage to come in due time.

Republicans expected Johnson to accept the compromise and sign the bills. They were wrong.

Johnson vetoed both measures as unconstitutional, charging that they encroached on powers rightfully belonging to the states. He publicly denounced Thaddeus Stevens and Sen. Charles Sumner as "traitors" and even accused his political enemies of plotting his assassination.

Johnson's actions drove the moderate Republicans into the camp of the Radicals, and for the first time in American history, Congress overrode the president's veto of a major piece of legislation—the civil rights bill. Later Congress submitted to the states the Fourteenth Amendment, which specified that "all persons born or naturalized in the United States . . . are citizens," and no state shall "deprive any person of life, liberty, or property without due process of law." That was followed by the Fifteenth Amendment, which extended suffrage to formerly enslaved male African Americans.

Republicans supported voting rights for blacks, in part, because blacks were critical to their power base in the South. Thus Congress made ratification of the Fifteenth Amendment a condition for readmittance of the seceded states to the Union.

Johnson regarded these bills as too harsh on the South and unduly interfering with the president's authority. Fighting back, he tacitly encouraged Southern opposition to congressional laws and campaigned vigorously in the 1866 congressional elections for congressmen who would support his policies. His plan backfired. His campaign style—attacking Republican opponents in vile and abusive language—cost his candidates about a million Northern votes and assured Republican victories. Nor did Johnson help his cause by appearing intoxicated on several occasions.

Congress, recharged by popular support, continued to whack away at Johnson's policies in 1867. Legislation removed the state governments Johnson had created and replaced them with military control, which was to continue until new governments based on equal civil and political rights were established.

Johnson fumed. He supported Southern resistance and, asserting his power as commander in chief, tried to block the military from enforcing laws protecting the rights of blacks.

Johnson's belligerent temperament, as well as his attempts to gain control of the army, alienated Stanton and led to a political feud between the two men. Johnson saw Stanton as seeking personal dictatorial power over the conquered South through the imposition of military control. Stanton had consistently argued that reorganization of the seceded states should be under federal authority, "that the conqueror and not the conquered should control the states," and that "to bring to life dead legislatures would bring endless trouble to the Government and to reconstruction."

Johnson and Stanton also were caught up in the controversy over the hanging of Mary Surratt. Stanton was plagued with revived talk of his alleged duplicity in hiding from Johnson the clemency petition to spare her life—the petition Johnson claimed he never saw. As was noted in chapter 13, the president blamed both Stanton and Holt for not calling the petition to his attention. Meanwhile, the feud between the two came to a boiling point, and Stanton's foes urged Johnson to fire him.

In the meantime, the Radicals sided with Stanton and jointly turned their vengeance upon Johnson. They decided to crush him and to oust him from office at any price and as soon as possible.

Early in 1867 Congress had passed the Tenure of Office Act over Johnson's veto. The act stripped the president of the power to remove federal officials without the Senate's approval. A law of dubious constitutionality, it was regarded by many historians as a vicious partisan effort to subvert constitutional guidelines on the separation of powers. The Radicals pushed through the act to protect Stanton's job and the jobs of others who supported their proposals and to punish Johnson and usurp his authority. Stanton was still a valuable commodity for the Radicals. They expected to run him for the presidency in 1868 and did not want any blots on his record.

On the steamy Monday morning of August 5, 1867, Johnson defied the Congress and demanded Stanton's immediate resignation. Stanton refused because he knew the Radicals in the Congress would support him. Such defiance galled Johnson, and one week later he suspended Stanton and appointed Grant in his place.

When the irate Senate reconvened in January, the Radicals ridiculed and attacked Johnson relentlessly and opposed Stanton's dismissal, calling it illegal, a violation of the Tenure of Office Act. Grant vacated the office, and Stanton returned but refused to attend cabinet meetings or associate with Johnson's colleagues. Outwardly cool, Stanton inwardly suffered severe emotional stress. He had an uncertain future; he was losing a lifelong battle with asthma; and he had lost his private fortune. Yet while eager to leave his irksome cabinet situation, he distrusted Grant's motives and feared the general might become a tool of Johnson.

If Stanton was unsure of his future, Johnson was more determined than ever to decide it for him and let the courts rule on the constitutionality of the Tenure of Office Act. He fired Stanton. To force the issue, Stanton—the great, brainy bulldog—refused to vacate his office.

Popular opinion was not in Johnson's favor. He had failed to explain adequately or defend his position and appeared to the public to have acted dictatorially. The Radical Republicans were now in a position to smash their despised foe. In a political power play in 1868, they moved to impeach the president for "high crimes and misdemeanors," the Constitution's mandated requirement for removing a president.

Thaddeus Stevens, the extreme Radical who ran the Republican machine in the House of Representatives, asserted: "Let me see the recreant who would vote to let such a criminal escape. Point me to one who will dare do it and I will show you one who will dare the infamy of posterity." With all

Republicans voting in the affirmative, Johnson was impeached by the House then brought to trial in the Senate.

The proceedings lasted three months. A two-thirds vote was needed to dismiss him from office. So sure were the Radicals of victory that the next person in line for the presidency, the president pro tempore of the Senate, Benjamin F. Wade, had already selected his cabinet. His secretary of state was to be Benjamin F. Butler, the chief prosecutor for the House Radicals. During the war he had been known as "Beast Butler" and described as the "vilest of scum" for his harsh policies and alleged looting for personal gain.

John F. Kennedy noted in his *Profiles in Courage* "the impatient Republicans did not intend to give the President a fair trial . . . but intended instead to depose him from the White House on any grounds, real or imagined, for refusing to accept their policies." The Senate vote on removing the president was expected to be close—so close that each vote was critical. Thirty-six votes were needed to convict. Only one vote was in doubt, and that vote would determine the outcome.

Astoundingly, it was the vote of Radical Republican Edmund G. Ross, who refused to disclose his position. Ross was a freshman senator from Kansas, appointed by the state legislature after the suicide of his predecessor, James H. Lane. He was expected to vote in line with the Radical agenda, which he regularly did. Ross did not like Johnson. He considered Stanton's removal to be unlawful. But after Ross told another senator that Johnson "shall have as fair a trial as any accused man ever had on earth," the word went out that "Ross was shaky." He was badgered by his colleagues and subjected to every imaginable form of pressure and abuse, from bribery to threats of political ostracism and assassination. A man not easily intimidated, Ross had had two horses shot out from under him while repelling an invasion of Fort Leavenworth by a Confederate army in 1864.

Among the leaders of the anti-Johnson movement were Mary Lincoln's friend Charles Sumner and Stanton. The war secretary issued threats from his barricaded headquarters and used his military contacts to lobby senators and to spy on Johnson's supporters. Attempts were even made to browbeat Secretary of State Seward to force him to withdraw his support for Johnson. Seward, who had written many of Johnson's veto messages, exploded: "I'll see you damned first; the impeachment of the president is the impeachment of his cabinet!"

Ten minutes before the vote was taken, Ross's Kansas colleague warned him that if he voted for acquittal, he would face trumped-up charges and his own political death. As the voting proceeded, it became clear that Ross's vote would determine the outcome. When his name was called, the room turned eerily quiet to wait for his response. He voted not guilty. The Senate failed to convict by that one vote.

Johnson's presidency was surprisingly saved on May 16, 1868, by a Republican from an anti-Johnson state. A Kansas Supreme Court justice wired Ross: "The rope with which Judas Iscariot hanged himself is lost, but [a] pistol is at your service." Ross's fellow Kansas senator, Samuel Pomeroy, who headed the Radical Republican impeachment caucus, found someone to falsely testify before a House committee that Ross had accepted a bribe to alter his vote. The same witness also testified that Pomeroy had offered to produce three acquittal votes for forty thousand dollars. A later investigation uncovered a letter from a senator willing to sell his vote to Johnson's supporters. That letter bore Pomeroy's signature.

Those who threatened Ross later gained their revenge by helping to defeat him for reelection. When Ross returned to Kansas in 1871, he and his family suffered social banishment and physical attacks. He became a Democrat, ran unsuccessfully for governor, then went to New Mexico, where President Grover Cleveland appointed him territorial governor. Twenty years after the impeachment trial, Congress repealed the Tenure of Office Act, and later the Supreme Court held the act itself to have been unconstitutional.

Failing by one vote to evict Johnson from the presidency, Sumner, Stanton, Stevens, and their fellow Radicals were outraged. Stevens, too feeble to

Edmund G. Ross of Kansas held the swing vote in the Senate trial to oust Johnson from office. He was subjected to every imaginable form of pressure and abuse.

Vinnie Ream, a young sculptor working on Lincoln's statue for the U. S. Capitol, was believed by Radical Republicans to have had enormous influence on Senator Ross's swing vote in the impeachment trial. A delegation of Radical Republicans visited Vinnie Ream's studio to attempt to persuade her to use her influence to secure Senator Ross's vote to remove Johnson from office.

LIBRARY OF CONGRESS

walk without help, was carried out of the Senate as he shouted, "This country is going to the devil!"

Hungry for vengeance, Representative Benjamin F. Butler, speaking for the House impeachment managers, soon charged that twenty-year-old Vinnie Ream had used her feminine charms to persuade the handsome forty-one-year-old Ross to support Johnson. Ross, seething with anger, blasted Butler from the floor of the Senate on July 27, 1868, charging that Butler was trying to make him "a scapegoat for the egregious blunders, weaknesses and hates which have characterized this whole impeachment movement; itself a stupendous blunder from its inception to the present time." Butler, he asserted, was "a shrewd and unscrupulous criminal lawyer of the most degraded and remorseless type [who] has added the sobriquet of 'persecutor of women' to his many laurels in the various grades of infamy."

Attractive Vinnie Ream was a sculptor who had created a bust of Lincoln when she was only seventeen years old. During the last year of his life, the president had given her periodic half-hour daily sittings for five months. She recalled later that she was "still under the spell of his kind eyes and genial presence" at the time he was assassinated.

At age nineteen she competed for a ten-thousand-dollar congressional commission to do a life-size marble statue of Lincoln for the Capitol. With the support of Johnson, cabinet members, and 141 current and former members of Congress, she was selected, winning over several distinguished male sculptors. She became the first woman and the youngest artist ever awarded a federal grant for a statue. The commission was a major career

LIBRARY OF CONGRESS

On the night before the trial, the Radical Republicans dispatched Gen. Daniel E. Sickles to the Ream family home, where Ross boarded. Sickles badgered Vinnie Ream from midnight to 4 A.M., while waiting to see Ross. But Ross refused to talk to him.

boost for this petite young lady, but she had already made her mark on Washington by sculpting numerous VIPs and through her work as a creative writer and a volunteer. She composed poetry and music, sang at concerts in military hospitals, helped wounded soldiers write letters, and did charity work for the blind.

All that aside, the angry Radicals of the House and Senate targeted this kind, compassionate young genius. They defiled her name, called her a coquettish and conniving wench, and branded her a "female lobbyist," a nasty bit of innuendo directed at women whose favors politicians sometimes traded among themselves. The House of Representatives even voted to evict her from her basement studio in the Capitol, where she had worked for two years on the Lincoln statue. The *New York World* took up her cause and wrote about the eviction campaign under the headline, "How Beaten Impeachers Make War On Women."

Johnson's supporters before and during the impeachment trial had held secret meetings in Ream's studio, where she served them tea, but her studio was also a gathering place for friend and foe with a common interest in her work on the statue. Ream recalled that at times "old feuds were forgotten, and they met on neutral ground." Biographer Glenn V. Sherwood commented, "Vinnie's presence and the spirit of Lincoln may have been enough to radically change American history."

The Radicals apparently based their presumption that Ream had influenced Ross on two facts: Ross was a boarder in the Ream family home, and the families had known each other in Kansas, where Ream's father was a

Vinnie Ream's statue of Abraham Lincoln stands in the Capitol rotunda.

ARCHITECT OF THE U.S. CAPITOL

surveyor before taking a government job in Washington. An 1869 issue of *Atlantic Monthly* reflected what the Radicals believed, noting "the assured, lively manner in which she holds a circle of men in conversation" and describing her as "one of those graceful, animated, bright-eyed, picturesque, undaunted, twinkling little women who can make men say YES to anything they ask."

Could this twenty-year-old artist affect the vote of a forty-one-year-old senator? The Radicals never doubted that she did.

For leverage, the Radicals sent Representative George W. Julian and others to Ream's studio to suggest that she exert her influence to secure Ross's vote for conviction. Furious at their intrusion, the sculptor went home distressed and anxious.

On the night before the vote, the Radicals dispatched Gen. Daniel E. Sickles to the Ream home to find out how Ross was going to vote. A devious character who courted notoriety, Sickles had ten years before been defended by Stanton on a murder charge for killing the dashing son of Francis Scott Key who had been having an affair with Sickles's wife. Stanton got him acquitted, using the first-ever temporary insanity defense. As a Union general at Gettysburg, Sickles had advanced his unit without authorization and lost half his men and his own leg. After the war he bitterly turned against Johnson for relieving him of command as a military governor in the Carolinas and was determined to retaliate by ruining Johnson's political career. Because Sickles had a reputation as a ladies' man, the Radicals hoped he might charm Vinnie Ream into allowing him to see Ross.

Sickles arrived at the Ream home after midnight. He observed lights in the front parlor and Ross's upstairs bedroom and knocked on the front door. Vinnie Ream answered it, and Sickles asked for the senator. She recognized Sickles and told him that Ross was out. The general said he would wait. When she did not invite him to enter, he pushed his way in.

"You know what I came here for," he said. "I came to save Ross. You can help me." He sat in the parlor and talked endlessly about Johnson's "crimes" and Ross's political suicide if he voted for acquittal. Ream said little. He asked her to sing. She tried to comply but burst into tears and ran from the piano.

At 4 A.M. she asked Sickles if he would leave, but he still demanded to see Ross. "No," she replied, "it would do no good." Sickles then asked if she knew if he had decided to vote for acquittal. Ream answered that Ross would support the president. As Sickles prepared to leave, he turned to her and said, "He is in your power, and you choose to destroy him." From the street, Sickles turned and looked back at the house. The light was still on in Ross's bedroom.

Ream eventually was allowed to return to her studio in the Capitol thanks to an unlikely defender—Thaddeus Stevens, who had led the fight in the House to impeach Johnson. Just before his death in August 1868, he convinced his fellow congressmen that it was the right thing to do.

During her lifetime Ream sculpted more than a hundred pieces, including a freestanding statue of Sequoya for Statuary Hall at the Capitol and the first major monument to a U.S. naval officer (Adm. David G. Farragut) to be built in Washington, D.C. Her legacy also includes several speeches. In a 1909 address to the International Council of Women, she stated that "women have at last burst their bonds," noting that women could have both a family life and professional careers—an idea much ahead of its time.

Vinnie Ream received numerous marriage proposals by mail, including one from the Mormon leader, Brigham Young. Lawyer Albert Pike showered her with poems and love letters for ten years and even conferred upon her several degrees in the Masonic order. At age thirty, Ream married Richard Hoxie, chief of the Corps of Engineers, and they had one son. She died in 1914 at age sixty-seven and was buried, along with her husband, in Arlington National Cemetery. The town of Vinita, Oklahoma, was named in her honor.

What then of Andrew Johnson, whose presidency Vinnie Ream apparently helped to save? He completed the rest of his term quietly, having ceased to interfere with the Congress in its reconstruction plans for the

South, and did not run for reelection. As a Southerner, he should have used his power and influence to convince white Southerners that amnesty for rebellion required fairness for black Southerners. Instead, he led them down a different path, requiring only the abolition of slavery. His racist views and his miscalculation of public support for his policies made it impossible for him to build a satisfying and just peace. He probably did more to extend national strife than to end it, having failed to act properly on Lincoln's words, "to bind up the nation's wounds [and] to do all which may achieve a lasting peace, among ourselves, and with all nations."

The American electorate changed dramatically with the ratification of the Fourteenth and Fifteenth Amendments. These laws not only extended citizenship and suffrage to African Americans but also denied the elective offices of senator or representative in Congress to anyone who engaged in insurrection or rebellion against the United States. Hundreds of black delegates participated in state constitutional conventions, and from 1869 until 1876 fourteen blacks served in the U.S. House of Representatives and two in the U.S. Senate. Such results were against Johnson's wishes, but the situation would change as the Old South rose again and white Southerners, with assistance from terrorist groups such as the Ku Klux Klan, found ways to reign supreme.

In his final weeks in office, Johnson did clean up some dirty business. In February 1869 he secretly ordered Booth's remains removed from its burial place at the penitentiary and delivered to the assassin's family for interment in the family plot at Green Mount Cemetery in Baltimore. Also in February he notified Frances Mudd to come to the White House to receive her husband's pardon. At the White House he personally put the papers in her hand and told her to guard them carefully "as they may be put away in some pigeon hole or corner." Then he added: "You think this is tardy justice in carrying out my promise made to you two years ago. The situation was such, however, that I could not act as I wanted to do." A few days later he pardoned conspirators Samuel Arnold and Edman Spangler.

At the end of his term Johnson went back home to Tennessee. He immediately sought to revive his political career but lost U.S. Senate and congressional bids in 1869 and 1872, respectively. In March 1875 he was finally elected to the Senate. Four months later he died of a stroke. He was sixty-six.

17

THE DETECTIVE
AND
THE DIARY

OF ALL THE MYSTERIOUS and devious characters associated with the events surrounding the assassination of Abraham Lincoln, none played his role better than Lafayette C. "Lafe" Baker. During the war, he commanded Stanton's National Detective Police, a large, undercover, anti-subversive organization.

Baker looked like a spy: grizzly face, thick red beard, and riveting eyes. A man of powerful physique, he was skillful and fearless, resourceful and intelligent, high strung and aggressive. Succinctly, his job was to root out disloyalty and corruption within the Union ranks. If he did his job well, Stanton told him, he would become one of the most hated men in the Union. The vicious epithets spoken and written about him should have earned him a superb job evaluation. Whenever Stanton needed quick action, he turned to Baker. No matter how influential his quarry, Baker never flinched.

Lafe Baker's early childhood offered little indication of what he would become. He was a sickly boy plagued with encephalitis and epilepsy while growing up on a farm in western New York. He feared his father, who disciplined him with a horsewhip. At age seventeen Lafe sprouted the courage for which he was later known. Pointing a hunting rifle at his father one day, he said, "I've got a temper, Pa, and I wouldn't want anything bad to happen to you if you touched me with that whip." His father dropped the whip and left the room. Less than a year later, Lafe left home for good.

While working in Philadelphia as a tinner and mechanic in 1852 he met and married Jane Curry. A short time later Baker moved to San Francisco and worked for one of his wife's relatives, owner of the House of Curry, a major dealer for gun manufacturer Henry Derringer. While in California, Baker gained notoriety as part of the Vigilance Command that cleaned up the crime-ridden city—a place where five hundred murders had been committed the preceding year and only five killers had been brought to justice. Baker and the vigilantes shadowed crooked politicians and broke up gangs of murderers, burglars, and thieves. Within four years, the city was civilized. Then, in 1860, when fake Derringer firearms flooded the market, Baker found the counterfeiters and traced shipments of their muskets to militia units in the South.

Returning to the East Coast to investigate, he was in Washington a few days after Fort Sumter was fired upon. He registered at Willard's Hotel in hopes of meeting Gen. Winfield Scott, the army's general in chief. Proprietor Joe Willard was so awed by the lean, muscular, self-assured young man that he put him in contact with Congressman William Kelly, a close friend of General Scott. Kelly then arranged a meeting with Scott, and Baker offered his services as a secret agent. With Union forces having occupied Arlington Heights and Alexandria, Virginia, and with newspapers and congressmen demanding, "On to Richmond," Scott desperately needed information about the strength and disposition of Confederate forces, especially at nearby Manassas and at Richmond. He assigned these tasks to Baker, and Baker headed into Virginia one week before the army was to march on Manassas.

Although disguised as an itinerant war photographer, Baker was arrested several times by friendly and enemy forces. In Manassas he bribed Confederate soldiers with twenty-dollar gold pieces for tours of encampments and information about entrenchments and troops. In Richmond, Baker claimed that Jefferson Davis interrogated him three times and released him after being convinced he was a Confederate. Having bluffed his way out of Richmond, Baker made it to Fredericksburg before being arrested again. Fearing execution, he broke two loose bars in his cell with a small knife hidden in his shoe.

When Baker finally reached Washington, the battle of First Bull Run was long over. If Baker had skipped his trip to Richmond and returned to Washington from Manassas, he might have helped the Union avoid its dev-

Lafayette C. Baker: Was he a "miserable wretch" or "one of the most remarkable men in his vocation"? As head of Stanton's spy organization, he had few friends and many enemies.

astating defeat at Bull Run. Regardless, Scott was sufficiently impressed to place Baker in charge of the army's intelligence service.

Edwin M. Stanton then recruited Baker to head his spy organization, the National Detective Police. At its center were the soon-to-be feared plainclothes detectives who wore black vested suits and usually made arrests without warrants since they operated outside the judicial system. Baker hired men who excelled at deception, disguise, and double-dealing. He also hired thieves, he said, because of their ability to catch others of their kind.

One example was Confederate smuggler Samuel Eakin, who had been arrested in Philadelphia. Baker assigned him to Baltimore to watch the movements of anyone aiding the Confederacy. Defending these qualifications, Baker wrote:

> It may be said that deception and misstatements . . . are demoralizing and corrupting. But . . . in war no commander fails to deceive the enemy whenever possible, to secure . . . advantage. Spies, scouts, intercepted correspondence, feints in army movements, misrepresentations of military strength and position are regarded as honorable means of winning victories over the foe. A detective's work is simply deception reduced to a science or profession. . . . War is a last and terrible resort in the defense of even a righteous cause and sets at defiance all the ordinary laws and customs of society. . . . And not until the nation learns war no more, will the work of deception and waste of morals, men, and treasure, cease.

Other divisions of Baker's organization included a cavalry unit; operatives such as maids, bartenders, and prostitutes; and couriers who secretly

visited the operatives to obtain information. Baker's office manager was Earl
Potter, an antisecessionist from North Carolina. Earl's younger brother
Andrew was in charge of the operatives. Many details of the operation
remained secret. Baker seldom used vouchers, paying almost always in
cash. The identities of his operatives were never made public.

One of Baker's first assignments was to hunt out subversives in southern Maryland. It was an area where nearly everyone was a Southern sympathizer. Baker discovered the secret postal service used by Confederates in
the North to move mail and dispatches to and from Richmond. He arrested
Thomas A. Jones for ferrying fugitives across the Potomac to Virginia and
incarcerated him in the Old Capitol Prison in Washington for six months.
Jones, whose main function was operating a Confederate signal station, was
the man who later assisted Booth and Herold while they hid in the woods
for six days after Lincoln's assassination.

Baker and Stanton kept the Old Capitol Prison full to overflowing with
some thirty-four thousand prisoners arrested for suspected acts against the
Union or statements of disloyalty. Baker's arrests included several Marylanders—men and women—for trading quinine to the Confederates. More valuable than gold to the South, quinine was badly needed as an antidote to fever.

Unknown to Baker, a number of people he arrested turned out to be
relatives of Postmaster General Montgomery Blair, a politically powerful
Marylander who had a reputation for burying his unlucky opponents. Blair
blasted Stanton in a cabinet meeting for allowing the arrests to occur, but
Stanton answered that nearly all postmasters in southern Maryland received
contraband letters and forwarded them to Richmond. Blair could not do
much about that. Stanton persisted, however, and further inflamed the situation by suggesting that each cabinet officer should be held responsible for
the loyalty and conduct of his employees and appointees. Stanton finally
acquiesced, probably with a nudge from Lincoln, and shortly ordered Blair's
relatives released. Stanton, however, kept their horses and wagons and 450
ounces of quinine. When Blair demanded restitution, Stanton refused. Blair
then asked Lincoln to dismiss Lafayette C. Baker. Lincoln advised Stanton
of the demand. Stanton ignored it, saying, "Mr. Blair's dismissal would be
more beneficial to the country than that of Colonel Baker."

Stanton gave Baker considerable leeway. Look for frauds, Stanton
advised, pursue crooks and traitors; capture spies; track down deserters;
unmask Union officers who misuse funds, rations, or equipment; and
punish anyone guilty of treasonable, corrupt, or dishonest acts. Baker later

wrote in his memoirs: "The true cause of the North's shortcomings was its inherent and almost universal corruption. Crooks, schemers, sharpers, dishonest businessmen saw in the war an opportunity to make a quick fortune. The army needed a thousand things, from horses to skillets, uniforms to food, and it needed them not tomorrow, but today. These men provided what the army needed and got away with ten—sometimes a hundred—times what it was worth."

In the ensuing months, Baker relentlessly performed his duties. He captured the notorious Confederate spy Belle Boyd. He arrested contractors who bribed government clerks to favor purchase of their wares or to make false entries for their mutual profit. He attempted to civilize the Union occupation of Manassas where soldiers were looting residents, insulting women, and carrying off chickens, turkeys, and pigs. He seized all liquor not properly conveyed to the army after concluding that important battles had been lost because soldiers had been half-drunk or worse. He shut down all gambling houses in Washington when he discovered that nine out of ten paymasters whose courts-martial were pending had lost government funds in the gambling halls. He intercepted blockade-runners taking shipments of guns and drugs from Baltimore to Richmond. He uncovered clerks in the Treasury Department who absconded at quitting time with sheets of uncut currency rolled up inside their stovepipe hats. He exposed bribes paid to Union officers in Norfolk, Virginia, to ignore the lucrative traffic in illegal cotton shipped north in exchange for supplies for the Confederacy.

In a series of sensational raids Baker squashed the schemes of New York City bounty brokers who bribed recruiting-office clerks to sell them forged enlistment papers, which the brokers used to collect money in payment for men they said they recruited. He rounded up bounty jumpers—men who collected their bounties for enlisting then promptly disappeared until they claimed more bounties elsewhere with forged papers.

Baker also was instrumental in foiling the grand conspiracy of Confederates in Canada to use well-trained saboteurs and Copperheads (radical antiwar Democrats) to burn Chicago and free Confederate prisoners there.

In all these accomplishments, Baker stepped on toes and made many enemies among the high and mighty, especially those whose colleagues wound up in the Old Capitol Prison. Nevertheless, Baker's record was impressive. *Leslie's Illustrated Newspaper* called Baker "one of the most remarkable men in his vocation. . . . [He] takes his place in our gallery, among other celebrities of history."

The unpopular draft induced local governments to offer generous bounties for volunteers. Bounty brokers illegally obtained forged enlistment papers to collect money for men they said they recruited. Baker squashed their scheme in a series of sensational raids in New York City.

Baker's critics—and there were many of them—claimed he was an ever-lurking evil shadow over the administration. They said he jailed those who refused to share their gains with him. A congressional committee described him as "a miserable wretch." The military disliked him because he constantly looked over the commanders' shoulders and exposed their faults. Generals accused him of unlawfully confiscating their private wines and liquors. In the Treasury Department, where Baker apparently had exposed a mountain of graft, Register of the Treasury Lucius E. Chittenden pictured Baker as "cruel and rapacious." He asserted, "Protected against interference from the judicial authorities, Baker became a law unto himself." Chittenden said Baker had "an abundance of money" and "always lived in the finest hotels," such as Willard's in Washington. Actually, Baker's suite at Willard's was retained by his wife, whose trust fund paid her about five thousand dollars a year.

Yet Baker had a well-earned reputation for telling a story to his own advantage. He often said that he was a trusted operative of the president and had conferred with him many times at Lincoln's request. No record, however, exists of any communication between Lincoln and Baker. Still, they might have conferred at the War Department, which Lincoln visited almost daily. Navy Secretary Gideon Welles was among those who despised Baker. He regarded him as "wholly unreliable . . . and zealous to do something sensational."

At the time of the Lincoln assassination, Baker was in New York. Stanton summoned him immediately back to Washington.

Baker, then thirty-nine, reached Washington on April 16. When he entered Stanton's office, he recalled that the war secretary said: "Well, Baker, they have now performed what they have long threatened to do; they have killed the president. . . . You must go to work. My whole dependence is upon you." Stanton implied rather strongly that he was aware of Booth's threats against Lincoln. If true, he had not done much about them.

As noted in previous chapters, Baker's force to pursue Booth was headed by his cousin, Luther B. Baker, and by Everton J. Conger. Before sending out the search party, Lafayette Baker spread out a map of Virginia and pinpointed Port Conway as the likely place the assassins would cross the Rappahannock and the site where they would land. Then, with his compass, he placed one point at Port Conway and drew a circle around it. He said that they should find the fugitives within that area, and events proved him to be right. As Luther Baker and Conger prepared to leave, Lafe Baker told his cousin: "You are going after Booth [and] we have got a sure thing." This force eventually cornered Booth and Herold in the shed on the Garrett farm near Port Royal, Virginia, where Booth was killed and Herold taken prisoner.

Baker, for organizing the pursuit of the conspirators, was awarded $3,750, a meager amount compared with the $15,000 given to Conger. Baker resented his treatment. Stanton privately made him a brigadier general, but told him he could not make it public because his enemies in Congress would never confirm it.

At the Garrett farm, one item supposedly removed from Booth's body was an 1864 appointment book he used as a diary. It was a small red book, about six by three and a half inches. Conger took the diary and other items to Washington and placed it in the hands of Lafayette Baker, who gave the diary to Stanton, reportedly on April 27. Then the diary disappeared.

The diary was withheld as evidence in the trial of the conspirators and was not seen again until Baker revealed its existence in a book on the Secret Service two years later. The revelation created a sensation and eventually tarnished the reputations of Stanton and Judge Advocate General Joseph

Holt. Initially, the news embarrassed Stanton and forced him to produce the diary, which had been stored in a "forgotten" War Department file.

Congress instructed its House Judiciary Committee to investigate the matter, and the committee called Lafayette Baker to testify. When he was shown the diary, Baker expressed surprise and set off another bombshell. He claimed that someone had removed eighteen pages. "Who spoliated that book?" asked Representative Benjamin F. Butler of Massachusetts, gesturing toward the White House. "Who suppressed that evidence?"

The committee then interviewed Stanton, but he denied removing the pages. Under oath, Baker responded to the committee's questions about the state of the diary when he gave it to Stanton:

> Q: Do you mean to say at the time you gave the book to the Secretary of War there were no leaves gone?
>
> A: I do.
>
> Q: That is still your opinion?
>
> A: That is still my opinion.
>
> Q: Did you examine it pretty carefully?
>
> A: I examined the book, and I am very sure that if any leaves had been gone I should have noticed it.
>
> Q: Did you examine it carefully?
>
> A: It did not require careful examination to discover the absence of so many leaves.

Except for Lafayette Baker, all others who had seen the diary testified that the pages were missing when Stanton received it. All of them, however, were connected to the War Department: Baker's cousin Luther; Assistant Secretary of War Thomas T. Eckert, who never disagreed with Stanton; and Judge Advocate General Holt. Conger, one of Lafayette Baker's trusted subordinates, swore that Baker had not examined the book, which seems highly unlikely for a professional detective.

Historians differ on who lied. As the former chief of the National Detective Police and the man Stanton chose above all others to organize the chase, Lafayette Baker obviously was highly respected by his superiors—at least until Booth was killed. After that he was widely condemned as a greedy liar and possibly as someone involved in the assassination.

It is difficult to separate truth from fiction in this "missing pages" mystery. Even the number of missing pages is disputed. Historian Thomas Reed Turner estimated the number at thirty-six, not eighteen. Two of the pages supposedly were torn out by Booth himself to write a sarcastic message to Richard H. Stuart on April 24. Some writers speculated that the other missing pages either revealed the identities of government officials and financial contributors who assisted Booth or named several prominent officials whose socializing with Booth would prove politically embarrassing. Others believed the pages may have contained evidence of collusion between Radical Republicans and the Confederate Secret Service. Another possibility was that the pages were meaningless, that perhaps Booth needed paper for purposes other than writing during six days in the woods. To one author who closely observed the book, however, it seemed evident to him that most of the pages were cut away at one time, either by scissors or a sharp knife.

While the missing pages aroused much public interest, the hiding of the diary from the public created a furor. The conventional wisdom was that the diary's contents had been kept secret because of the dramatic impact they would have had on the conspirators' trial. While hiding in the woods during his escape, Booth had recorded his thoughts and justifications for killing Lincoln. In one passage, he said: "The little —the very little I left behind to clear my name, the [Government] will not allow to be printed. . . . I have . . . almost a mind to return to Washington and in a measure clear my name which I feel I can do."

"How clear himself?" exclaimed Butler upon hearing Booth's words. "By disclosing his accomplices? Who were they?" Lewis Paine had told one of his jailers the detectives had not "got half of [the conspirators] yet!" Strangely, no one followed up on Paine's statement. No one offered him a deal to trade his life for naming others who were involved. Butler said if the diary had been presented in 1865, it might have been possible to learn "who it was that changed Booth's purpose from capture to assassination, who it was that could profit by assassination who could not profit by capture and abduction of the President." Butler clearly implied that the guilty party was Andrew Johnson. Yet a special congressional assassination committee, as noted previously, found no evidence against Johnson.

The meaning of Booth's statement has been debated for decades. Could he have cleared his name by naming important officials and dignitaries in Washington who supported his plot, as Butler implied? Or would Booth simply have explained his motives as the act of a patriotic Confederate?

Booth looked daily in the newspapers for "what he left behind to clear his name" without avail. Some historians believe he was referring to the letter he allegedly gave to fellow actor John Mathews to deliver to the *National Intelligencer*—the letter Mathews said he read and burned to avoid being implicated in Lincoln's murder. The diary makes no reference to Mathews, and Herold later said that Booth never mentioned Mathews to him.

Other historians believe Booth may have left a letter to be discovered among his belongings—a letter Stanton could have censored and/or destroyed. There is insufficient evidence to support either possibility.

Stanton testified that, after he examined the diary, he gave it to Maj. Thomas T. Eckert, who later delivered it to Judge Advocate General Holt, the chief prosecutor at the conspirators' trial. Stanton claimed not to have seen it since.

The Judiciary Committee then asked Holt why the diary was not introduced at the trial. "There was nothing in the diary which I could conceive would be testimony against any human being, or for anyone except Booth himself, and he being dead, I did not offer it to the Commission."

Holt's testimony paralleled that of Stanton, who testified the previous day that he had examined the diary with great care and could find no evidence identifying any other person as connected with Booth in the assassination conspiracy. There was, however, strong evidence that several persons charged in that conspiracy were involved only in the plot to capture Lincoln. What neither Holt nor Stanton admitted was that they played down the kidnapping plot so that they could falsely tie all the conspirators to murder. Their case would have fallen apart if the court had seen Booth's passage: "For six months we had worked to capture. But our cause, being almost lost, something decisive & great must be done." To achieve his desired ends, Stanton could not allow the court to see those words.

Stanton's and Holt's actions were criminal: preempting material evidence in a capital trial. Doing so meant that the court never had the opportunity to rule on the diary's admissibility. Doing so meant that Stanton and Holt concealed the knowledge that the decision to kill Lincoln was made within days of the act, not months before. Holt's statement to the judiciary committee that he did not release the diary to the court "because it contained nothing germane" established a clear conflict of interest. He appeared either oblivious to the significance of Booth's words or incapable of contriving a better excuse.

Holt obviously tried to shift the focus of the committee from Stanton, but his collaboration with Stanton on withholding the diary from the trial resulted in unjust verdicts, not the least of which were the hanging of Mary Surratt and the imprisonments of Arnold, O'Laughlin, and Spangler.

Strangely, someone had leaked the existence of the diary to the *New York Times* shortly after it had been discovered. The *Times* reported on April 28, 1865, that Booth had a diary in which he had jotted down notes related to the assassination. Since the diary presumably was removed from Booth's body on April 26, Conger, the Bakers, or someone in Stanton's office disloyal to him must have told a *Times* reporter about it. More strangely, why did the defense lawyers at the conspirators' trial not know about the item in the *Times*? They should have, and if they did, why did they not attempt to have it introduced during the trial?

Also puzzling is the mystery surrounding another diary—the 1865 diary of Congressman George W. Julian of Indiana, a Radical Republican, who, like his colleagues, was relieved that Lincoln was no longer president. Alleged notes in the Julian diary contradict Stanton's assertion that pages were missing from Booth's diary when he received it. According to Julian's notes, when he was summoned to the War Department on Monday, April 24, 1865, he found Stanton and several Radicals in an uproar. The war secretary was "pacing up and down," and Sen. Zachariah Chandler of Michigan was reading a small book with "a dour look on his face." Stanton told Julian, "We have Booth's diary, and he has recorded a lot in it."

Alleged notes in the diary of Congressman George W. Julian contradicted Stanton's claim that pages were missing from Booth's diary when he received it. Julian supposedly wrote: "Booth knew much which they are deathly fearful that he, even from the grave, will tell."

BOTH: LIBRARY OF CONGRESS

Booth's diary allegedly contained information that connected Stanton and Radical Republicans Zachariah Chandler (*left*) and John Conness (*right*) to the assassin.

Shortly afterward, Sen. John Conness of California arrived. While reading the diary, he kept mumbling, "Oh my God, Oh my God, I am ruined if this ever gets out!"

When Julian declined to read the diary since he had not met Booth, Stanton said, "It concerns you for we either stick together on this thing, or we will go down the river together."

Chandler declared, "We cannot let it out."

The others agreed. Then, wrote Julian, "Stanton placed the book in an envelope and sealed it, giving it to [Maj. Thomas Eckert] with instructions to place it in his safe and release it to no one without his order."

Four days later, according to Julian's notes, Conness stopped by Julian's office and was "mortally fearful about his association with Booth. . . . He tried to make it appear that he really did not know Booth too well when it is common knowledge in the Congress that he not only on more than one occasion shared a room with him but even his bed and his women. The man is an immoral swine and he makes me sick." Julian had a reputation for being brutally blunt, so the language of the diary entry is consistent with his style and personality.

Forty-four-year-old Conness reportedly was a "skirt chaser" who had been seen with Booth on many occasions. Conness had no known connection with Booth's plots, but he obviously would have been humiliated and

disgraced by any disclosure of Booth's writings that referred to their friendship and shared women. Their association may or may not explain the
franked envelope from Conness's office that was found in Atzerodt's room
after the assassination. For whatever reason, the popular senator did not
seek reelection, and near the end of his life was committed to an insane
asylum. When Conness left office in 1869, Mark Twain described him as
"one of the pleasantest men, socially, and one of the best hearted that exists;
and by the same token a man that has worked hard for the coast, done his
duty faithfully, and accomplished all that any man could have done." A
mountain in California was named after him.

The Julian diary includes the allegation:

> I, like so many other Radical Republicans, felt that Lincoln must be removed
> from office for he had taken it upon himself to run the country like a king,
> making decisions which should have been made by Congress, the body
> charged by the Constitution and the people to make such decisions. But I have
> the feeling that many of my colleagues know more about his removal than I
> was at first aware. I know that they were not in concert with Booth but I do
> know that Booth knew much which they are deathly fearful that he, even from
> the grave, will tell. Stanton is so nervous that he is unable to function in his
> usual deliberate manner. Chandler is so upset that he is unable to eat or sleep.

Julian did not spell out what he thought his colleagues knew about Lincoln's
death, and he failed to comment on why he thought Stanton and Chandler
were in an uproar and concerned about going "down the river together."

If Julian's notes are genuine, and if he recorded the meetings correctly,
three startling conclusions can be drawn: (1) The missing pages from
Booth's diary were in Stanton's possession, since nothing in the diary's public
version would have elicited the comments from Chandler, Conness, and
Stanton recorded by Julian; (2) Booth's diary was in the hands of detectives
before the events at the Garrett farm took place; and (3) both Stanton and
Lafayette Baker lied when they stated that Baker gave the diary to Stanton at
the war secretary's home on Thursday afternoon, April 27. Officers in the
National Detective Police would later report that the diary had been found
and returned to Washington on Sunday morning, April 23 (not Thursday,
April 27), and their statement is consistent with the information in Julian's
diary. Since Stanton regularly worked long hours at his office, it is not likely
that he was home on a Thursday afternoon—but he would have been home
on a Sunday.

If the April 23 date is correct, how did Stanton obtain the diary before Booth's apprehension and death? A possible explanation is that the diary was found at one of Booth and Herold's campsites. Another possibility is that Booth left his diary with Thomas Jones on Friday, April 21, or with John J. Hughes on April 22. Either man might have surrendered the diary to avoid prosecution. By sheltering the fugitives for six days, Jones did more than anyone to aid Booth's escape, and he was never prosecuted. Furthermore, Booth seemed to be writing for posterity; he therefore may have wanted the diary's contents revealed. Jones or Hughes would have complied with his wishes. Also, Booth's last entry in the diary is dated April 21. If he had kept the diary until April 26, would he not have added more notes during those five days? He certainly had time to do so at the Garrett farm. Yet if Booth left his diary with Jones or Hughes, where did he get the paper—if he did not rip it out of his diary—for his April 24 message to Dr. Richard Stuart? In fact, paper was not that scarce, especially in a doctor's home. Charley Lucas, who conveyed Booth and Herold to Port Conway, could also have provided the material.

The reputations of Stanton, Conness, and Chandler hinge mightily on the authenticity of Julian's notes. Excerpts from Julian's 1865 diary were published in *Lincoln Log* (March–April 1977) and freely paraphrased in David Balsiger and Charles E. Sellier's *The Lincoln Conspiracy* (1977). The book, which was the basis for a movie, is tainted because it contains material that many historians believe to be based on hoaxes. Whether or not the alleged Julian notes are an elaborate forgery has not been proven.

Balsiger and Sellier claimed to have obtained a transcript of the diary from newspaper reporter Claude G. Bowers, who wrote *The Tragic Era* (1929). Bowers had borrowed the actual diary from Julian's daughter, Grace Julian Clarke. She had told Bowers that her father meant to destroy the diary and that she felt "a little guilty in sending it forth, even for your friendly eye." Thus, when Bowers returned it to her, she allegedly burned the parts relating to the Civil War and gave the remainder to the Indiana State Library. Because Bowers, an anti-Radical, did not use any of the incriminating information in his book, and because portions of Julian's diary copied in the *Indiana Magazine of History* in 1915 contained no reference to Booth's diary, historians William Hanchett and William C. Davis concluded that the alarming quotes were fabrications.

Ray A. Neff takes the opposite position. A retired professor at Indiana State University, Neff has researched various aspects of the Lincoln assassination over the past forty years. In the introduction to the 1992 reprint of Lafayette Baker's *History of the United States Secret Service* (1867), Neff clarified the Clarke-Bowers issue with numerous observations, a summary of which follows.

Clarke loaned her father's diaries to Bowers "with the explicit understanding that certain parts not be used or disclosed to anyone," but just after Bowers received the diaries, she demanded their return. He complied after photostating them so he could study them at his convenience. When his book manuscript was finished, Bowers sent a copy to Clarke. She accused him of acting in bad faith, threatened to sue him, and insisted that he delete certain items he had included from the 1865 diary. Both Bowers and Clarke hired attorneys. In the resulting settlement, Bowers removed the objectionable material, which is why the incriminating notes were not used in his book. Clarke's attorney retained possession of the 1865 diary, apparently for safekeeping, and it was in his hands when she died. The attorney died soon after she did. In the late 1960s the building in which the attorney's office was located was demolished, and the wrecking crew discovered in a locked closet several boxes of papers, including Julian's 1865 diary and Bowers's photostats. In 1974 the diary was offered for sale. Neff was allowed to examine it and to have the photostats transcribed but not photocopied. They were copied by a notary public, who proofread and notarized the transcripts on April 4, 1974, and declared them to be the exact copy of a photostatic copy of Julian's diary. Julian's signature on the front of the diary was photographed. In June 1974 a collector from Illinois paid twenty-five hundred dollars for the original diary, and the photostatic copy was acquired by Hugh Smith of Indianapolis, who has since died. Excerpts of Neff's transcribed version were published for the first time in the introduction to the 1992 reprint of Baker's book.

Regarding the omission of the controversial material in a 1915 edition of the *Indiana Magazine of History,* Neff noted that Clarke had censored the text before delivering it. He compared his notarized text with the printed text, and in his published version he underlined what she had eliminated. It included the material quoted earlier.

All of this intrigue began because Lafayette Baker revealed the existence of Booth's diary in his book on the Secret Service and noted the missing pages during his interrogation before the House Judiciary Committee. In doing so, he drove a permanent wedge between Stanton and himself. Not one to maintain good relationships with the right people, Baker essentially ended his career when he spied on a woman who was a friend of Andrew Johnson's. This episode is yet another hard-to-believe-but-true sidebar of the Lincoln assassination.

New on the Washington scene in the postwar years were pardonbrokers. Usually these pardonbrokers were attractive, fashionably dressed women who flirted (among other things) with government officials in exchange for pardons for former Confederates. Southerners worth twenty thousand dollars or more needed official pardons to regain the right to hold public office and to reclaim seized property. To get these pardons, many Confederates employed pardonbrokers, the most successful of whom were women. They charged a high commission, but they earned it. It was soon rumored that these brokers were giving part of their fees to influential officials close to President Johnson—including his son, Robert—and that Johnson seldom refused the lady brokers who wanted to see him.

Baker, supposedly concerned about a possible scandal, decided to expose the lady brokers and terminate their access to the president. Through one of his detectives assigned to the White House, he learned that a broker, Lucy Cobb, was "at the president's office at all hours of the day and night" and that she boasted she "could get pardons from the president as easy as falling off a greased log." Cobb told detective S. S. Jones that she had an "understanding" with the president and "on a good day [made] a thousand dollars in commissions."

Baker brought in an operative to contact Cobb for a pardon, which she delivered the next day, signed by the president. She was paid six hundred dollars in marked bills. When the operative questioned the amount, Cobb claimed that she had to "pay off certain friends in the government." After the transaction, Baker hauled Cobb in for questioning. She advised him not to do anything rash, saying, "The president is a good friend of mine." Baker demanded the money she had received that morning, and she surrendered the marked bills but threatened, "Arresting me is going to cost you your job! The president is going to dismiss you. And I'm going to the grand jury and have you indicted for false arrest."

Cobb remained in custody while Baker went to the White House, briefed the president, and showed him the marked bills. He intended to charge Cobb with forging pardons, but Johnson exploded in rage. The president ordered Baker to cease interfering in the business of the White House. "Bring Mrs. Cobb to see me tomorrow evening," Johnson ordered the detective.

Baker appeared at the White House the following evening without Cobb, because he had not been able to find her after her release. Johnson again assailed him for his conduct and commended Cobb as a respectable, virtuous—and innocent—woman. Baker was determined, however, to prosecute Cobb and instructed his detective at the Executive Mansion to refuse admittance to her. Lucy Cobb, however, refused to be bullied by Baker and, being denied the front entrance, she used the backstairs to the president's office.

Johnson demanded to see Baker and gave him another tongue-lashing, this time denouncing Stanton, Baker's superior. "I know your motives," said the president, "and they aren't what you say they are; they're despicable. You and your friend Stanton want to embarrass and discredit me. Well, go tell Stanton that he isn't going to succeed!"

Reporting back to Stanton, Baker incurred another reprimand. "I can't approve of your actions," the secretary of war told him. "They amount to a serious lack of tact. . . . You should have ignored this woman's comings and goings, suspect though they might be. . . . Moreover, you have managed to bring my name into it, and in a most unpleasant way. Before it is too late you must realize that principles are principles, and politics politics."

It was too late for Baker. Johnson dismissed him as head of the National Detective Police on February 8, 1866.

Lucy Cobb followed through on her threat to charge Baker with false arrest and extortion, and he was indicted and brought to trial. With none of his friends willing to take the stand as character witnesses and newspapers excoriating him for "numberless oppressions and indignities," the jury reached a verdict after ninety minutes. They found him guilty of false arrest but not guilty of extortion. The judge, before pronouncing the sentence, said that Baker "in his zealousness to discharge his duty, may have gone a hair's-breadth too far in committing an act which could not be justified in law. Yet, from a moral point of view, it could not be said to be culpable." He sentenced Baker to "pay to the United States the sum of one dollar and the costs of the prosecution"—a total of thirty-six dollars. That night, Baker took the late train for his home in Philadelphia.

The former head of the National Detective Police did not return to Washington until January 1867 to testify before the House Judiciary Committee as part of the case to oust Johnson from office. Baker swore he had seen and could obtain correspondence between Johnson and Jefferson Davis that proved Johnson had been a Confederate spy, but he could not prove his allegations. A committee member exclaimed, "It is doubtful whether he has in any one thing told the truth, even by accident."

After Baker's appearance before the committee, he became convinced that someone was trying to murder him. Newspapers reported attempts to silence him. His wife, Jenny, wrote in her diary on January 2, 1868: "He'd been shot at just before Christmas. Splinters hit him in the shoulder. [It] is healing but he complains of soreness." Later testimony at a hearing revealed that his life had been threatened for the last seven or eight months of his life. Not only had shots been fired, but he also had been stabbed and beaten.

Baker had made numerous enemies as head of the National Detective Police, and perhaps some of them were seeking revenge. Jenny Baker's diary, however, reveals another possibility. It seemed that every time Baker's brother-in-law, Walter G. Pollock, visited him and brought German beer, Baker became ill. Pollock, it should be noted, was a detective in the War Department. Nearly a hundred years later, Ray Neff's chemical analysis of a lock of Baker's hair indicated with certainty that the detective had been exposed to toxic levels of arsenic.

On July 3, 1868, Baker was found dead at his home in Philadelphia. Officially, he died of meningitis. He was forty-two. His physician, Dr. William Rickards, testified that his symptoms were typical of arsenic poisoning, but he did not believe Baker had been poisoned because "no one had the opportunity."

In April 1868—three months before his death—Baker wrote a letter to Hiram Walbridge of New York and stated that both Stanton and Johnson were involved with the conspirators who killed Lincoln. Yet, according to Neff, Baker was apparently mentally unstable at that time from overdosing on belladonna drops to suppress frequent epileptic attacks. The detective probably also suffered from bromism, a disease caused by the long-term ingestion of bromides. Thus statements he made under these conditions should be weighed accordingly.

President Ulysses S. Grant, who succeeded Andrew Johnson in 1869, became concerned about what seemed to him to be a high mortality rate among persons who had served the federal government during the Civil War. He appointed Gen. Lew Wallace, one of the judges at the Lincoln conspirators' trial, to investigate. Wallace's report was based on a study involving hundreds of depositions and reviews of countless documents in federal and state files. Wallace found no evidence of foul play, with one exception—the death of Lafayette C. Baker. On February 7, 1877—shortly before

Gen. Lew Wallace was appointed by President Grant to investigate the high mortality rate among significant government officials who had served during the Civil War. He found only one evidence of foul play—the death of Lafayette Baker.

LIBRARY OF CONGRESS

Grant left office—Wallace sent a report to the president naming five suspects who could be indicted for Baker's murder:

1. Walter G. Pollock of Tansboro, New Jersey, Baker's brother-in-law and the War Department detective who may have slowly poisoned Baker with arsenic.

2. John McGinnis Jr. of Chicago, son-in-law of a former Illinois governor, who was one of Baker's two partners in the Henry J. Eager Company that Baker created to sell cotton to raise money for the National Detective Police.

3. Robert D. Watson* of Hickman, Kentucky, from whom conspirator John H. Surratt had received a March 19, 1865, letter stating that Watson wanted to see him on important business. The letter, found in Surratt's room after the assassination, was rushed to Baker in New York. The "important business" had nothing to do with the assassination, and Baker soon realized that. It concerned Watson's efforts to work with agents from both the North and South in Montreal to execute a contract for an exchange of pork for cotton. The transaction would have netted the Watson family millions of dollars. Baker wanted in on the deal, but he had nothing to offer Watson—

---

*Watson has been incorrectly identified in numerous books. His identity here is based on material from the Turner-Baker Papers in the National Archives. Lafayette Baker regularly received his orders from Levi C. Turner, special judge advocate in the War Department and a legal adviser to Stanton. The Turner-Baker Papers were closed to historians until the 1950s. Edwin C. Fishel, an authority in intelligence analysis with the National Security Agency, regards the Turner-Baker Papers as having "considerable value" even though they are less sensitive "than their previous cautious treatment implied."

until he had Watson's letter to Surratt in his hands. Baker sent McGinnis to see Watson and, in effect, to blackmail him. In a "deal with us or hang" arrangement, Baker's company took the contracts away from Watson for 75 percent of the deal and a promise not to arrest Watson as a conspirator.

4. Dr. Henry Megill of Owensboro, Kentucky, Watson's brother-in-law, who bought pharmaceuticals in bulk from New York and then repacked them for shipment to drugstores throughout the South. He was obviously furious with Baker for "stealing" millions from the Watson family.

5. James V. Barnes of Eaton, Indiana, about whom little is known.

Wallace's communiqué to Grant indicated that if indictments were pursued, Barnes would become the star witness for the government in exchange for immunity from prosecution. Wallace, however, recommended that no action be taken and that the report be sequestered: "The political implications are staggering to imagine. . . . Who knows what direction the testimony might take and just what previously undisclosed secrets might be dislodged by astute defense." Grant agreed, and according to Neff, the report ended up in "the inner recesses of Grant's confidential papers."

Jenny Baker remained concerned about the mystery surrounding her husband's death but took comfort from a letter she received from an army chaplain who had served with Baker:

I feel it a duty to say, first, it is scarcely possible to estimate the good he accomplished in strengthening the Union armies. Second, in weeding out the vicious and the worthless. Third, in making Copperheads, scoundrels, and traitors feel the secret war at home. I believe him to have done more during the late war to save the country than any other single man. His name carried with it a dread that made evil-doers tremble.

About certain facts your husband might have stated about men high in the Government—the half he would not tell. . . . I hope to see the truth come. Let it cut where it may!

18

STANTON'S
MANY FACES

URING THE LAST YEAR and a half of his life, Stanton was in frail health from congestive asthma, the stressful years of the Civil War, and the controversies surrounding Mary Surratt's hanging and President Johnson's impeachment trial. His unsuccessful efforts to remove Johnson left Stanton no choice but to resign as secretary of war in May 1868 and to return to a private law practice.

That fall Stanton supported U. S. Grant for president and made speeches praising him even though he was too feeble to stand through an entire address. On September 25, at his hometown of Steubenville, Ohio, Stanton declared: "General Grant stands this day before you the foremost military commander of the world, with peace for his watchword. What reason has any lover of his country for not voting for him?"

After Grant's election, Stanton's health improved and his public appearances increased. Rumors circulated that Stanton wanted and expected a major appointment from Grant. Instead, Grant dipped from the bottom of the diplomatic barrel and offered him an assignment to Mexico to deal with claims arising from wartime border problems. Appalled by what he considered ill treatment, Stanton curtly turned the offer down and immersed himself in legal cases.

Shortly after that, influential Massachusetts Sen. Charles Sumner visited Stanton. Four years later, on the floor of the Senate, Sumner recalled their conversation and quoted the former war secretary: "I know General Grant better than any other person in the country can know him. It was my duty to study him, and I did so day and night, when I saw him and when I did not see him, and now I tell you what I know, he cannot govern this country."

One of Stanton's steadfast friends, Sen. Matthew Hale Carpenter of Wisconsin, found this statement hard to believe, but asserted, "If there is a word of substantial truth in [it] then Mr. Stanton was the most double-faced and dishonest man that ever lived."

In 1869 word came to Stanton from Edwards Pierrepont, a Grant appointee and close friend, that the president had taken him aside at a dinner "and spoken several times of you with marked favor." Julia Grant also had indicated "how much was due to you and that the General had made a mistake in not giving you a place of the highest grade, and that it ought to be done now." Yet nothing was done then.

Stanton considered touring the Rocky Mountain country that summer but chose not to because he could not afford it. Instead, he and his wife, Ellen, departed on August 3 for New Hampshire, but the mountain weather turned unsuitable, and they journeyed to Boston then to Cape Cod, where they were hosted by friends.

On September 18 Stanton wrote to his mother: "I have this summer been diligently seeking health on mountains and the seashore, hoping to find some place where we could be free from asthma. But my search has been in vain and tomorrow I start home scarcely as well as when I set out." His condition deteriorated, however, with uncontrollable spasms of coughing, and he and Ellen remained at Cape Cod where he slowly recovered but remained almost invalid. He sat near a hearth, wrapped in blankets, listening to the nearby surf.

In late September he was well enough to return to Washington but so poor financially that he had to borrow money and request the return of a loan he had made to a friend years before. He commented to a political friend, Roscoe Conkling, that his health had improved significantly but he probably would "never regain my former vigorous strength." Persistent coughing was the only outward sign of a health problem.

That fall Stanton learned that a justice of the Supreme Court planned to step down. It was a position he coveted, so he asked a person Grant trusted, Methodist bishop Matthew Simpson, to intervene with the president on his

U.S. ARMY MILITARY HISTORY INSTITUTE

Edwin M. Stanton had a national reputation before the war as a shrewd attorney—he pioneered the temporary insanity defense in the murder trial of Daniel E. Sickles, later a Union general—and had served as attorney general during the Buchanan administration. Many of the wartime successes of the War Department under Stanton are attributable to his overpowering and ruthless personality.

behalf and to assure the president that the former war secretary was physically and mentally able "to manage the high judicial responsibility." Grant was almost persuaded to nominate Stanton for the position, but a wealthy Philadelphia banker, George W. Childs, dissuaded him. Years earlier Stanton had canceled a major contract Childs had with the War Department, and Childs seized this moment to retaliate.

Still there was hope for Stanton. The Supreme Court had not one vacancy but two. Moreover, Radical Republicans such as Benjamin F. Wade reassured Grant that reports of Stanton's illness were greatly exaggerated.

The first week of December Stanton was well enough to plead an important patent case before the Supreme Court, and he did so with skill and energy. Returning from the Court, he responded to a request from Grant and stopped by the White House. The president informed him that he was going to submit his name for one of the openings. Stanton was jubilant.

On Sunday, December 19—Stanton's fifty-fifth birthday—Grant and Vice President Schuyler Colfax visited Stanton to officially inform him of the submission. The Senate confirmed the nomination one hour after receiving it, by a vote of forty-six to eleven. Stanton's lifelong ambition had been fulfilled. He wanted to personally thank Grant at the White House, but his physician refused to allow him to go out on that cold, damp, and windy day. Instead, the newest Supreme Court justice penned a note of acceptance, and his wife, Ellen, delivered it.

In thanking Grant, Stanton said: "It is the only office I ever desired and I accept it with great pleasure. The appointment affords me the more pleasure coming from you, with whom for several years I have had personal and official relations such as seldom exist among men. . . . I have the honor to be truly your friend."

The next day, Stanton experienced severe coughing and was too weak to work. A group of doctors tried various medications and treatments. Rousing briefly from his affliction, he asked when the next Supreme Court session was scheduled so he might prepare for it. After midnight he had a relapse and became unconscious. A few hours later, in the early morning of December 24, 1869, he died. Before midnight, none of his doctors had any serious apprehension of immediate danger for the ill Stanton. He had had these respiratory attacks many times and recovered.

Strangely, Ellen closed their house before the funeral and admitted only family members and a few close friends. The element of secrecy spawned rumors that Stanton had committed suicide out of remorse for Mary Surratt, perhaps cutting his own throat as his brother Darwin had done. Other rumors noted that Ellen had the coffin sealed to prevent public observation of the wound. Only a day earlier Stanton had whispered to his friend, Col. William P. Wood: "The Surratt woman haunts me so that my nights are sleepless and my days miserable. . . . I cannot endure the pressure."

President Grant offered a full state ceremony with the body on display in the Capitol Rotunda. Ellen, however, declined his generosity and insisted on as much simplicity as possible.

On April 16, 1879, after the death of Stanton's wife and eldest son, surgeon general Joseph K. Barnes, who had attended Stanton at his death, responded to a letter about Stanton's rumored suicide in the *Philadelphia Press:*

> In reply to your inquiry, the late Mr. Edwin M. Stanton was for many years subject to asthma in a very severe form, and when he retired from the War Department, was completely broken down in health. In November of 1869 the "Dropsy of Cardiac Disease" manifested itself (after a very exhausting argument . . . in a legal case), and from that time he did not leave the house, rarely his bed. For many days before his death I was with him almost constantly, and at no time was he without most careful attendance by the members of his family or nurses. On the night of December 23rd the dropsical effusion into the pericardium had increased to such an extent, and the symptoms were so alarming, that the Rev. Doctor Starkey, rector of the Epiphany, was summoned and read the service appointed for such occasions; he, with Mrs. Stanton, Mr. E. L. Stanton, the three younger children, Miss Bowie, their governess, myself and several of the servants were by his bedside until he died at 4 A.M. December 24, 1869.

It is incomprehensible to me how any suspicion or report of suicide could have originated, except through sheer and intentional malice, as there was not the slightest incident before, or during, his long sickness indicative of such a tendency, nor a possibility of such an act. Fully aware of his critical condition, he was calm and composed, not wishing to die, while unterrified at the prospect of death. During the lifetime of his widow and his son, Mr. E. L. Stanton, I did not feel called upon to make any written contradiction of the infamous and malignant falsehood you allude to; but now, in view of your letter of April 14th, and in behalf of Mr. Stanton's minor children, I do most emphatically and unequivocally assert that there is not any foundation whatever for the report that Mr. Edwin Stanton died from other than natural causes, or that he attempted or committed suicide.

Was Barnes telling the truth or trying to preserve Stanton's legacy? In an 1873 speech, former President Andrew Johnson asserted that Mary Surratt had been executed by trickery and that Stanton had committed suicide out of remorse for the deed. If Johnson had any information to support his statement, he never provided it; it does not exist in his private papers.

Many secrets and unanswered questions died with Stanton. Among them:

1. Why did he refuse to honor Lincoln's request for Thomas T. Eckert to accompany him to the theater as a bodyguard?

2. Considering Stanton's history of severely punishing soldiers for neglecting their duties, why was he not interested in John F. Parker's failure to remain at his post outside the State Box at Ford's Theatre?

3. Why were Samuel Cox and Thomas Jones released after questioning since both men played major roles in Booth's escape, and yet three others— Arnold, O'Laughlin, and Spangler—who had nothing to do with the assassination were tried, convicted, and imprisoned?

4. Were at least eighteen pages of Booth's diary missing when Stanton took possession of the book, or did he remove them? Did Stanton obtain Booth's diary before or after the assassin was killed? Did the controversial pages from George W. Julian's diary accurately describe a meeting in Stanton's office with Radical Republicans during which Booth's diary was passed around? If so, what was in the diary that frightened so many of them and Stanton?

5. Why did Stanton and Joseph Holt withhold Booth's diary from the trial of the conspirators, especially since knowledge of its contents would have had a distinct affect on the trial and its outcome?

6. With the military commission apparently voting not to hang Mary Surratt, to what extent was Stanton involved in the plan to change the vote?

7. Did Stanton know if the judge advocate general discussed the clemency petition with President Johnson? If they did not discuss it, was Stanton a party to a scheme to hide the petition from Johnson?

8. Why did Stanton not pursue John H. Surratt Jr. in Europe when he had earlier targeted him as a major conspirator?

As Manton Marble wrote in a *New York World* obituary on Stanton: "All men die, and death does not change faults into virtues." In Stanton's case, it is sometimes difficult to distinguish between faults and virtues. What one person calls a fault, another might call a virtue. One thing is clear: To understand the events surrounding America's greatest murder mystery—Lincoln's assassination—one must seek to understand Stanton and his relationship with Lincoln. Was Stanton the government official most likely involved in conspiracy and betrayal, as many conspiracy theorists believe? Or was he steadfastly loyal to Lincoln and incapable of evil deeds against him, as many historians contend? Both parties can only establish reasonable doubt or reasonable likelihood. The whole truth of who conspired to kill Lincoln may never be established beyond any doubt. The cover-uppers did their work well.

Stanton was a man of iron and a man of mystery. No one questions his administrative brilliance in building and supporting the complex military machine that won the Civil War. Grant described him as "one of the great men of the Republic." Yet nearly everyone on Lincoln's cabinet disliked him. Navy Secretary Gideon Welles believed that Stanton lacked sincerity,

Robert Lincoln may have destroyed incriminating information about his father's assassination. When two friends called upon him at his summer estate in Vermont in 1923, they found him burning papers in the fireplace. One of the men, golfing partner Horace G. Young, related that Robert explained that he was destroying certain papers because they contained evidence of the treason of a member of his father's cabinet. The other visitor, Nicholas Murray Butler, president of Columbia University, understood that Robert was burning private family papers. With widespread speculation in the twentieth century that Edwin M. Stanton may have been involved in the conspiracy against Lincoln, it is worth noting that Robert Lincoln kept a large, ornately framed portrait of Stanton at his summer estate.

practiced duplicity, engaged in intrigue, and was "deep in conspiracy." As the years passed, this image of the "terrible Stanton" prevailed in the public's mind.

Author Frank A. Flower's flattering biography of Stanton included this interesting description:

> No man in American history has been so thoroughly misunderstood as Stanton. Much as he loved and trusted certain men, he really trusted no man fully. One friend or counselor was permitted to know all about this or that matter, and another all about something else; but he was completely confidential with no two persons on the same subject. Each man who knew him at all intimately knew things not known to anyone else, and thus arose the many differing views which, however, are all essential to the final picture which shall have some approach to completeness and correctness.

Even Gen. N. P. Chipman, who worked closely with Stanton and admired him, confessed that "well as I felt I knew him, yet he is a stranger to me."

Stanton had no sense of humor. He often irritated people, partly because he was abrasive and inconsiderate of the feelings of others, but also because his snap judgments were often more accurate than the careful considerations of others.

Lincoln first felt the sting of Stanton's bite in 1855 when they were on the same legal team defending the John H. Manny Company against a suit filed by Cyrus H. McCormick for patent violations. Fortunes were at stake because of the rich wheat empire of the West and the heavy demand for reapers and mowers. Stanton was rude and snobbish toward Lincoln. He wondered where "that long-armed baboon" came from and criticized his dirty linen duster whose back, he said, was splotched with perspiration like "the dirty map of the continent." According to journalist Don Piatt, Stanton declared, "If that giraffe appears in the case, I will throw up my brief and leave." Although Lincoln had prepared a written argument he planned to present to the court, the lead attorney in the case, Peter H. Watson, told him that he would not be asked to speak. Lincoln gave him his written speech, thinking his colleagues might find it useful. Without looking at it, Watson threw it into a wastebasket. As Lincoln watched from the background, the Watson-Stanton team used gross chicanery and fraud in their presentation. Nevertheless, they won the case, and the verdict was upheld in the U.S. Supreme Court.

Stanton's rise in the legal profession caught the attention of President James Buchanan, who appointed him attorney general for the last four months of his administration, which preceded that of Lincoln's. During the months between Lincoln's election and his inauguration, Stanton urged Buchanan to strengthen the U.S. Army, but Buchanan refused. In a clear case of insubordination, Stanton went around Buchanan and made the same request to the Committee on Military Affairs in the House of Representatives. The Democrats, however, backed their president and turned down Stanton's proposal, saying that if there were any real need for it, the president would request it.

After Lincoln's inauguration, Buchanan returned to Pennsylvania but asked Stanton to keep him informed. In letters to the former president, Stanton severely criticized the Lincoln administration: There is "a strong feeling of distrust in the candor and sincerity of Lincoln personally and of his Cabinet. . . . No one speaks of Lincoln or any member of his Cabinet with respect and regard."—April 11, 1861. "The dreadful disaster of Sunday [battle of First Bull Run] can scarcely be mentioned. The imbecility of this administration has culminated in that catastrophe, and irretrievable misfortune and national disgrace are to be added to the ruin of all peaceful pursuits and national bankruptcy as the result of Lincoln's 'running the machine' for five months."—July 26, 1861. In a June 11, 1861, letter to Gen. John A. Dix, who had been secretary of the treasury in Buchanan's cabinet, Stanton again referred to "the painful imbecility of Lincoln."

Meanwhile, Lincoln's Secretary of War Simon Cameron demonstrated little competence, but Stanton was his confidential legal adviser. Cameron had dominated Pennsylvania politics for thirty years and supported Lincoln in 1860 in exchange for a cabinet post promised by Lincoln's subordinates. As secretary of war, Cameron presided over massive fraud and corruption in appointments and procurement. In November 1861 he embarrassed Lincoln by publicly advocating the freeing and the arming of the slaves. It cost him his job; Lincoln made him minister to Russia. Ironically, Stanton, who had written the report on freeing and arming the slaves, was named the new secretary of war. Lincoln was unaware of Stanton's involvement with Cameron's statement and apparently did not know that the iron-willed tiger he was putting into his cabinet was more stubbornly in favor of arming the slaves than the man he was putting out, but Stanton's devious double role did not surprise anyone who knew him.

Lincoln, however, recalled Stanton's snooty treatment of him six years earlier. Before placing Stanton in charge of the War Department, the president told an acquaintance: "I have made up my mind to sit down on all my pride—it may be a portion of my self respect—and appoint Stanton." He realized that Stanton would be hard to manage—being hot-tempered, blunt, sometimes unstable, and usually not amiable—but he also knew that Stanton would be a superb manager.

When Rep. Henry L. Dawes congratulated Lincoln for Stanton's appointment, he added some words of caution, but Lincoln acknowledged that he had been warned by others that Stanton might try to dominate the administration. The president added: "We may have to treat him as they are sometimes obliged to treat a Methodist minister I know of out West. He gets wrought up to so high a pitch of excitement in his prayers and exhortations that they are obliged to put bricks in his pockets to keep him down. We may be obliged to serve Stanton in the same way, but I guess we'll let him jump a while first. Besides, bricks in his pockets would be better than bricks in his hat."

Stanton found chaos throughout the War Department. "On the day he was sworn in, his department resembled a great lunatic asylum more than anything else," said Col. A. P. Heichold of Pennsylvania. Fortifications around Washington were sparse and flimsy. Enlistments were down. The streets of the capital swarmed with officers who should have been with their regiments at the front. Most city residents and hundreds of government employees were secret aiders and abettors of secession. Many army divisions had passed several paydays without meeting the paymaster. The North itself was contentious, with a considerable number of its people siding with secession. France and England were watching for an excuse to recognize the Confederacy as an independent nation. Lincoln was up to the task, but he needed strong leaders to work with him. The president was counting on Stanton to be such a man. He was.

Stanton's hair-trigger mind produced instant actions and effective results. He efficiently manned, equipped, and reorganized the military, instituted harsh security measures such as arbitrary arrests, and strengthened Washington's fortifications to the point where they were reputed to be the most extensive fieldworks known. It was said that after Stanton took office, no Union general wanted for soldiers and no Union soldier wanted for food, ammunition, or clothes by his fault. When the war ended, the

Union possessed a reserve adequate to have equipped another army as large as the one already in the field.

Standing behind a long, high desk, Stanton held late morning sessions for everyone from contractors and claimants to office-seekers and parents of punished soldiers. He disposed of their cases with ruthless snap judgments. If he did not like a contract, he would tear it up and fling the pieces in the contractor's face. When mothers of captured deserters pleaded for their sons not to be shot, he would turn them away without flinching. He could be quick and kind on other matters, but it was typical of him to be tactless and abrasive. When these morning sessions ended, Stanton routinely washed his face and sprayed cologne into his beard. He wanted no traces of the unpleasant breaths blown at him.

Treading on constitutional rights, Stanton effected press censorship and controlled press coverage of the war, doing so because he believed that the press was subordinate to national safety. He so disliked the press that he once wrote, "Newspaper reports are lies, invented by knaves for fools to feed on." On February 26, 1862, he decreed, "All newspapers publishing military news, however obtained, not authorized by official authority, will be excluded thereafter from receiving information by telegraph and from transmitting their publications by railroad." This order was modified the next day "permitting newspapers to publish past facts, leaving out all details of military forces, and all statements from which the number, position, and strength of the military forces of the United States can be inferred." Stanton required all communications about the war to be sent through the War Department. He prohibited all department subordinates from giving information even of a personal nature to reporters and correspondents. "No newspaper reporter ever came to Mr. Stanton or to any officer of the War Department for news," said Maj. A. E. H. Johnson of Stanton's staff. "He held all officials to a rule of strict non-intercourse with reporters and correspondents. Of all the branches of government, the War Department was the last resort of reporters. For this the newspapers reveled in denunciation and abuse of Mr. Stanton." Thus war coverage came from only one source—Stanton. Each night he summarized that day's military events and movements and issued the summary over his own signature to the press. The marches, battles, losses, captures, conditions, and achievements of every command in the army were condensed and published the following day in newspapers throughout the country. What the people read about the war was what the government—Stanton—gave them to read. Supposedly, Stanton's objectives were to suppress fabricators of sensational rumors and peddlers of false reports and to wipe out the power of hostile and quasi-disloyal papers to weaken the war effort or harass the administration.

This so-called war diary was Stanton's only direct communication with the public during his six years in office. According to biographer Frank Flower, Stanton "submitted to no interview, prepared no magazine articles, made no defense, wrote no book, and held his subordinates rigidly to the same line of decorous military conduct." Further, he made no journal of his activities and retained few or no private copies of his letters. After Lincoln's assassination, Stanton did, however, respond to an article by Horace Greeley in the *New York Tribune* by retaining an attorney to prosecute Greeley and the newspaper for what Stanton strangely regarded as "Greeley's persistent effort the last four weeks to incite assassins to finish their work by murdering me. Please . . . secure copies of all *Tribunes* published since the night of the president's murder; also the names of the owners. I propose to prosecute criminally and by civil suit. I shall not allow them to have me murdered and escape responsibility without a struggle for life on my part." A few days later Stanton chose not to follow through.

In Stanton's thoroughness to control communications he did not stop with the press. His method of controlling the telegraph lines was also peculiarly autocratic and independent. He gained management of all telegraph lines in the country by a February 26, 1862, order that concentrated the control of the telegraphic machinery next to his own office. Previously, the telegraph bureau had been managed by Gen. George B. McClellan, who never forgave Stanton for what he termed "his humiliation." Men in whom Stanton had implicit confidence were placed in command of the bureau. They invented and used a cipher code that the Confederates were never able to break, and which the operators and translators never betrayed. Stanton even deprived Lincoln of the use of a special code. The president had to send and receive messages through the common channel. Maj. A. E. H. Johnson, who was placed in charge of telegraph records, said that Stanton ordered him "to let no person see the telegraphs." The war secretary screened telegrams he thought the president should see and personally delivered them to the White House two or three times daily. Johnson added:

> Although the president frequently went into the telegraph office to send telegrams, the operators would not show him the telegrams coming in from the armies, until later during the war, when the rule was relaxed and a box for

his use was provided. [Then] he came over from the White House several times a day and thrusting his long arm down among the messages, fished them out one by one and read them. When he had secured the last one he invariably made some characteristic remark—generally something that caused laughter—and then proceeded to consult with Secretary Stanton.

Historians generally agree that Stanton's early contempt for Lincoln eventually gave way to respect and that the two men developed an excellent working relationship. If true, Stanton sometimes had a strange way of showing it.

In one instance, when Lincoln approved a petitioner's request and sent him to Stanton with a written order to execute the request, the man returned to the White House to report that Stanton not only refused to do so but had also called Lincoln "a damn fool."

The president, looking surprised, asked: "Did Stanton call me a damn fool?"

"Yes," replied the petitioner.

"Well," Lincoln remarked drolly, "I guess I had better step over and see Stanton about this. Stanton is usually right."

On another occasion Lincoln provided a pass to a speculator so that he could go through the Union lines to buy cotton. The speculator took it to Stanton to have it countersigned. Stanton tore it to pieces, threw the pieces on the floor, and stomped on them. When the speculator reported this action to Lincoln, the president said calmly: "Well, you go back and tell Stanton that I will tear up a dozen of his papers before Saturday."

A would-be chaplain carried the following correspondence back and forth between Lincoln and Stanton:

Dear Stanton: Appoint this man a chaplain in the army—A. Lincoln

Dear Mr. Lincoln: He is not a preacher.—E. M. Stanton

Dear Stanton: He is now.—A. Lincoln

Dear Mr. Lincoln: There is no vacancy.—E. M. Stanton

Dear Stanton: Appoint him chaplain-at-large.—A. Lincoln

Dear Mr. Lincoln: There is no warrant in law for this.—E. M. Stanton

Dear Stanton: Appoint him anyhow.—A. Lincoln

Dear Mr. Lincoln: I will not.—E. M. Stanton

Lincoln gave up and did not pursue the matter further. On other, more important issues, the president stood firm, however. For example, some Confederate prisoners requested their freedom so they could fight for the Union. It seemed like a good idea to Lincoln, so he issued an order for it to be done. When Stanton learned about it, he dashed over to the White House and stated his objection. He said that if the men were captured by the Confederates, they would probably be tried as deserters and hanged or shot. "Now, Mr. President, those are the facts," said Stanton, "and you must see that your order cannot be executed." Lincoln looked solemnly at Stanton and said: "Mr. Secretary, I reckon you will have to execute the order." Stanton shot back: "Mr. President, I cannot do it." Lincoln responded firmly: "Mr. Secretary, it will have to be done." Stanton issued the order.

Lincoln was not above deceiving Stanton when he thought it advisable to do so. One such occasion involved a young soldier who had been sentenced to be shot for sleeping at his post on the picket line. The soldier's mother was a constituent of Rep. Thaddeus Stevens, a powerful Pennsylvania Republican. On the morning of the day fixed for the execution, she applied to the congressman to help save her son, and he immediately took the case to Lincoln.

"I am sorry, but I cannot help you," said Lincoln. "Mr. Stanton says I am destroying discipline in the army, and I have promised him I will grant no more reprieves without first consulting him."

Stanton ordered the rocking chair in which Lincoln was shot brought to his office. He kept it there for a year and looked at it daily. The crimson tufted walnut chair had come from Harry Ford's home, and Ford had it placed in the State Box specifically for the president's use on the fateful night.

Looking at the clock, Stevens rejoined: "There is no time to consult anybody. There is not an hour to spare."

Sorrowfully Lincoln replied, "It is too bad, but I must keep my promise to sign no more reprieves without first referring them to Mr. Stanton."

Stevens then picked up a telegraph form, wrote a reprieve, and asked Lincoln if the wordage were correct. Lincoln said that it was, whereupon Stevens signed "A. Lincoln" to it and dispatched a messenger on the run to the telegraph office to have it sent to the officer in command where the soldier was to be shot.

A few minutes later Stanton steamed into Lincoln's office and exclaimed, "I see, Mr. President, you have signed another reprieve contrary to your agreement not to do so without first consulting me."

"No," responded Lincoln, "I have signed no reprieve. I have kept my word."

"But," said Stanton, "I just now saw one going over the wires"—for Stanton ordered all messages to be recorded in the War Department so he could know instantly everything that was going on in the armies—"and your name is signed to it."

"But I did not write it," persisted Lincoln.

"Did not write it! Then who did write it?" demanded Stanton.

"Your friend, Thad Stevens," Lincoln replied.

Stanton, who had been neatly circumvented, took his hat and left without another word.

Lincoln's first objective as president was to preserve the Union, which he stated in his first inaugural address: "I have no purpose, directly or indirectly, to interfere with slavery in the states where it exists. I believe I have no lawful right to do so." The president clearly opposed the expansion of slavery into the territories, but while he hated slavery he believed that any attempt to interfere with it in the South would be unconstitutional.

Stanton, however, wanted to abolish slavery immediately. In an act of insubordination, Stanton declared in his first formal report to Congress: "It is, in my opinion, the duty of those conducting the war to strike down the system and turn against the rebels the productive power that upholds the insurrection." The secretary of war sought to recruit thousands of escaping slaves into Union armies. Not to do so, he wrote on May 5, 1862, "would be a failure to employ means to suppress the rebellion and restore the authority of the Government."

Four days later Gen. David Hunter issued a proclamation declaring all slaves in his territory—Georgia, Florida, and South Carolina—"forever free." Lincoln promptly set it aside as void, but the slaves regarded it as valid and flocked by the thousands to Hunter. He made use of them as if they were freedmen. When Congress asked Stanton if he had permitted certain generals to use the services of blacks and to issue arms and clothing to them, the war secretary gave an interesting but devious answer: He had no "official" information as to whether Hunter had organized a regiment of "black men, fugitive slaves," and that while Hunter had "not been authorized to organize and muster" those black men, he had been furnished with clothing and arms for the forces under his command "without instructions as to where they should be used." Thus, against Lincoln's wishes, Stanton was silently and effectively equipping black soldiers for the Union army.

At a cabinet meeting on July 21, 1862, Stanton presented letters from Hunter advising the War Department that "the withdrawal of a large portion of his troops to reinforce General McClellan rendered it highly important that he should be immediately authorized to enlist all loyal persons without reference to complexion." Lincoln again strongly objected to arming blacks. At the next cabinet session, Stanton persisted in his opposition to the president's position, arguing without success for three hours for "immediate emancipation."

Disagreeing with Lincoln, Stanton disregarded the president and made every possible use of slaves in the army. In another example, Gen. Benjamin F. Butler asked Lincoln about black recruitment to supplement his forces in New Orleans. The president replied that he was not prepared to discuss such a policy. Butler then went to Stanton, and according to the general, Stanton told him "to hold, equip, employ, or arm all the Negroes who came to me." Butler said that he was "about to do so openly when the news of Lincoln's voidance of Hunter's proclamation arrived."

In August 1862, Gen. Rufus Saxton succeeded Hunter and received instructions from Stanton to "enlist, enroll, arm, equip, and drill for military service" up to five thousand black volunteers. Stanton clearly continued to ignore the president's position.

At the beginning of the war, Lincoln refused to include blacks in the war effort because he wanted to keep the crucial Border States—Missouri, Kentucky, and Maryland—in the Union. These states were largely settled by Southerners, and Lincoln was concerned that the enlistment of thousands

LESLIE'S

Stanton was one of more than ninety people, including sixteen doctors, who visited or stood vigil in the small room where Lincoln died at 7:22 A.M. The secretary of war said through his tears, "He belongs to the angels now." This epitaph was soon amended to, "Now he belongs to the ages."

of black troops might turn these states against the Union and cause them to throw their substantial resources to the Confederacy. As the war progressed, Lincoln considered it politically unwise to move on African American recruitment and emancipation until his armies produced major victories— victories he believed would generate public support for such a drastic measure. Stanton, on the other hand, saw the need for black troops to help achieve those victories.

The opportunity Lincoln sought came in September 1862 when McClellan stopped Lee's invasion of Maryland and forced him to withdraw to Virginia. Lincoln then drafted an Emancipation Proclamation, which became effective on January 1, 1863. It irrevocably notified the world that the war was being fought not just to preserve the Union but to put an end to slavery. It also secured support for the war from abolitionists and black leaders; it enabled Union armies to free thousands of slaves as they occupied Southern territory; and it officially opened the army and navy to

African American volunteers. By the end of the war, nearly two hundred thousand black recruits strengthened the Union's military forces and helped to win the war.

"Mr. Stanton's impatience with the slowness of President Lincoln to proclaim emancipation was great," proclaimed Charles A. Dana, "and was expressed more freely to the president than to anybody else. When the proclamation finally came, his delight and his gratitude to God were unbounded. Now, at last, he felt that no blunder and no disaster could avert the ultimate triumph of our arms."

Stanton apparently drew no lines between political plots and legitimate political activities during the presidential campaign of 1864. New York's Democratic governor, Horatio Seymour, opposed allowing soldiers from his state to cast their ballots in the field, assuming most of them would vote for Lincoln. So when the legislature passed a bill enabling the soldiers to vote, Seymour vetoed it. Not to be outdone, the Unionists in the legislature outflanked him by amending the state constitution. The governor followed up by sending a commission to Washington to garner Democratic votes and to ensure that all Democratic soldiers voted. When Stanton heard of this plan, he threw the commissioners in prison and kept them there until the election was over.

So far as is known, no member of the Lincoln or Johnson cabinets—save William Seward and Salmon P. Chase—ever spoke kindly or favorably of Stanton. His colleagues hated him. The short, stocky war secretary was a brainy bulldog in the cabinet and an irresistible force in the War Office.

Generally, Lincoln tried not to interfere with Stanton, but he wrote to a friend, "I can overrule his decision if I will, but I cannot well administer the War Department independent of the Secretary of War." Lincoln and Stanton worked out a system that Lincoln summed up by saying: "I cannot always know whether a permit ought to be granted, and I want to oblige everybody when I can; and Stanton and I have an understanding that if I send an order to him that cannot be consistently granted, he is to refuse it. This he sometimes does." Whenever Stanton turned down a request Lincoln thought important, the president overruled him, saying, "Let it be done."

Thus Stanton could inflict strict military punishment for sentries who fell asleep or soldiers who disobeyed orders, and Lincoln, if he saw fit, could pardon them. For Lincoln, there were moral, ethical, and political issues he had to consider; for Stanton, the only issue was the prosecution of the war, which included whatever ruthless measures he deemed necessary. Some say that Stanton could stand unmoved by the pleas of parents whose sons were condemned to be shot for desertion because he knew that Lincoln might commute the sentence. The administration appeared more efficient and popular when Lincoln was perceived as pardoner while Stanton wore the undeviating mantle of severity. As David Homer Bates, a cipher operator, pointed out, Stanton's austere and sometimes imperious official manner was "a necessary armament of the hour."

Grant observed that "Stanton required a man like Lincoln to manage him"—a man with "gentle firmness." Lincoln was calm, unruffled, forgiving; Stanton was merciless, secretive, impatient, always in a hurry. Lincoln tended to delay major decisions in hopes the problems might resolve themselves—a habit that pushed Stanton into pungent temper tantrums that usually passed as quickly as they struck.

After the fall of Richmond, Stanton, feeling feeble because of congestive asthma, submitted his resignation to Lincoln. The president tore it up and put both of his hands on Stanton's shoulders. "You cannot go," he said. "Reconstruction is more difficult and dangerous than construction or destruction. You have been our main reliance; you must help us through the final act. The bag is filled. It must be tied and tied securely. Some knots slip; yours do not. You understand the situation better than anybody else, and it is my wish and the country's that you remain."

While Stanton seldom showed his good-natured, gentlemanly side publicly, one example is worth sharing. The wife of Gen. Rufus Saxton wrote of Stanton's being their guest at Beaufort, North Carolina, in January 1865.

On arriving he said that fatigue would compel him to retire early; but after dinner . . . he sat down [in front of the fireplace] and chatted brightly. Examining the books on the table, his face grew animated and he exclaimed: "Ah, here are old friends," and taking up a volume of Macaulay's poems he turned to me, saying: "I know you love poetry. Pray read us something—anything. Poetry and this fire belong together." I read "Horatius at the Bridge," and returning the book to him, [I asked him to] please read to us. He at once complied, reading finely "The Battle of Ivry" and other poems. The next morning we drove him out on the "Shell Road," where the live-oaks were draped with graceful gray moss, the birds singing and the air was soft and bland. He leaned back silent in the carriage, gazing at the blue sky, seeming in spirit to "soar with the bird and flutter with the leaf." The Titan War Secretary was replaced by the genial companion, the man of letters, the lover of nature—the real Stanton, who expressed again and again his rapturous enjoyment of the surroundings.

Was she right? Was this the real Stanton? Opinions differ dramatically. Was Navy Secretary Gideon Welles correct when he called Stanton "deep in conspiracy"? Was John Hay right when he told Stanton "no honest man has cause to quarrel with you" and "your hands have been clean and your heart steady every hour of this fight"?

Is it not strange that two of the people closest to Lincoln—Stanton and Mary Todd Lincoln—had peculiarly constituted, abnormal personalities? It's one thing to imagine Stanton's supervising the dressing of Lincoln's dead body. It's another to imagine him dressing and redressing the body of his first wife, who died in childbirth, until he was satisfied that she looked just as she did seven years before at the marriage altar. "She is my bride and shall be dressed and buried like a bride," said Stanton, who threw her valuable jewelry into her coffin.

Stanton also had acted strangely after the death of his young daughter Lucy two years earlier. After she had been buried about a year, he had the remains exhumed, placed them in a metal box made for the purpose, and soldered it shut. He kept the box in his bedroom for a year. This is the same Stanton who unleashed a smear campaign of malicious lies against

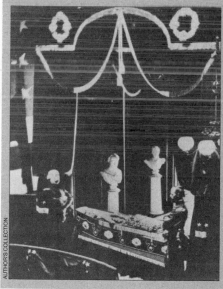

A New York City photographer, Jeremiah Gurney Jr., received permission to photograph Lincoln's body while it lay in state in City Hall. Stanton, however, erupted angrily when he heard of this and ordered the photographic plates broken and the prints destroyed. This was done except for one small print sent to Stanton. He hid it among his papers, where his son Lewis discovered it twenty-two years later. Lewis mailed it to Lincoln's personal secretaries John Nicolay and John Hay, who were working on a ten-volume history of Lincoln's life. They chose not to use the print, and again it disappeared. The image was not found until 1953, when a fifteen-year-old boy came across it among Nicolay's papers at the Illinois State Historical Library. The haunting photograph has since been published many times.

William T. Sherman; who lied to Lincoln about Thomas T. Eckert's availability to accompany him to the theater; who used underhanded and illegal tactics to bring about the hanging of Mary Surratt; who barricaded himself inside his office after being fired by President Johnson; and who described Lincoln as a long-armed baboon.

Col. Horace Porter, Grant's aide-de-camp, commented that Stanton "had a wide reputation for extreme brusqueness . . . even with his friends, and seemed determined, as an officer once expressed it, to administer discipline totally regardless of previous acquaintance. A Frenchman once said that during the Revolution, while the guillotine was at work, he never heard the name of Robespierre that he did not take off his hat to see whether his head was still on his shoulders; some of our officers were similarly inclined when they heard the name of Stanton."

Col. William P. Wood observed that "when Secretary Stanton gave orders to his trusted men to perform a given service, he expected them to succeed or die in the attempt, and they acted accordingly." On October 31, 1862, Wood, supposing he was acting under independent instructions from Stanton, refused to obey orders from Gen. John A. Dix in relation to prisoner exchanges. Dix telegraphed Stanton, who replied: "Wood should have been put in the guard-house. When you think a man deserves it, shoot him on the spot."

CONCLUSION

———◆◆◆◆◆———

BASED ON THE EVIDENCE currently available, John Wilkes Booth is now seen to have been a Confederate spy assigned to capture the president of the United States. Abraham Lincoln was to be exchanged for thousands of Confederate prisoners—men desperately needed to replenish the dwindling ranks of the Southern army. When Booth's mission failed, Confederate leaders resorted to more desperate measures to disrupt the Union command and create chaos advantageous to the Confederacy.

A team of demolition experts was dispatched to Washington to blow up the White House. That team, headed by Thomas F. Harney and aided by Mosby's Rangers, was captured a few miles outside the capital.

By this time Richmond had been evacuated, Robert E. Lee had surrendered, and communication between Booth and Confederates on the run was nonexistent. Yet Booth believed that the Confederate cause was still not lost. Lee had surrendered only one-sixth of the forces in the field. Thus Booth took it upon himself to carry out Confederate objectives as he had understood them to be just two weeks earlier: a wartime attack against the enemy's leadership—Lincoln, Vice President Andrew Johnson, and Secretary of State William H. Seward.

Booth expected that he would escape afterward, and he planned accordingly. Since his weapons consisted only of a single-shot pistol and a knife, he likely knew who would or would not be guarding Lincoln. Booth's friends apparently included Radical Republican leaders in the House and Senate, and he may have had an informant in the White House or the War Department. Some actions of Secretary of War Edwin M. Stanton and First Lady Mary Todd Lincoln are illogical, irresponsible, and unexplainable. Because there was no investigation of major governmental figures, there is no concrete evidence tying any of them directly to Booth's plans to assassinate the president.

Seventeen persons aided Booth during his escape. Fourteen of them were associated with or connected to an underground Confederate network. They carried out their responsibilities to protect Booth and keep him out of Union hands. Once Booth was cornered, however, at the Garrett farm, with no way out, it is possible that one of Booth's protectors may have killed him, or he may have killed himself. It is not an uncommon practice in clandestine operations that a spy will kill himself rather than be caught. Such action is usually undertaken because it is in the best interests of other agents, for their lives are at risk if one of their own is captured and interrogated successfully. Further, would any Union official not associated with Booth's plots want him dead?

Dr. Samuel A. Mudd and Mary Elizabeth Surratt remain the most controversial of the eight conspirators brought to trial. There is little doubt that Mudd was an associate of Booth who helped him to organize his team. While Mudd may not have known of Booth's plan to kill the president, he certainly contributed to the assassin's escape. Similarly, Mary Surratt was well acquainted with Booth and undoubtedly aware of his earlier scheme to kidnap Lincoln. She also knew something sinister was afoot on the night of April 14, 1865, and apparently contributed to it by telling John Lloyd at her tavern in Surrattsville to "get the shooting irons out." A major piece of evidence not available at the trial—George Atzerodt's confession discovered years later—left the court with only circumstantial evidence from a drunkard and a family friend whose testimony may have been perjured to save his own life. Mary Surratt should not have been hanged and would not have been except for the underhanded maneuvering of the president, the secretary of war, and the judge advocate general.

Back in the 1920s a historian wrote that it was unlikely anything new could be written about Lincoln or his assassination. The subject had been thoroughly covered, he said. How wrong he was. Even today there still is no full agreement among historians as to what happened in 1865. Yet since 1988 more has come to light about the Lincoln assassination than had been learned the previous century. This book, for example, could not have been written before the 1990s. What the record will become in the decades ahead cannot be predicted anymore than what historians in 1990 could have predicted for today. Undiscovered revelations may yet lie buried in obscure archives or private collections—revelations that may shed blinding light on the assassination and the individuals involved in it. Thus where we stand today on the assassination may not be where we stand tomorrow or a thousand tomorrows from now. The possibilities will depend upon the perseverance and dedication of those individuals searching for the truth—and on their various degrees of sophistication and integrity.

"At every step we must be true to the main purpose," Lincoln said. "The struggle of today is not altogether for today—it is for a vast future also." One might add, the struggle is also for a better understanding of our uncertain past.

SELECTED SOURCES

Arnold, Samuel Bland. *Defense and Prison Experiences of a Lincoln Conspirator.* Hattiesburg, Miss.: The Book Farm, 1943.

Baird, Nancy D. "The Yellow Fever Plot." *Civil War Times Illustrated,* November 1974.

Bak, Richard. *The Day Lincoln Was Shot.* Dallas: Taylor, 1998.

Baker, Lafayette C. *History of the United States Secret Service.* Philadelphia: L. C. Baker, 1867. Reprint, Bowie, Md.: Heritage Books, 1992.

Beale, Howard K., ed. *The Diary of Gideon Welles.* New York: Norton, 1960.

Benedict, Michael Les. *The Impeachment and Trial of Andrew Johnson.* New York: Norton, 1973.

Bishop, Jim. *The Day Lincoln Was Shot.* New York: Gramercy Books, 1955.

Blair, Walter, ed. *The Sweet Singer of Michigan: Poems by Mrs. Julia A. Moore.* Chicago: Pascal Covici, 1928.

Busch, Francis X. *Enemies of the State.* Indianapolis and New York: Bobbs-Merrill, 1954.

Campbell, Helen. *The Case for Mrs. Surratt.* New York: G. P. Putnam's Sons, 1943.

Carter, Samuel, III. *The Riddle of Dr. Mudd.* New York: G. P. Putnam's Sons, 1974.

Chamlee, Roy Z., Jr. *Lincoln's Assassins: A Complete Account of Their Capture, Trial, and Punishment.* Jefferson, N.C.: McFarland and Company, 1990.

Clampitt, John W. "The Trial of Mrs. Surratt." *North American Review* 131 (1880).

Clarke, Asia Booth. *The Unlocked Book: A Memoir of John Wilkes Booth by His Sister.* New York: G. P. Putnam's Sons, 1938.

Cottrell, John. *Anatomy of an Assassination.* New York: Funk & Wagnalls, 1966.

DeWitt, David M. *The Assassination of Abraham Lincoln and Its Expiation.* New York: Macmillan, 1909.

———. *The Judicial Murder of Mary E. Surratt.* Baltimore: J. Murphy & Co., 1895.

Dillon, David, ed. *The Lincoln Assassination: From the Pages of the Surratt Courier (1986–1999).* 2 vols. Clinton, Md.: Surratt Society, 2001.

Eisenschiml, Otto. *In the Shadow of Lincoln's Death.* New York: Wilfred Funk, 1940.

———. *Why Was Lincoln Murdered?* Boston: Little, Brown, 1937.

Fishel, Edwin C. *The Secret War for the Union.* New York: Houghton Mifflin, 1996.

Flower, Frank Abial. *Edwin McMasters Stanton, The Autocrat of Rebellion, Emancipation, and Reconstruction.* Akron: Saalfield, 1905.

Ford, John T. "Behind the Curtain of a Conspiracy." *The North American Review.* 1889.

Fowler, Robert H. "Album of the Lincoln Murder: Illustrating How It Was Planned, Committed, and Avenged." *Civil War Times Illustrated,* July 1965.

Frank Leslie's Illustrated History of the Civil War. New York, 1895.

Frank Leslie's Illustrated Weekly. 1861–65.

Grant, Julia Dent. *The Personal Memoirs of Julia Dent Grant.* Ed. John Y. Simon. New York: G. P. Putnam's Sons, 1975.

Grant, Ulysses S. *Personal Memoirs of U. S. Grant.* Ed. E. B. Long. Cleveland: World, 1952.

Gray, John A. "The Fate of the Lincoln Conspirators: The Account of the Hanging Given by Lieutenant-Colonel Christian Rath, The Executioner." *McClure's* 37 (1911).

Hall, James O. *The Surratt Family and John Wilkes Booth.* Clinton, Md.: Surratt Society, 1984.

———. "The Dahlgren Papers: A Yankee Plot to Kill President Jefferson Davis." *Civil War Times Illustrated,* November 1983.

———. "John Wilkes Booth Escape Route." *Surratt Society News,* 1984.

———. *The Mary Surratt House.* Clinton, Md.: History Division, Maryland–National Capital Parks and Planning Commission, 1979.

———. "The Saga of Sarah Slater." *Surratt Society News,* February 1982.

Hanchett, William. *The Lincoln Murder Conspiracies.* Urbana and Chicago: University of Illinois Press, 1983.

———. "The War Department and Booth's Abduction Plot." *Lincoln Herald* 82, no. 4 (Winter 1980).

Harper's Weekly. 1861–65.

Harris, Thomas M. *The Assassination of Lincoln: A History of the Great Conspiracy.* Boston: American Citizen Company, 1892.

Headley, John W. *Confederate Operations in Canada and New York.* New York: Neale, 1906.

Higdon, Hal. *The Union vs. Dr. Mudd.* Chicago: Discovers Press, 1964.

Jones, John Paul, ed. *Dr. Mudd and the Lincoln Assassination, The Case Reopened.* Conshohocken, Pa.: Combined Books, 1995.

Jones, Thomas A. *John Wilkes Booth.* Chicago: Laird & Lee, 1893.

Jones, Virgil Carrington. *Ranger Mosby.* Chapel Hill: University of North Carolina Press, 1944.

———. "The Story of the Kilpatrick-Dahlgren Raid." *Civil War Times Illustrated,* April 1965.

Julian, George Washington. *Political Recollections, 1840 to 1872.* Chicago: Jansen, McClurg, and Co., 1884.

Katz, D. Mark. *Witness to an Era: The Life and Photographs of Alexander Gardner.* 1991. Reprint, Nashville, Tenn.: Rutledge Hill Press, 1999.

Kauffman, Michael W. "David Edgar Herold, the Forgotten Conspirator." *Surratt Society News,* November 1981.

———, ed. *In Pursuit Of . . . Continuing Research in the Field of the Lincoln Assassination.* Clinton, Md.: Surratt Society, 1990.

———. "John Wilkes Booth and the Murder of Abraham Lincoln." *Blue and Gray Magazine,* April 1990.

Keller, Allan, "Canada and the Civil War." *Civil War Times Illustrated,* November 1964.

Kennedy, John F. *Profiles in Courage.* New York and Evanston: Harper & Row, 1956.

Kimmel, Stanley. *The Mad Booths of Maryland.* New York: Bobbs-Merrill, 1940.

Klapthor, M. B., and P. D. Brown. *The History of Charles County, Maryland.* La Plata, Md.: Charles County Tercentenary, 1958.

Kunhardt, Dorothy Meserve, and Philip B. Kunhardt Jr. *Twenty Days.* New York: Harper & Row, 1965.

Laughlin, Clara E. *The Death of Lincoln: The Story of Booth's Plot, His Deed and the Penalty.* New York: Doubleday Page, 1909.

Leech, Margaret. *Reveille in Washington.* New York: Harper, 1941.

Lewis, Lloyd. *Myths After Lincoln.* New York: Harcourt, Brace, 1929.

Luvaas, Jay. "An Appraisal of Joseph E. Johnston." *Civil War Times Illustrated,* January 1966.

Maione, Michael, and James O. Hall. "Why Seward?" *Lincoln Herald,* Spring 1998.

Manakee, Harold R. *Maryland in the Civil War.* Baltimore: Historical Society, 1961.

McHale, John E. *Dr. Samuel A. Mudd and the Lincoln Assassination.* Parsippany, N.J.: Dillon Press, 1995.

McPherson, James M. *Ordeal by Fire.* New York: Knopf, 1982.

Mills, Robert L. *It Didn't Happen the Way You Think: The Assassination: What the Experts Missed.* Bowie, Md.: Heritage Books, 1995.

Monteiro, Arisides. *War Reminiscences by the Surgeon of Mosby's Command.* 1890. Reprint, Gaithersburg, Md., n.d.

Moore, Guy W. *The Case of Mrs. Surratt.* Norman: University of Oklahoma Press, 1954.

Mosby, John S. *Mosby's Memoirs.* Boston: Little, Brown, 1917.

Mudd, Nettie. *The Life of Dr. Samuel A. Mudd.* Washington: Neale, 1906.

Mudd, Richard D. *Dr. Samuel Alexander Mudd and His Descendants.* Saginaw, Mich.: Self-published, 1979.

―――. *The Mudd Family of the United States.* 2 vols. Saginaw, Mich.: self-published, 1951.

Munson, John W. *Reminiscences of a Mosby Guerrilla.* New York: Moffat, Yard & Co., 1910.

National Archives Records Administration, Washington, D.C. Papers Relating to Suspects in the Lincoln Assassination, Records of the Provost Marshal's Office. Record Group 110.

―――. Records of the Judge Advocate General's Office (Army). Record Group 153. Court Martial Case File, MM 2513.

―――. Report of Col. William P. Wood, superintendent of Old Capitol Prison, on Louis J. Weichmann. Bureau of Military Justice Records.

Neely, Mark E., Jr. "Some New Light on Thomas A. Jones and the Mysterious Man Named Mudd." *Lincoln Lore,* no. 1721 (July 1981).

Oldroyd, Osborn H. *The Assassination of Abraham Lincoln.* Washington: self-published, 1901. Reprint, Bowie, Md.: Heritage Books, 1990.

Orrmont, Arthur. *Mr. Lincoln's Master Spy, Lafayette Baker.* New York: Julian Messner, 1966.

Ownsbey, Betty J. *Alias "Paine": Lewis Thornton Powell, the Mystery Man of the Lincoln Conspiracy.* Jefferson, N.C.: McFarland & Co., 1993.

————. "The Military Career of an Assassin." *North & South,* November 1998.

Pitman, Benn. *The Assassination of President Lincoln and the Trial of the Conspirators.* Cincinnati: Moore, Wilstrach & Baldwin, 1865.

Poore, Ben Perley. *The Conspiracy Trial for the Murder of the President.* 4 vols. 1865. Reprint, New York: Arno Press, 1972.

————. *Perley's Reminiscences.* Philadelphia: Hubbard, 1886.

Posey, Calvert R., and Judith L. Posey. *A History of the Role Charles County Played in the Civil War.* La Plata, Md.: Times Crescent, 1960.

Pratt, Fletcher. *Stanton, Lincoln's Secretary of War.* New York: Norton, 1953.

Ramage, James A. *Gray Ghost: The Life of Col. John Singleton Mosby.* Lexington: University Press of Kentucky, 1999.

Reck, Emerson. *A. Lincoln: His Last 24 Hours.* Columbia: University of South Carolina Press, 1994.

Rhodenhamel, John, and Louise Taper, eds. *"Right or Wrong, God Judge Me": The Writings of John Wilkes Booth.* Chicago: University of Illinois Press, 1997.

Richmond (Va.) Sentinel, March 5, 1864.

Riddleberger, Patrick W. *George Washington Julian, Radical Republican.* Indianapolis: Indiana Historical Bureau, 1966.

Roscoe, Theodore. *The Web of Conspiracy.* Englewood Cliffs, N.J.: Prentice-Hall, 1959.

Schultz, Duane. *The Dahlgren Affair.* New York: Norton, 1998.

Searcher, Victor. *The Farewell to Lincoln.* New York: Abingdon Press, 1965.

Sears, Stephen W. "The Dahlgren Papers Revisited." *Columbiad* 3 (Summer 1999).

Sefton, James E. *Andrew Johnson and the Uses of Constitutional Power.* Boston: Little, Brown, & Co., 1980.

Shelton, Vaughan. *Mask for Treason.* Harrisburg, Pa.: Stackpole, 1965.

Sherwood, Glenn V. *Labor of Love, The Life and Art of Vinnie Ream.* Hygiene, Colo.: SunShine, 1997.

Siepel, Kevin H. *Rebel: The Life and Times of John Singleton Mosby.* New York: St. Martin's Press, 1983.

Smoot, Richard. *The Unwritten History of the Assassination of Abraham Lincoln.* Clinton, Mass.: Coulter, 1908.

Steers, Edward, Jr. *Blood on the Moon: The Assassination of Abraham Lincoln.* Lexington: University Press of Kentucky, 2001.

————. "Dr. Mudd and the 'Colored' Witness." *Civil War History* 46, no. 4 (December 2000).

————. *His Name Is Still Mudd: The Case Against Dr. Samuel Alexander Mudd.* Gettysburg, Pa.: Thomas, 1997.

————, and James O. Hall. *The Escape and Capture of George Atzerodt.* Clinton, Md.: Surratt Society, 1980.

Stern, Philip Van Doren. *The Man Who Killed Lincoln.* New York: Literary Guild of America, 1939.

Swanson, James L., and Daniel R. Weinberg. *Lincoln's Assassins: Their Trial and Execution.* Chicago: Arena Editions, 2001.

Taft, Charles Sabin. "Abraham Lincoln's Last Hours." *Century Magazine,* February 1895.

Thomas, Benjamin P., and Harold M. Hyman. *Stanton: The Life and Times of Lincoln's Secretary of War.* New York: Knopf, 1962.

Tidwell, William A. *April '65: Confederate Covert Action in the American Civil War.* Kent, Ohio: Kent State University Press, 1995.

————, James O. Hall, and David W. Gaddy. *Come Retribution: The Confederate Secret Service and the Assassination of Abraham Lincoln.* Jackson: University of Mississippi Press, 1988.

Townsend, George Alfred. *The Life, Crime, and Capture of John Wilkes Booth.* New York: Dick & Fitzgerald, 1868.

The Trial of John H. Surratt in the Criminal Court for the District of Columbia. Washington, D.C.: Government Printing Office, 1867.

Trial of the Assassins and Conspirators for the Murder of Abraham Lincoln. Philadelphia: Barclay and Company, 1865. Reprint, Port Tobacco, Md.: James L. Barbour, 1981.

Trindal, Elizabeth Steger. *Mary Surratt: An American Tragedy.* Gretna, La.: Pelican, 1996.

Turner, Thomas R. *The Assassination of Abraham Lincoln.* Malabar, Fla.: Krieger, 1999.

———— *Beware the People Weeping.* Baton Rouge: Louisiana State University Press, 1982.

U.S. Congress. House. *Report on the Assassination of Abraham Lincoln.* 39th Cong., 1st sess., July 1866. Washington, D.C.: Government Printing Office, 1866.

Verge, Laurie. "A Portrait of Mary E. Surratt." *Surratt Society News,* May 1981.

————, ed. *The Body in the Barn.* Clinton, Md.: Surratt Society, 1993.

Walter, J. A. "The Surratt Case." *Church News.* Washington, D.C., August 16, 1891.

Wearmouth, John M., and Roberta J. Wearmouth. *Thomas A. Jones: Chief Agent of the Confederate Secret Service in Maryland.* Port Tobacco, Md.: Stones Throw Publishing, 2000.

Wearmouth, Roberta J. *Abstracts from the "Port Tobacco News and Charles County Advertiser"* Vol. 2, 1855–69. Bowie, Md.: Heritage Books, 1991.

Weckesser, Elden C. *His Name Was Mudd.* Jefferson, N.C.: McFarland and Co., 1991.

Weichmann, Louis J. *A True History of the Assassination of Abraham Lincoln and of the Conspiracy of 1865.* Ed. Floyd E. Risvold. New York: Knopf, 1975.

Wert, Jeffrey D. *Mosby's Rangers.* New York: Simon & Schuster, 1990.

Whiteman, Maxwell. *While Lincoln Lay Dying.* Philadelphia: Union League of Philadelphia, 1968.

Wiatt, R. W., Jr. *Libby Prison, Richmond, Virginia.* Official Publication No. 12. Richmond: Richmond Civil War Centennial Commission, 1961–65.

Williams, T. Harry. *Lincoln and the Radicals.* Madison: University of Wisconsin Press, 1941.

Williamson, James J. *Mosby's Rangers.* New York: Ralph B. Kenyon, 1896.

Willing, Richard. "Fight to Clear Mudd's Name May Affect Terror War." *USA Today,* August 23, 2002.

Wilson, Francis. *John Wilkes Booth*. New York: Houghton Mifflin, 1929.

Winik, Jay. *April 1865: The Month That Saved America*. New York: HarperCollins, 2001.

Winkler, H. Donald. *The Women in Lincoln's Life*. Nashville, Tenn.: Rutledge Hill Press, 2001.

Winston, Robert W. *Andrew Johnson, Plebeian and Patriot*. New York: H. Holt & Co., 1928.

Wood, Gray. *The Hidden Civil War*. New York: Viking Press, 1942.

INDEX